Immortal for Quite Some Time

IMMORTAL
for Quite Some Time

Scott Abbott

for David

an inspiration for
three decades —
an activist + friend

THE UNIVERSITY OF UTAH PRESS
Salt Lake City

The Defiance House Man colophon is a registered trademark of the University of Utah Press. It is based on a four-foot-tall Ancient Puebloan pictograph (late PIII) near Glen Canyon, Utah.

20 19 18 17 16   1 2 3 4 5

LIBRARY OF CONGRESS CATALOGING-IN-PUBLICATION DATA
Names: Abbott, Scott H., author.
Title: Immortal for quite some time / Scott Abbott.
Description: Salt Lake City : University of Utah Press, 2016.
Identifiers: LCCN 2016011034| ISBN 9781607815143 (pbk. : alk. paper) |
  ISBN 9781607815150 (ebook)
Subjects: LCSH: Abbott, Scott H. | Mormons—United States--Biography. |
  Abbott, John Herbert, 1951-1991. | Homosexuality—Religious
  aspects—Mormon Church.
Classification: LCC BX8693 .A23 2016 | DDC 289.3092 [B] —dc23 LC record
available at https://lccn.loc.gov/2016011034

Printed and bound by Edwards Brothers Malloy, Inc., Ann Arbor, Michigan.

For John (Jay)

It can fool me but once
my grandmother used to say
death can fool me only once
then it'll be my turn to laugh

—ALEX CALDIERO

And our faces, my heart, brief as photos

—JOHN BERGER

Contents

This is not a memoir. This is a fraternal meditation on the question "Are we friends, my brother?" The story is uncertain, the characters are in flux, the voices are plural, the photographs as troubled as the prose. This is not a memoir.

1

Autopsy

Greek *autopsia*, a seeing for oneself:
auto-, auto- + *opsis*, sight

— The American Heritage Dictionary

23 JULY 1991, 425 WEST JEFFERSON, BOISE, IDAHO

NO CHILDREN, NO PETS
LILA & DEAN, MANAGERS

I'm Lila, the heat-drugged woman announces, edging her weight out of an overstuffed room into the hall. How can I help you? I explain we are his family. She says she is sorry. He seemed like such a nice man.

We follow her up two flights of wooden stairs. Her key opens #41.

A battered refrigerator labors in the heat. Slick white maggots unsettle a thin layer of garbage under the sink. A double bed crowds the bedroom. Soiled latex gloves sprawl atop a trash can next to the bed. Beneath them a desperate spattering of vomit. Cigarette butts. A peach can. An applesauce can. Six beer cans. Containers for aspirin, amoxicillen, Alupent.

French doors lead me out onto a tiny balcony dominated by a single kitchen chair. I sit down, stretch my legs across two milk crates, and try to imagine him gazing across Jefferson Street at the well-tended gardens and white dome of Idaho's state government. Dark clouds bunch over the mountains to the north. Purple thread dangles from a needle thrust into the chair back. Under the chair squats a can of "turpentine replacement paint solvent." The words feel weighty. I repeat them to myself: Turpentine. Replacement. Paint. Solvent.

In the slope-roofed living room, Christy holds up a cardboard box. The shapes of feet have been cut out of one panel. Jill pulls grease-soaked work shoes from under the bed. They are lined with new cardboard.

A W-2 form tucked into a manila envelope reports last year's total wages as $13,235. A cash-register tape lists his recent purchases: a case of Doral cigarettes, a six-pack of Olympia beer, a bottle of Listerine, two bars of soap, a can of applesauce and one of peaches.

We stuff his things into plastic garbage bags, pile them into the van. A bearded man and a pregnant woman approach from the sidewalk. Are you the family of the deceased? the woman asks. My husband was the one who went into the room and found him. The café called the managers here and asked them to check why he hadn't come to work. My husband helps take care of the place, so he went up. It's the second one he's found.

We drive to his workplace, where a gray-haired woman is putting salt and pepper shakers on tables. We tell her who we are. I'm Alice, she says. She bursts into tears. Ted, a big man in suspenders, sits us down at a table. He worked for us for two years. Sometimes he slept in Saturday mornings. We'd send a waitress to wake him up, and he always came right over. One night he asked me for a hundred-dollar advance on his wages. The next day he walked in with flowers for all the waitresses. That's the way he was.

We leave the café and drive to a mortuary. The mortician greets us and offers sincere condolences. I say I would like to see him. He explains that most family members, especially after an autopsy, find it better to wait until the body has been worked on. I explain that I need to see him now. We walk down a flight of stairs to the basement. The smell of pizza and the sound of laughter from a side door. Three bodies laid out on tables. The mortician points to a clear plastic bag on the center table. I pull open the folded plastic. Don't touch him, he warns.

His face is drawn. An open eye leers upward. A scraggly growth of beard and a thin mustache. The sagging jaw reveals uneven teeth.

My teeth.

A surgical Y from shoulder to shoulder, down the chest to the hips. The top of the skull has been sawed off. Severed locks of hair litter the forehead.

I stand before his body. It is unspeakably present. His feet are livid.

2

Incalculable Territory

Every image of the past that is not recognized by the present as one of its own concerns threatens to disappear irretrievably.

—Walter Benjamin

Recognize as a characteristic of all human striving for truth that it is fragmentary, and that it is precisely this which distinguishes it from nature's infinite coherence.

—Søren Kierkegaard

His feet are livid, I wrote.

Bags of his things lurk in the garage. They once reeked of cigarette smoke. Now they fail to retain even his most pungent odors. I'm losing him. Molecule by molecule.

I want to know him in ways I never did.

I worry about contagion.

I worry about worrying about contagion.

I turn to our notebooks, his and mine. I gather photographs and documents. I let my mind slide back. I want more than the pale patterns memory settles into. I don't want to remember him—I want to smell his breath, thump his back, hear his voice.

I'll have to make do with memory. My memories, not his. The memories of a brother.

His feet were livid.

* * *

MARCH 1950, FARMINGTON, NEW MEXICO

In what will become our home-town, good citizens report seeing flying saucers for three days running. Between eleven and noon each day, the alien craft thrill residents of this border town.

I was born seven months before aliens were sighted in Farmington. John was born fourteen months after the sightings.

I have never seen a flying saucer. Nor, to my knowledge, did John.

SEPTEMBER 1954, PAONIA, COLORADO

A little engine leaves the tracks to frolic in meadows. Wildflowers snagged in his wheels betray him. Pedagogical engineers hide in a meadow and jump up with red flags when he turns their way. He gives up frolicking, stays on the tracks, and grows into a good puller-of-trains.

I put down my Golden Book and watch boxcars loaded with fruit rattle past our little log house. In the early evening my mother leads me across the street to a warehouse. She knocks at a side door. It slides open. Through the opening she hands her warm bread and a pot of steaming pinto beans to a dark-eyed woman with a brown-skinned baby at her breast.

1957, MONTPELIER, IDAHO

Pots, rings, or chase. We lay out our marble games on the playground. I drop my winnings into a bulging blue-and-white-striped bag my mother sewed from an overall leg.

I watch a girl with patent-leather shoes swing so high the chains go slack. Her shoes flash in the sun. Her black hair flies in the wind. She knows I watch her.

1958, MONTPELIER

Our third grade teacher has enrolled us in a reading contest. I speed through dozens of little paperbacks. My list of titles and authors grows and grows. Mrs. Sharp awards me a steel medal engraved with my name and the number of books I have read: 129.

1960, FARMINGTON

If it weren't for our breakneck soccer games on the school's dirt field, I would gladly skip lunch to listen to our fifth grade teacher read an extra chapter of *Little Britches*. Little Britches is tough. Determined. Good with horses. Ingenious. Saves his wages.

1963, FARMINGTON

Standing next to the east goal post of the Hermosa Jr. High football field after practice, a fellow seventh grader gleefully informs me that there are creatures in the world called "homaphrodites." Incredulous, yet credulous, I recoil from those hitherto unknown, still faceless, but now named abominations: "homaphrodites."

1964, AZTEC, NEW MEXICO

Regional competition between junior high bands. I carry my clarinet, she hers. We suck our reeds to keep them moist. We hold sweaty hands, speak in low tones, wish there were no end to the day.

1965, LONG BEACH, CALIFORNIA, AND FARMINGTON

Escorted by Mormon leaders, our Explorer Scout troop travels to Southern California. Words fail me the next Sunday when I try to describe what we saw on the beach. I cup my hands to indicate breasts, tanned breasts, enormous breasts barely restrained by tiny scraps of cloth. My Sunday-school classmates erupt. The teacher struggles to restore order, to banish the breasts.

1966, FARMINGTON

At four o'clock two mornings a week I drive to a warehouse where a truck has dropped off bundles of the *Albuquerque Journal.* I load them into our family car, deliver them to every café and restaurant and motel in town, empty coins from locked tubes, and fill the racks with new papers. I drop bundles at houses where paperboys still sleep and finally head home to slip back into bed for a half-hour nap before breakfast and seven o'clock seminary at the church.

One morning, out on the Bloomfield Highway at about five, the black sky explodes. Hundreds of brilliant flares slash through the darkness, five or ten at a time above where I stand on the empty highway next to the idling car.

Two years later John drives this same route. The five dollars per morning gave us a taste of independence. What did he see in the night sky?

1966, FARMINGTON

Late-afternoon light diffuse in the old Mormon chapel. The man standing at the pulpit intones the word of God. Sixteen-year-old boys and girls sit thigh to thigh in the back row, pass notes, play games on paper, whisper warmly into eager ears.

JULY 1967, FARMINGTON

DR. GENE SMITH, ORTHOPEDIC SURGEON.

I have swept Dr. Smith's parking lot, watered his shrubs, cleaned his office, transcribed his tapes, and once almost fainted while holding a basin of warm water into which he squirted fatty yellow fluid drawn through an enormous needle from deep inside a man's sweaty knee.

Today, in the red glow of the darkroom, I pull the X-ray film from the chemical bath and hang the sheets to drip dry. I turn on the fluorescent screen behind them.

Glistening reproductions of Claudia Cannon's spine. The knobbed line curves gracefully from the delicate vertebrae of her neck down to where it disappears between the bright wings of her hips.

The bright wings of her hips.

I trace the ghostly scoliotic curve. The line deviates suggestively from the strictly vertical. I study the dim arcs of ribs that frame her spine, the cunningly articulated vertebrae. I picture Claudia in the next room, naked under the examination gown. The images arouse me, confuse me. I'm feeling something like what I've learned to distinguish as the fire of the Holy Ghost. I worship these pale images.

The door opens. It's Dr. Smith. So, what have we got?

OCTOBER 1967, PROVO, UTAH

Calculus, chemistry, political science, English composition, the Book of Mormon—I'm a somewhat dutiful student at best. But in the honors room of the library among talented and curious colleagues, I come alive. The director of the Honors Program, freshly graduated in philosophy from Yale, is the dynamo at the center of the energetic group. Last night he introduced us to a friend of his, actor Anthony Zerbe. For an hour Zerbe performed poetry by e. e. cummings, and for an hour I was transfixed.

"Eternity's a Five Year Plan," Zerbe sang, and then growled, "Who dares to call himself a man?" Philosophers and priests have taken "sweet spontaneous earth" onto their scraggy knees, he chanted, but earth answers only with spring. "All lose who find." "Progress is a comfortable disease." Something about being wrong even if it's Sunday. Young love and naked girls better than statues. What an evening!

JANUARY 1968, PROVO

And here's to you, Mrs. Robinson,
Jesus loves you more than you will know…

Accompanied exuberantly by Simon and Garfunkel, the graduate and his girlfriend flee her seductive and wrathful mother. I leave the theater happy for them, free with them, disgusted with them by social convention. Still, as I strive to be clean, I wish Jesus's love and the seduction that had my full attention (Mrs. Robinson's spreading knees!) weren't so snugly intertwined in the joyful song.

FEBRUARY 1968, PROVO

A cold night. I stand with friends outside Brigham Young University's "Smith Family Living Center." Students dance inside the plate-glass windows. A young black man approaches, looks through the window, moves on.

I know him, someone claims. He's LDS. Can't hold the priesthood. Can't marry in the temple. Seed of Cain. Curse of Ham.

We enter the Family Living Center to join the dancers.

His testimony of the true Gospel, I think, commits him to a difficult life now, but in the eternities... My mind skids from the impotent thought to the warm, firm thighs of the tall girl from Idaho who is holding me as close as I her.

MARCH 1968, PROVO

We had a nice conversation with Dr. Wilkinson, Bobby Kennedy tells thousands of students packed into the Smith Field House. I assured him that all Democrats would be off the BYU campus by sundown. Our diminutive and emphatically conservative university president sits dour-faced on the podium behind the presidential candidate.

JUNE 1968, FARMINGTON

I have a summer job installing metal bins in the warehouse of the new Four Corners Power Plant on the Navajo Reservation. My boss is Navajo, and I greet him with the *ya tah he hosteen* I learned from my gregarious grandpa Hilton, a Farmington businessman. When I ask, my boss teaches me how to say "Good-bye. I'm going home now." It sounds something like *hagaohnee howan cu*, and when I say it at the end of the day, he nods good-bye. I ask him how to say "Good morning. How are you?" *Doh nah'l ish da*, I hear him say.

When I greet him in the morning—*Doh nah'l ish da*—he laughs. He has me repeat the phrase and laughs again.

30 JULY 1968, SALT LAKE CITY

I am a new missionary, and I have a new name. In the Salt Lake Temple today, part of a solemn ritual that reenacts scenes with Adam

and Eve and Satan and God in the Garden of Eden, a man whispered
a new name into my ear. He said to remember it always. He said it
would be needed at the Resurrection. He warned me to keep it utterly
secret. On our bodies we traced the penalties for breaking the oath
of silence: slit throat, disembowelment.

I repeat the name in my mind, spell it, whisper it between tongue
and teeth. It's a key to the universe, a sacred symbol that I am a new
person, a magical token of knowledge and power and glory. I have
a new name.

NOVEMBER 1968, LANGUAGE TRAINING MISSION, PROVO

Missionaries have been assembled in a large lecture hall to learn
advanced techniques of "motivational psychology." A young, bald,
and energetic man named Stephen Covey shows us a double-sided
drawing and asks us if we see the face of an ugly old woman or of a
beautiful young woman. Your conditioning determines what you see,
he explains. The keys of influence depend on the point of view, he tells
us. When we criticize, judge, and reject, we freeze a person's point of
view, and they become defensive and hostile. If we understand and
accept, they will be open, teachable, and fluid.

Then we're back to German verb forms: *er glaubt, er glaubte, er hat
geglaubt, er hatte geglaubt*. He believes, he believed, he has believed,
he had believed.

7 APRIL 1969, COLOGNE, GERMANY

The young couple invites us into their book-lined apartment near
the university, curious about our American religion. She asks about
the war. I explain we aren't political, that as missionaries we are
trying to make the world better one person at a time by teaching the
Gospel of Jesus Christ. He argues that persons can't flourish unless
political and social institutions make that possible. He sings protest
songs, bangs on his battered guitar. We read together from the Book
of Mormon. Their little boy succumbs to the sandman. Nephi cuts
off Laban's head to get the brass plates inscribed with family history:
"It is better that one man should perish than that a nation should
dwindle and perish in unbelief."

What?

That's Nephi, my companion responds. The Lord commanded him. It was an exceptional case, I argue. God ordered Nephi to break the law because his people needed to know their family history and God's law.

I've seen violence in the service of God, our host explains, and in the service of dialectical history for that matter. "Exceptional case" means "the end justifies the means."

What are those books on your shelves? I ask, pointing at a rainbow-colored row of paperbacks.

It's a series published by Suhrkamp: Brecht, Marcuse, Frisch, Benjamin, Weiss, Adorno, Hesse, Bloch. Do you know them?

Not yet.

Before the week is out I am carrying a slim purple edition of Bertolt Brecht's *Mutter Courage und ihre Kinder*. I bend over the dialect-strewn text on the streetcar, reading my way into a radical new world. I savor the vinegary words on my tongue

> Eia popeia
> Was raschelt im Stroh?
> Nachbars Bälg greinen
> Und meine sind froh.

MAY 1969, COLOGNE

My companion agrees to accompany me to the Wallraf Richartz Museum. It will be my first art museum, just as Cologne performances of *Aida* and *Lohengrin* have been my first operas.

Just inside the entrance, an oversized, bulbous, winged, and brightly colored female figure stands balanced on one leg. I can't help but smile. This is fun already. *Nana*, Niki de Saint Phalle.

Bright flashes of color draw me across the room. Vivid blue sky and water. Grasses flame yellow. A delicate drawbridge spans a canal, its counterweights reaching back like wings. A woman crosses the bridge holding an umbrella. I struggle with unexpected emotions, like Moses standing before the burning bush. The label says *Zugbrücke*, Vincent van Gogh, May 1888.

DECEMBER 1969, COLOGNE

"Der verdammte bleierne Morgen eines Winterregentages"—The damned leaden morning of a rainy winter day. I repeat the words from Herman Hesse's novel *Steppenwolf*, strange in their sound, strange in their meaning, strangely familiar. It is a mood I know but have never named.

JANUARY 1970, COLOGNE

Cursed with a black skin?

I explain to the young man who has been reading the Book of Mormon prayerfully that the Lamanites were wicked and "the Lord God did cause a skin of blackness to come upon them." But if they overcome their wickedness, I add, the Lord will bless them to become "a white and delightsome" people again. He shakes his head skeptically. I skip to another passage: "Think of your brethren like unto yourselves, and be familiar with all and free with your substance, that they may be rich like unto you." Yes, he says. Yes.

OCTOBER 1970, PROVO

The lights go down, and the play begins: "Years ago, bloody years, a governor named Georgi Abashwili ruled this damned city. He was as rich as Croesus."

They skipped Brecht's prologue set on the Soviet collective farm! I whisper.

This is BYU, she whispers back.

The mother leaves her child. The servant girl saves the child. A stagehand walks aimlessly across the stage.

Alienation effect, I whisper. The top of her foot grazes my calf.

The war ends. The mother returns and wants the child she abandoned. The judge suggests a Solomonic solution.

The warm foot again. And again.

MAY 1971, NORTHWEST OF MOAB, UTAH

Will you marry me? I asked. She looked at me quizzically—and said yes.

I borrowed my roommate's Pontiac GTO, an aging but full-throated beauty. We drove from Provo to Farmington, where I asked her father for her hand in marriage. My father embraced her warmly.

Now, after having climbed under the car to adjust the transmission linkage at a Moab gas station, we're barreling along Interstate 70 toward Green River.

She unzips my pants.

When I return to the task of driving, the speedometer reads an ecstatic 105 mph.

Do you mind if I take off my shirt? she asks.

No, I whisper.

JUNE 1971, PROVO

"When I'm loving you more than I can stand I have to get you something and a book is all I can think of. As you grow with the contents of these pages and others I will be with you always." She inscribes the Anchor paperback of Kierkegaard's *Either/Or* with her love. I mark two early passages:

> One ought to be a mystery, not only to others, but also to one's self.

> Every individual, however original he may be, is still a child of God, of his age, of his nation, of his family and friends. Only thus is he truly himself. If in all this relativity he tries to be the absolute, then he becomes ridiculous.

JULY 1971, SAN FRANCISCO

We lie spooned in her single bed. I'm not ready to be married, I say. It's too soon, I say. This won't work out in the long run, I say. It will be better for both of us, I say. Get out of my bed, she says.

16 JULY 1972, ELOY, ARIZONA

Pipe in the derrick, Howard says. Time for a trip.

We climb steep stairs to the doghouse, change into work clothes, pull on steel-toed boots, grab gloves and hard hats, and step out onto the floor where the first ninety-foot stands of pipe already thrust up from the floor to the derrick's catwalk. While the daylight tour ("tower") dresses, Rudy and I check the water and oil in the draw-works' diesels, the diesels in the powerhouse, and the three pump engines. When we return to the floor, Steve is already in the derrick.

Let's do it, girls, Howard says.

Rudy slams the elevators shut around the tapered tool joint. Howard guns the draw-works engine, and the derrick settles under the weight of nearly two miles of drill pipe. One thirty-foot pipe rises, then another, then a third. I kick the slips into the hole around the pipe, and it settles into their tungsten embrace. Rudy swings his tong onto the bottom tool joint, levers it tight. I swing mine onto the top joint, lean into one handle, and pull on the other to make it grip and break loose the tightly torqued joint. Rudy grabs the mud box dangling from a boom line and wrestles it around the pipe. Howard reverses the rotary table and spins the bottom pipe from the top one. Mud (Bentonite gel with barite for weight and cottonseed hulls to fill the salt formation we drilled through earlier in the week) explodes into the mud box and down onto the rotary table. I press my thigh against the warm, abrasive metal to guide the descending pipe across the floor. High above us, Steve leans out against a safety belt to unlatch the elevators. He maneuvers the pipe back along the catwalk and moors it between steel fingers with a slipknot. Howard lowers the elevators, and Rudy latches them around the next tool joint.

A dozen stands of steaming pipe … two dozen … three … methodically we raise the pipe out of the hole. The sun drops behind thick clouds to the west. We work on in bright pools of artificial light. Four bodies move rhythmically, steadily, in concert. A full moon rises from behind Picacho Peak. We grow warm, then weary. Clouds obscure the moon. The derrick thrusts upward amid desert rock and vegetation; engines roar and fall silent in predictable intervals; the rig floor sways and creaks. A breeze intensifies to gusts. Fat drops of rain splatter the rig floor; rainsqualls shudder the derrick. The gathering ranks of pipe drone like the organ pipes they resemble. Taut cables whistle high notes.

The dark monotony of rising drill pipe is interrupted by massive drill collars, the final stand punctuated by the worn drill bit. We break the bit loose from the drill collar with our tongs.

I drag a safety plate over the hole. Rudy waddles out of the doghouse, his fist clenched inside the hollow center of the new Hughs diamond-studded bit that hangs between his legs. I brush drill-collar dope onto the bit's threads, and Rudy and I, holding the bit between us, circle the hanging drill collar, screwing the bit up into the waiting orifice.

Let's get something to eat, Howard shouts over the wind, waving at Steve to come down from the derrick. In the doghouse we sit in a row against the lockers, eat our food mindfully, drink as if we were working in the desert. Howard adjusts his hard hat, hikes up his drooping Levi's, and walks out to the controls.

The return trip commences. First the bit and drill collars, gingerly, ponderously. Then the first stands of drill pipe. We settle into a new rhythm, faster than the trip out. Revving engines raise the open elevators into which Steve thrusts the drill pipe. I catch the abruptly rising pipe, let it jerk me across the muddy floor to where Rudy stands with the chain coiled three times around the waiting tool joint. I stab the descending pipe into place, and Rudy swings his arm and snaps his wrist, and the chain snakes up from the bottom tool joint, grips the pipe, and spins it down into the pipe below. We tighten the connection, pull out the slips, watch the pipe descend, kick in the slips, unlatch the elevators, dope the pipe threads, throw the chain, spin down the pipe . . . on and on and on, deeper into the hole, farther into the stormy night.

Midnight. Five stands of pipe still in the derrick. The last of the clouds blow over. The moon is cold and bright. The wind dies. The last stand of pipe disappears into the hole. Howard resumes drilling, the new bit ten thousand feet below us. Steve descends from the derrick. We clean up and change clothes. The morning tour arrives.

John also knew these men and these extended, choreographed sequences set in the "oil patch." We worked or we didn't go to college. We were proud to be workingmen.

2 AUGUST 1972, SEAL BEACH, CALIFORNIA

The rig is being moved, and on our off day I have traveled with Steve to visit his sister. I wake up early, sit alone in the kitchen, watch the light through the lens of Joni Mitchell's song "Chelsea Morning," sniff the fragrant yellow skin of a lemon.

14 AUGUST 1972, WICKENBURG, ARIZONA

We're drilling an exploratory well a few miles north of town, and I've taken a room in a ramshackle motel crammed into the elbow of a highway-railroad intersection. My next-door neighbor is a wizened ex-contortionist who looked deeply into my eyes the first time I said hello and offered to read my palm if I would come into her room. I claimed to have a vague palm. Her name is Maria, and in the cool of the evenings she maneuvers a hose to sprinkle a tiny plot of grass and flowers. She wears a sleeveless blouse, a pair of loose shorts, and sneakers with no socks. She ties white rags around her deeply tanned left calf and her equally brown left bicep, bright semaphores that accentuate the contrast between the almost theoretical lines of her emaciated limbs and their pronounced joints. When I stare at her bulbous elbows (galls, burls), she responds with a practiced explanation of how her mother tied her in knots when she was a baby so she could be an acrobat. She has never regretted it, she says, for it led to her eventual fame and the chance to mingle with the truly great people of this century. She is resigned to living out her days in Wickenburg, where the desert heat eases her arthritic joints.

16 AUGUST 1972, WICKENBURG

Scott, Rudy says while he boils tripe for our dinner, I like you. You work hard. I help you.

What kind of help, Rudy?

The guys like you better, the sheepherder-turned-roughneck explains, the guys like you better if you cuss a little. Just a little. A few *hell*s and *damn*s. That's all. It's the way we talk. Just a little.

FALL 1972, PROVO

German poetry has caught my fancy, so much so that I've changed my major from premed to German literature. The ideas arouse me in ways math and science never have. Thales Smith and I sometimes skip class, bored by mechanical classification: this is a sonnet, this is a dactyl, this is political poetry. Yes, of course, but what the hell does it mean! Why don't we use the form to talk about the content? About why and how the poem moves us?

One day we walk into class together (we have calculated how many classes we can miss before losing credit), and Thales sits down in the standard-issue wood-and-steel desk. He jumps up as if he sat on a rattlesnake. He points at the thick wooden seat molded for a human butt. Bird's-eye maple, he whispers. The bastards have used bird's-eye maple. It's rare. It's unpredictable. You can't tell until you've cut into the tree that it has bird's-eyes. It's expensive. Only a half-wit would use it for a school desk. My best mandolin is made of bird's-eye maple.

SPRING 1973, PROVO

I have quit attending my beginning Latin class to write a short story. The main character is an aspiring poet who works as a roughneck in the oil field. Like Jim Casy in *The Grapes of Wrath*, I give him Jesus's initials. Like the Trappist monk Thomas Merton whose *New Seeds of Contemplation* I've been reading, my character balances the active life with the contemplative. And like jazz pianist Thelonius Monk, he can be cool and passionate, playful and edgy, dissonant and mellow. *Misterioso*.

The contest requires that I submit my entry under a pseudonym. The new name pleases me even more than the story I'm writing: Thelonius Merton.

I'll conjugate the ancient verbs next semester.

FEBRUARY 1974, PROVO

John and I are renting an apartment with two other students, a middle-aged macho theater student who advertised for roommates and a bright homosexual English major. After our sometimes vicious fights at home and after having ignored one another for long stretches, it feels good to share this habitation with my brother.

In the student ward we attend on Sundays, I meet a thoughtful young woman with whom I have long and intimate conversations. One Saturday we drive to Huntsville, a small town in northern Utah where monks from Thomas Merton's Kentucky monastery have made a new home. We eat their bread and honey, listen to their celebration of the hours, marvel at their commitment to meditative silence.

Driving back to Provo, I lay out a set of ideas I have been exploring: "The glory of God is intelligence, or, in other words, light and truth" (the Doctrine & Covenants); the declaration in the Book of Mormon that "men are, that they might have joy"; and apostle Parley P. Pratt's admonition that we should pray "that every affection, attribute, power and energy of your body and mind may be cultivated, increased, enlarged, perfected."

She points out that my celebration of intelligence and affection is at odds with scriptures in the Book of Mormon asserting that "the natural man is an enemy to God," "carnal, sensuous, devilish." We fall silent, and I wonder how well my brother is dealing with this conundrum. He has been spending a lot of time with a sultry divorcée.

10 JUNE 1974, TOCITO OIL FIELD, NAVAJO RESERVATION, NEW MEXICO

I kick at rabbitbrush to break the evening's silence. The derrick has been lowered, the doghouse packed with equipment. Cactus Drilling Company is paying me time and a half to stand guard for the night.

In the solitude I retrace the events of April that followed the exquisite months of February and March. She left me to marry an older, more settled man.

I browse through Farmington's *Daily Times*:

Juveniles Sentenced to Springer
All three youths charged in the mutilation murders of
three Navajo men in April were sentenced to terms at the
New Mexico Boys School at Springer following an all-day
hearing in San Juan County District Court Friday.... Medical

and psychiatric testimony at the hearing revealed that in
the opinion of the authorities, none of the three youths was
insane and that they would be "amenable to treatment."

Violence Erupts, Policeman Injured:
Coalition Stops Posse Parade
A traditional Sheriff's Posse Parade through downtown
Farmington Saturday erupted after a peaceful beginning
into an afternoon of violence which saw a Farmington
policeman struck by an automobile and crowds of hundreds
flee from police tear gas when members of the Coalition
for Navajo Liberation attempted to stop the parade.... The
leaders, who seemed to be supported by an estimated 40
to 50 more Indians on the sidewalk, objected to allowing
a six-man contingent of horsemen to proceed. Dressed in
cavalry uniforms of the late 19th Century, the horsemen were
members of the U.S. Army's Ft. Bliss, Tex. drill team.... One
middle aged Fruitland Indian, speaking just after the violence, said in a voice heavy with alcohol, "I care for my
people. It should not happen."

I watch a sidewinder leave its track in the sand, a sinuous sentence
with ellipses. The snake progresses almost by regress. I sleep fitfully
in the back of my car, dream of vengeful, heavy-voiced Natives in
the gray dawn.

SPRING 1975, MANTI, UTAH

It's a perfect day, a perfect spring. We picnic in a park with a view
of the nineteenth-century Manti Temple where we'll be married in
August after her USO trip to Europe. I write a poem about sunlight
and cheese, apples and Jesus, love and joy.

OCTOBER 1976, PRINCETON, NEW JERSEY

Inside our graduate-student apartment, little Joseph wails his
hunger. I lean over my bicycle to replace the front wheel. A sharp
pain in my lower back drops me to the grass.

At the university clinic the doctor gives me pills for the pain and asks what sort of stretching exercises I do.

Stretching exercises?

You're not fifteen anymore, she says.

21 MARCH 1977, FARMINGTON

Jeff wears a neck brace. Mom sits on a folding chair, weak from the operation that took her ruptured spleen. The casket disappears into the ground. People express condolences.

The chapel and the adjoining recreation hall were packed with church members and coworkers and students from the junior high school where Dad was the principal. Marlo Webb, president of the LDS Stake in which Dad served as bishop, spoke at the funeral.

The generous man had given Mom a new car from his Chevrolet dealership to replace the one destroyed in the wreck. Now he spoke briefly of Dad. Then, to comfort the Mormons and instruct those of other faiths, he laid out the "Plan of Salvation." Heaven, he said, is organized by families, fathers and mothers who bear spirit children. Born to earth, those spirit children take on physical bodies. During our mortality we undergo trials, make choices, prove ourselves worthy of returning to our Heavenly Parents.

The theological schema he laid out was as little comforting to me as was the American flag draped over the veteran's coffin. Comfort me rather, I thought, with memories however faulty, with the quick skip Dad took to begin running, with his wry "cogitation," with the day he brought home his first reading glasses, with the unforgettable sermon he once gave: We read the teachings in the Book of Mormon about caring for the poor and decide they don't apply to us, he said, then ripped a page out of the holy book, crumpled it into a ball, and threw it over the pulpit.

JUNE 1979, PRINCETON

Dissertation done, eager to provide for our growing family (Joseph, Maren, and a third child due in July), I applied for thirty-five jobs at colleges and universities across the United States. I made promising but ultimately unrequited campus visits to Stanford and Texas-Austin. I looked into a bleak future. And then, by some strange twist of fate, the chair of Princeton's German Department offered me a one-year lectureship to fill an unforeseen vacancy. Thirteen thousand dollars for the year. The downside: I'm now ineligible for graduate-student housing.

We find an ad in the *Town Topics*: Companion needed for older gentleman. Free rent in exchange for cooking, gardening, and personal care.

In a large house on a tree-lined street, we meet ninety-three-year-old Walter Furman and his sixty-four-year-old son. They are sipping bourbon in a sunny room.

Could I get you a drink? the younger man asks.

No, thank you.

Don't you drink? asks the older man.

No.

Why not?

We are Mormon.

You're Mormons! I have an aunt who is Mormon. She spends her free time tracing our family lines. Marvelous stories. Do you do that sort of thing?

Not as much as we should.

I used to live in Vermont near Brigham Young's birthplace. I've always admired his virility.

I change the subject. What will be expected of us if we move in?

The younger man answers. Minimal yard work, light housecleaning, availability at night in case help is needed, cooking dinner. A homemaker will come each morning to get Father up, bathed, and dressed. She'll get him breakfast and clean his rooms. A woman will come from New York when you go on vacation.

Will our small children be a bother?

Certainly not, interjects the older man. I like children. I have always liked children. If they get too loud, I can take out my hearing aid.

Can you get around? I ask, eyeing the aluminum walker standing next to him and his right leg encased in a complicated brace.

Pretty well. Thirteen years ago, I was eighty then, I fell down the last step into the garage. Broke my leg in two places. When it didn't heal right, the doctor decided I was so old it wasn't worth resetting. And, so you know exactly what you are getting into, let me tell you about my ulcer.

He sips bourbon from his glass.

My ulcer began in 1912 when my business failed. I was married, with a small son. 1912. That makes it, today, the oldest living ulcer. My doctor told me he could trace every ulcer to a Greek restaurant. Do you eat in Greek restaurants?

Not often enough. We'll take the job if you want us.

24 NOVEMBER 1979, FIRESTONE LIBRARY, PRINCETON

A disheveled man of maybe fifty works and reworks papers scattered on a long table in the library's main hall. Later he leans against a column in front of the library and sucks impatiently on a cigarette. He returns to his table and writes with haste, as if this is his last chance, as if the memories are fading.

7 DECEMBER 1979, PRINCETON

The Elders Quorum president has assigned me to visit Alfred Bush, a lapsed Mormon who works in Princeton's Firestone Library. Brother Bush declines to be visited at home but says I can come by any time he is at the library. He is the curator of the Western Americana Collection and shows me some of his treasures: a copy of the Book of Commandments (an early and rare version of the Doctrine & Covenants), a letter from Brigham Young entreating one of his wives to return from Denver, and the pièce de résistance, a "seer stone" used by Joseph Smith. This is a recent acquisition, he tells me. After a break-in and attempted murder, its owners wanted interested parties to know it was here and not in their possession.

The stone, a geode, rests solidly in my palm. A fairly large opening invites my gaze into the crystalline center. A smaller opening admits light from the opposite end. It is a direct connection to the prophet

Joseph Smith, I think, a material link. With the stone in my hand I contemplate the difference between myself and the man who believed it had magical powers.

7 FEBRUARY 1980, PRINCETON

I am overjoyed to be a guest at Princeton University for a third time, Peter Brown begins, and once again to have the great pleasure, the great pleasure of renewing old acquaintances. Unfortunately, you have had two . . . two years to think about what I said the last time I was here. In private conversations with several of you today, I have been forced . . . have been forced . . . slowly and painfully to eat my own words.

The fourth century AD is a dark age in my mind, but from the moment the first stutter breaks from Peter Brown's lips, I hang on the laborious birth of every utterance. He speaks of politicians and their steady withdrawal from active life. He addresses the inexp-p-p-p-plicable. A Latin term is untransla-transla-la-la. . . . St. Elmo's fire fli-fli-fli-fli-flickered.

With faltering lips and faultless style, Peter Brown speaks of careful gesture, of well-formed sentences, of subtle restraints, and of meticulous grooming. He tells of the man so perfectly schooled that he committed suicide after he farted in a public lecture. A holy man was thought to have arrived at the most enviable prerogative to which an inhabitant of the later empire could aspire: parhe-he-he-he-parrhe-he-parrhesia—freedom to speak before the awesome majesty of God. Plotinus was so ashamed of his body that he would not speak of his parentage or of the date or place of his birth. Anthony blushed when he had to eat. Infe-fe-fectious serenity. D-d-d-d-d-death. A description of how the philosopher gains his superior qua-qua-qua-qua-(then softly), qualities. And finally, the Greek word *m-m-m-m-m-m-meschane*, the humiliated ones.

I walk back to the library. I worshipfully stutter that last Greek word, ritually defer d-d-d-death between my tongue and palate, savor broken words of my own making. To speak or write eloquently *and* to manifest the body.

1 MARCH 1980, PRINCETON

Two dreams last night. In the first I stood onstage, in costume, ready to say my lines. The audience waited, but I couldn't remember a word. In the other dream I also stood onstage, this time wearing a long beard. Words flowed from my mouth, and the beard dissolved, leaving me naked.

2 MARCH 1980, PRINCETON

I pour Walter's afternoon bourbon and tell him about the chain-smoking man outside the library. He reminds me of my brother, I say. Or, rather, the sight of him turns my mind to John. I'm not sure why.

How does he dress?

Old slacks. A wrinkled shirt.

Is he thin? Intense?

Yes.

Sounds like John Nash. He used to be a promising economist or mathematician. He had some sort of breakdown.

2 APRIL 1980, PRINCETON

For a second year in a row, after several dozen applications, after two campus interviews (Pittsburgh and North Carolina), I'm left with no job. I have papers to grade, and Thomas has been crying for two hours. I've just read an essay about new PhD's forced out of the profession. I escape to my office, drink a Coke marked "Kosher for Passover," and work like a madman.

1 MAY 1980, PRINCETON

John called this morning from Houston. He's cooking at a place called "Steak and Eggs," says he is doing well.

Late this afternoon, a colleague on leave to learn Greek so he can finish a book about Hölderlin called the department chair from a bar in Laredo to announce he won't be returning to Princeton. My lectureship will be extended for a year. The Wharton Business School's PhD retraining course can wait.

13 MAY 1980, PRINCETON

John called again yesterday. He made twenty thousand dollars last year, he said. He is going to enter a writing contest. He has heard the Russians are planning to let the Iran hostages loose just before the November election so Carter can take credit, win the election, and continue to be a pushover.

FALL 1980, PRINCETON

Michel Foucault lectured here today. I was lucky to find a standing place in an auditorium electric with anticipation. The French thinker stood at the room's center, his bald head radiant with reflected light. His lecture was dense with references to classical texts unfamiliar to me. Nonetheless, I left knowing I had been part of something important and with a single sentence echoing in my thoughts: "What constituted ethical negativity for the Greeks was being passive with regard to the pleasures."

5 JANUARY 1981, PRINCETON

Back from four days in Houston for the annual convention of the Modern Language Association, job interviews for the third year in a row. I sit by the fire, leaf through pages of *The Honorable Schoolboy*, watch football on TV, play games with the children. And sleep.

I stayed with John in Houston. He has changed his name to Jay. From the airport he drove me to the fire-damaged brick house his friend Lee is restoring in Houston's Montrose district. I slept on a narrow cot in a stuffy room half filled with boxes. The next morning I donned my suit and in ten minutes exchanged the tenderloin for Houston's high-rise monuments to economic virtues.

That evening Jay and Lee and I attended a potluck dinner in the basement of a Unitarian church. A muscular man sporting cropped blond hair, a steel chain, and engineer's boots seemed to be in charge. Between bites of fried chicken Jay told me his secret, putting into words what the kiss I heard the night before had already confirmed. Uncomfortable with the attention I was attracting from the all-male crowd, I focused on my brother. A handsome man.

Back at Lee's house, Jay offered me things: a set of knives, a cook-book, a fountain pen. I asked if he was still drawing. He told me about his new business venture: Shaklee vitamins that would make him (and me, if I wanted) healthy and rich. I asked him about fading bruises around his eyes and nose. He said he had won a drinking game called "Pass-out." He claimed Lee had an original da Vinci drawing somewhere in a box. We spent the evening playing cards. And we reminisced.

Do you remember when Mom broke her toe trying to kick Carol? The squirrel your arrow nailed to a tree trunk? Driving Grandma's riding mower in Colorado? Remember the neigh-bors who dismem-bered the lizards we sold them? When you fell off the top bunk and smashed your nose? And when you got your nose broken in Little League?

For seventeen years John and I played and punched and pounded one another in our shared bedroom. Brothers.

6 JANUARY 1981, PRINCETON

I call Mom to tell her about seeing John in Houston and about the job search. I skip the details of John's relationship and don't mention my postinterview depression. I tell her that this year I have more experience and new publications.

I prayed for you to do well, Mom says.

Thanks, I say.

It will only work if your faith is strong enough, she points out. You'll never get a job if you don't have faith in yourself.

Are you talking about faith or the power of positive thinking?

You know what I am talking about.

21 FEBRUARY 1981, PRINCETON

Job offers! How will I decide between Bucknell, Columbia, and Vanderbilt? I won't even make the invited campus visit to Washington University. Columbia's offer is for six years, but not tenure track. The small-town environment of Bucknell is inviting. Vanderbilt has a graduate program.

29 MARCH 1981, PRINCETON MEDICAL CENTER

Nathan was born today at eleven in the morning. Will he relish the fact that he was born in the same medical center where Einstein died? Where Einstein's brain was famously removed for examination?

4 JUNE 1981, COLUMBIA PRESBYTERIAN HOSPITAL, NEW YORK CITY

Yesterday morning we sent two-year-old Thomas into open-heart surgery. Several hours later we were allowed to see him in intensive care: cadaver white, his orifices crammed with tubes. He was breathing with the help of a respirator, every heartbeat monitored, every cc of urine measured. After a long hour he opened his eyes for the first time. Later he grasped my finger. The night passed silently. About midday the battered little boy nodded yes to my question: Are we still friends? From his window he and I watch airplanes drop out of the sky to land at La Guardia and count buses as they pass the abandoned dance hall below.

17 JULY 1981, PRINCETON

Scott. Oh Scott. Could you help me?

What's up, Walter?

I'm wondering if you could help me get my...my...you know, my...it's in the sitting room. I've had trouble with this word before...How do I remember it? I think of the Civil War, Sherman's march through Georgia. Only it wasn't a march it was a raid...radio! Would you get my radio?

I'm going to miss this man.

SPRING 1983, NASHVILLE

Vanderbilt's new provost tells 150 members of the faculty of the College of Arts and Sciences that he is readjusting the library's budget to focus on periodicals rather than books. I stand and tell him that his decision contradicts the report just issued by our faculty committee on the future of the library. My long experience, the provost intones, tells me that faculty committees tend to reaffirm the status quo. Have you read our report? I ask. No, he says. My experience . . . We have experience as well, I break in. We considered several options; we studied the issue carefully; we drew careful conclusions. You are a psychologist and administrator. What experience have you had with library collections? He points his index finger at me and asks: Who are you? Then more forcefully: Who are you! Scott Abbott, I answer. Department of Germanic and Slavic Languages.

29 MAY 1983, TÜBINGEN, GERMANY

I cower on the floor under a blanket. In the dark above me a cat spits and hisses and rips at couch fabric. I hug my legs to form a smaller target. The cat screams its outrage. Time crawls on. The cat springs like God through the dark and slams onto my head. I strike out wildly, but he is too quick for me.

From the bedroom comes Libby's sweet voice: Anything wrong?

At breakfast, Kitty rubs affectionately against my legs.

You're good with animals, Bruce says.

3 JULY 1983, TÜBINGEN

My mother and grandmother arrived yesterday after two weeks in "the Holy Land." Tomorrow we'll drive to München, where they want to visit the memorial at Dachau, and then to Zürich, where my brother Paul is being released from his mission.

I wish we had picked up John after his mission, Mom says over dinner. It might have made things less complicated for him.

5 JULY 1983, DACHAU

GERMAN WOMEN DON'T SMOKE.

Tavern owners should allow no jazz music to be played in their taverns in the future; if questions arise as to what constitutes jazz, they will be decided by Dr. Gerhard Schneider, Gmelinstrasse 6.

HOMOSEXUALS ARE ANIMALS.

Please burn all the filthy, Godless, Marxist, Jewish books you own; refer to the accompanying list.

JEWS ARE PIGS.

Protect the honor of your wives and sisters and daughters.

PLEDGE ALLEGIANCE TO FLAG AND FÜHRER.

Buy German; the job you save may be your own.

We are mostly quiet after the revelations of the concentration camp. Before bed, I give Mom a copy of a story I've been working on.

> The Hairy Turkey
>
> The station wagon climbed steeply between rocky hills, past the inventory of Four-Corners Auto Salvage. Bill's mother read a church magazine in the front seat. His sister slept next to him in the back. Bill looked out at riverside farms and oil refineries. Historical markers announced INDIAN PETROGLYPHS and MORMON SETTLEMENT. His father set the automatic station finder whirring up and down the radio dial. This early on Sunday morning the radio was the realm of Navaho disc jockeys, their guttural speech littered with English brand names.
>
> The hogback marking the reservation's eastern boundary came into sight. An occasional hogan appeared and receded beside the highway. Long-haired horses and scruffy dogs warmed themselves in the late November sun. Away from the river's cottonwoods the landscape was lunar. Shiprock's sharp towers rose in the west.
>
> Bill's father asked if he knew why the Indians call it Shiprock? They have a legend about a big ship that brought their ancestors across the ocean, he explained. Some say it is a remnant of the Book of Mormon story.

The highway drew them south from the volcano's massive core to Tocito, where busy pump jacks levered oil from the ground. The dark, conifer-covered slopes of the Lukachukai Mountains rose to the west. Bill's father turned the car onto a gravel road, then into a hard-packed yard surrounding a cinder-block house. A scraggly dog snarled at them from the top of an overflowing garbage drum: empty soup cans, stew cans, bean cans, canned chicken cans, hominy cans, spam cans. And bottles. It surprised Bill to see whiskey bottles here. Under the direction of the Southwest Indian Mission President, the McMasters had come to hold a sacrament meeting with Brother and Sister Begay.

Bill's father knocked on the door of the little house. A cold wind blowing off the mountain ruffled his thin hair. The door opened and he half entered the house. There seemed to be some discussion, then he leaned out and motioned for his family to follow.

As Bill approached the door, a confusing creature rounded the corner of the house and advanced on gnarled, all-but-toeless feet. Feathers scattered sparsely on its wings and body did little to hide scabrous folds of skin. From the bird's bare chest hung five or six long hairs, their ends dragging on the ground.

A hairy turkey?

Bill stumbled into the overheated house. Before his eyes had adjusted to the semi-darkness, his father was introducing him to Sister Begay: This is my son William, recently returned from a mission to Germany. The emaciated woman bobbed her head and smiled. McMasters led his son over to a long-haired man in a rusted wheelchair. This is Brother Begay. Brother Begay, this is my son William, just returned from a mission to Germany. Scattered white hairs dangled from the old man's chin and cheeks. He stared straight ahead. *Yá-át-ééh*, he said. Bill said *ya-ta-hay* and shook the man's bony hand.

The McMasters stood in the middle of the room. Sister Begay continued to nod. Brother Begay stared straight ahead. Bill's father motioned his family over to the double bed in one corner. His sister and mother sat down. Bill pulled his hand from the old man's grasping fingers and sat down next to them.

At a signal from her husband, Bill's mother stood up with her hymn book. Let's sing "We thank thee oh God for a prophet," she suggested. Sister Begay sang along quietly. When they finished, Bill's father began to pray. He stopped short, however, when Sister Begay interrupted: Spencer Kimball told us to join God's church. We'll see our son when we die. She lifted herself from her chair and limped over to a shelf. Cradling a photo of a young man in full dress uniform of the United States Marines, Sister Begay tearfully described the death of her only son, far from the reservation.

Bill's father announced that they would now bless and pass the sacrament. Bill broke small pieces of bread onto a plate and filled six tiny paper cups with water from a thermos. His father knelt to read the prayer on the bread, after which Bill offered each person the symbols of the body of Christ. He watched Brother Begay's yellow fingernails grope blindly across the plate in search of a piece of bread. His father said the prayer on the water. Handing each person a cup of water in remembrance of Christ's blood shed for them, Bill kept his head bowed and tried to think of his Savior.

Brother Begay broke the stillness to ask Bill a question: You drive past Shiprock?

Yes.

The People call it *Tsé Bit'a'í*, Winged Rock, the old man said. One end is the blood of Cliff Monster. He catches men with claws and throws them from sky to children in rocks. You see Shiprock? he asked again.

Yes, we saw it, Bill replied.

Dine' é, the People, call it Winged Rock. Cliff Monster has a long beak, very large eyes. Feathers on his shoulders. He catches prey and carries it to the high rock and throws it down to wife and children. Monster Slayer carries a pouch with blood. He hunts Cliff Monster. Cliff Monster sees Monster Slayer and catches him and carries him high and drops him on cliff. Monster Slayer doesn't die. He's saved by a life feather from Spider Woman. Blood from pouch makes monster think he's dead. Monster Slayer hides in nest with Cliff Monster's young. He learns parents' names from children, then kills mother and father. He tosses them to children to eat. Cliff Monster becomes Winged Rock and his blood turns to slippery rock on end. You call it Shiprock.

Bill's father stood and greeted the Begays on behalf of the Mission Presidency and the Stake High Council. He announced he would speak on the death and resurrection of Jesus Christ. While he described the crucifixion in grisly detail, pointing out that spikes were driven into the wrists rather than the hands, Bill looked around the room.

His father stood at the kitchen table, clear except for his scriptures and the quickly drying remains of the sacrament bread. A wood-burning stove squatted in the center of the room. His mother's head nodded in the close heat. Photos lined the shelf: the Marine son, an old picture of the Begays wearing traditional Navaho clothing and jewelry, and in a plastic frame an autographed glossy photo of Elder Spencer Kimball. Several white votive candles bracketed the photographs. Just above hung a plastic crucifix and a cluster of feathers.

The crucifixion of Jesus Christ, Bill heard his father saying, was a tragic event. As members of Christ's church we choose to remember the glorious resurrection that took place three days later. That is why you never see a crucifix in one of our chapels. Worshipping a cross is a form of pagan idolatry.

Bill looked at Brother and Sister Begay. How were they taking this call to repentance? Sister Begay was smiling, nodding her head. Brother Begay's sightless eyes were closed.

Slowly the scene changed from the crucifixion to the Second Coming. And on that grand millennial day, Bill's father was saying, Christ will come again. The just will rise from their graves to meet Him, their bodies made whole, "yea, and every limb and joint shall be restored to its body; yea, even a hair of the head shall not be lost; but all things shall be restored to their proper and perfect frame."

Closing his Book of Mormon with a flourish, Bill's father spoke in a gentle voice: I know that we will be resurrected on that great and glorious morning. You, Brother Begay, will see again and walk again. You, Sister Begay, will be reunited with your son, and the three of you can dwell together throughout all eternity. But behold, Bill's father concluded, reopening his Book of Mormon, "but behold, an awful death cometh upon the wicked,... they are cast out... and they drink the dregs of a bitter cup."

The whiskey bottles outside, Bill thought.

Gathering his books together, McMasters asked his wife to lead them in a closing hymn, called on Bill to offer a closing prayer, and sat down heavily on the corner of the bed. The frame gave way, and the McMasters found themselves sprawled on the floor.

The closing song and prayer were forgotten in the confusion. Bill picked up Brother Begay's hand from the arm of the wheelchair and said good-bye.

The cold air outside was refreshing. Bill scanned the yard for the turkey. They climbed into the car. The hissing turkey tottered at full speed around the corner of the house. Bill's father jerked the wheel around and stomped on the accelerator. The turkey pressed its attack on the chrome monster, weaving and feinting with its snakelike neck. The big car shuddered, careened out of the yard.

Damned turkey, Bill's father muttered.

8 JULY 1983, ZÜRICH

Driving across the German-Swiss border, I had to ask twice before Mom would comment on the story.

That's not the way it was, she declared.

That's how it felt to me.

Dad wasn't like that, Mom asserted. Why are you so critical of the church? So bitter and cynical?

25 JULY 1983, TÜBINGEN

Done with my work on Masonic ritual routes in Goethe's *Wilhelm Meister*, I've been trying to write a story based on my experiences in this town whose university is five hundred years old. My wandering fragments need the guidance of eros. That's simple enough if this is simply a story. But with a wife and four children at home, I can hardly let eros lead me by the nose through the streets of Tübingen.

Discovering himself and America in *Montauk*, Max Frisch uses a young American woman as a mirror. My new friends Žarko and Zorica act as wonderfully revealing counterbalances to my American perspective. But how to access the erotic complexities that guide a good story and a life?

4 AUGUST 1983, TÜBINGEN

A letter today from my friend Steven Epperson, working on a degree in religious studies at Temple University:

> Dear Scott—Last week was awful, living under the fan. I sleep poorly, and then, too tired to read, I watch late movies until, bored to tears, I wander the house, step on creaking floorboards, listen to cockroaches, the children softly snoring, Diana talking in her sleep.
>
> In the evening fireflies rise and fall with glowing abdomens. A neighbor two doors up sits in Bermudas and pork-pie hat and smokes a slow cigar. My confidence waxes and wanes.
>
> I think of you a lot and worry over you not a little. That solitude of yours. The estrangement and separation, emotional, spiritual, physical, from your wife. Maybe we are different, you and I, our chemistry. I'd die with homesickness, with loneliness and incompletion. I'd yearn for solace and maybe would seek it from damning sources. Who comforts and supports and fulfills you? Who binds your wounds and who hers? It's so

incomprehensible to me, for nothing but the flesh and blood and soul of woman—mate—lover could fill the open gaps in my life. No consolation except in her. Not in God. Not in a book. Not in writing. Those are threads that hang loose without a woman's body, without her knowing and loving presence.

I hope this letter is all right.

It's all right, Steven, yes, it's all right. It's a gift. Thank you. You have cut my throat.

7 AUGUST 1983, TÜBINGEN

I sit at my desk revising, inventing, questioning, throwing out misbegotten paragraphs, envisioning readers. I hear clocks strike the passing hours. The Coke I drank at midnight and the press of my thoughts keep me at my task.

Visiting Schiller in Weimar one day, Goethe opened a drawer in Schiller's desk and was shocked to find it full of rotting apples, the sudden scent of which Schiller used as a stimulant. Goethe would have never drunk a Coke (nor would he sniff rotten apples, drink coffee, wear glasses, or use a telescope). We should live within whatever boundaries nature imposes, he thought. Direct observation of the thing itself was his task, unaided and thus unhindered by devices or stimulants.

I drink Coke, but I don't drink coffee, which is forbidden by Joseph Smith's "Word of Wisdom." As a missionary I taught that alcohol and tobacco and coffee would veil the whisperings of the Holy Ghost—analogous, perhaps, to Goethe's bold and impossible search for unmediated experience.

From Walter Jens's history of the University of Tübingen: "In 1810 a student reported to the dean that a fellow student had saved him from drowning. The majority of the University Senate voted to award the Samaritan, but Chancellor Autenrieth refused: first, he stated, one must know what risk was involved; for given no risk the rescue was to be expected, 'even if the object of the rescue was a foreigner.'"

This morning I sent off an essay for a collection Žarko is planning as an appendage to his translation of Peter Handke's *Child Story*.

> *From the Diary of a Father of Six and Husband of One*
> *(both numbers reprehensibly low in the nineteenth-century*
> *Mormon tradition the author's ancestors helped establish)*

Dream: Each morning between ten and ten thirty an aging man in short pants pushes a baby carriage past the office window. He is average height. His upper body is heavy, his legs thin and hairy. He wears a sleeveless white undershirt, a wife beater. His socks are brown. His slippers are open at the back. A soft cap embraces his head. A child, three or four years old, sits upright in the carriage. Every morning the man shuffles past, between ten and ten thirty, pushing the frilly baby carriage and the oversize, dull-eyed child.

Dream: It is evening. The children are in bed. His wife makes advances. It has been months. A marvelous sense of being loved and needed washes through him. They kiss. A child appears at the bedroom door. His wife puts the child back in bed. She returns. They take off their clothes and sink onto the bed. There lies another child. He sends the child to her own bed. He and his wife begin to make love. While he tries to finish their task, he sees that she is reading a newspaper. He can read the headline through the paper: "!xamilC lauxeS." He lays back and waits for her to notice. The alarm rings.

> Jacob of Saanas (community Stenbrohult in Smaland) lived badly with his wife. One Christmas...she breaks through ice, holds on, 1/4 hour, to the edge of the ice with her hands, calls for help. Her husband stands on the bank, for it happened close to the yard, and says he doesn't dare to venture out on the ice (because he would be happy

to lose her). She drowns. Five years later Jacob's fingers begin to rot, the fingers with which he could have helped his wife; and they continue to rot on both hands. Finally he dies of the disease. Carl von Linné's *Nemesis Divina*.

His six-year-old boy gives him a big hug and sits down for breakfast. Dad, he says, I had a dream last night. I was in a tent with a rifle. You were in a tree, and so was the rest of the family. When I turned around, you had a hole in your head. Then I turned around again and Mama had a hole in her head. Then everybody had holes in their heads.

He squats next to a Colorado wheat field with his father and grandfather. There has been a drought. Between the little boy's hands wheat separates from prickly chaff. A puff of breath leaves wizened grains on his palm. They stare across the fields and his grandfather says: Needed rain the first week of June. His father nods and chews on a wheat stalk. A dry month later, after a meager harvest, the little boy plays happily in the warehouse, jumping from unbelievable heights into what seem to him unending hills of grain.

Please excuse this intrusion. I can't help but respond to your self-centered thoughts. You are very hard on your wife. You have appropriated your joint experience and shaped it to your own indulgent ends. There is another side to this story. You allude to it, and as a Mormon woman I could almost tell it myself. But when a reader looks over your notebooks, there will be only your side. She deserves better.

I can't argue with that. Had I written these fraternal meditations ten years earlier, they would depict a very different relationship. Nevertheless, I'm trying to tell these stories as fairly as I can, to question while declaring, to give irony its full due.

You're good at theory.

And you are proof of my intent.

24 AUGUST 1987, NASHVILLE

Home from a family reunion, the mountain-rimmed Utah landscape still working in me. On our last afternoon together, John, Grandma Hilton, and I cut up chickens for dinner. Trained in the kitchen of the Hotel Utah, John wielded his quick knife like the professional he is. We had no warning of the deadly salmonella shifting from chicken to bare hands, bacteria later rendered harmless for the rest of the family by dutch-oven heat. Through the night our stomachs heaved and knotted and cramped until our bodies were purged.

29 MARCH 1988, NASHVILLE

My manuscript *Fictions of Freemasonry* was accepted for publication by Wayne State University Press. On that basis, Vanderbilt awarded tenure, and BYU offered me a job. When I told the Vanderbilt dean of arts and sciences I was going to take the job in Utah, he asked if a higher salary would have kept me at Vanderbilt. I miss the scent of sage, I answered, and I want to contribute to the education of the next generation of my fellow Mormons.

24 MAY 1988, NASHVILLE

Spent a quiet day going through the book manuscript one last time. On Saturday, warmed by the late-afternoon sun, I enjoyed the smooth chugging of my VW engine, testimony to new plugs, points, and condenser and to my fledgling skill at timing, at finding that perfect 5 DEGREES BEFORE TOP DEAD CENTER.

Over the weekend there were other pleasures as well. The sting of a baseball in the pocket of my leather mitt, the ball thrown by nine-year-old Thomas in a straight, true line. The thud of a foot against a soccer ball and then shouts of excitement as Nathan, seven, kicked his team's only goal. Laughter when Joseph told us about the cottonmouth that dropped into his canoe from an overhanging branch on the Buffalo River. The fat boy on whose lap it landed made an uncharacteristically swift dive out of the canoe. The adult toward whose end of the canoe the snake slithered also bailed out. And I, Joseph said, caught it by the neck with my paddle.

25 MAY 1988, NASHVILLE

My fingers are battered and back muscles sore from a late-night wrestle with our now defunct dishwasher. In moments like this Walter Furman blamed the utter depravity of all inanimate objects. The depraved dishwasher gave me plenty of occasion to try out vocabulary I first heard as a roughneck.

Our anticipation of life in Provo is tempered by thoughts of the good friends and fragrant magnolias we'll be leaving behind. Still, I look forward to working at a Mormon university, to family proximity, and to the mountain-and-sagebrush-and-sandstone landscape whose child I am.

Our anticipation, you write. Your wife, I would wager, has no wish to leave friends, familiar surroundings, her volunteer work. This will be, for her, a move forced by her husband's decision to work someplace else. Your wife wants roots, stability, long-lasting relationships, tradition. You are a man, a nomad, and can hardly understand.

Hardly understanding cuts two ways. What sense can be made of the repetitive disappointments of this (and every?) marriage? For whatever reasons, despite my hopes and expectations and efforts, I am not a very good partner. We are not very good partners.

14 AUGUST 1988, AMERICAN FORK, UTAH

For your birthday, Mom announces, I'd like to buy you two suits. Why suits? I ask.

You are teaching at BYU now. You'll need suits.

I reply with some glee: To avoid the dangers of priestcraft, I'll have to avoid priestly dress. What I'd really like are two pair of Levi's.

I'll think of something else, she says. But you'll need suits.

8 MAY 1989, NEW YORK–TO–FRANKFURT FLIGHT

Despite my economy ticket, by some inexplicable grace I have been assigned a clipper-class seat on the New York–to–Frankfurt flight. A wide seat with unlimited legroom. A single quiet neighbor. Directly in front of me, in the nose of the 747, sit the first-class passengers. Even grace can't bring a regular passenger that far.

While the plane drones across the Atlantic, I read Peter Handke's novel *Repetition*. The protagonist, Filip Kobal, studies his brother Gregor's notebook while searching for him in northern Yugoslavia. If someone were to notice Handke's book and ask me about my trip, I would say I am a writer planning to travel in the Austrian and Slovenian landscapes of the novel.

In the next-to-last row of the first-class seats, a barrel-chested man works with an oversize hand-bound book whose text has exploded across pale-green pages. Strong blue strokes cross out entire unruly sections. Powerful red strokes underline and lend weight to flighty passages. A black silk shirt and a green-and-red sweater vest stretch across the reader's broad belly. Measured against his girth, his arms are an afterthought. He holds the book up to weak eyes. A florid man with thick glasses.

An hour later, the man accepts a glass of wine from a flight attendant and for the first time sets the book aside. I can read the gold-stamped title: *Tannhäuser*. Several first-class passengers note the turn from book to wine and gather around him. Engine noise keeps me from hearing the conversation, but I can follow the admiring gestures: Stupendous! Magnificent! Marvelous!

My clipper-class neighbor sleeps the entire journey.

9 MAY 1989, FRANKFURT AM MAIN

At the Frankfurt airport I'm waved past without even a glance at my passport. They so blithely assume my innocence.

A cheap hotel, one hundred meters from the train station. Police sirens, streetcars, jackhammers. The manager gives me a key and explains that the front door will be locked at eleven o'clock. I watch his one good eye jump from side to side while his other eye stares straight ahead. He hands me a registration form with his left arm. There is no right arm. He is a small man with a humped back. My six-by-twelve coffin of a room has a twelve-foot ceiling. I am not making this up.

In the evening I see a film called *La Lectrice*. The pleasure of the text and the text of pleasure. Reading as sexual provocation. The beautiful professional reader offers her clients the GOLDEN FLEECE. I contemplate Europe as an erotic text, as a mysterious mistress. Intercourse with the abstraction "Europe," I suppose, will not harm my marriage, such as it is. To experience this part of Europe with curiosity, openness, and sensitivity, I will have to risk conceiving intellectual and emotional children. Or will I keep my insular self intact prophylactically ("guarding against")?

Your marriage? Such as it is? You're willing to risk your family for openness and pretend it's an act of courage? Doesn't this drivel embarrass you?

Yes, this is the stuff of overwrought novels. David Lodge makes the dichotomy clear: Literature is mostly about having sex and not having children. Life is the other way around.

Feverish dreams. Shouts during the night in German, Turkish, and English. A violent thunderstorm. Finally I sleep long and well despite riots on the street and in my subconscious (where a naked man reads into an expanding condom until it bursts—freeing letters and word fragments to conceive monsters, impregnate the universe).

11 MAY 1989, TÜBINGEN

Quiet rain outside the train from Frankfurt. Along the tracks stretch colonies of meticulously tended *Schrebergärten*, tiny plots of paradise. Candide leaves Eldorado to tend his garden. In Handke's novel Gregor Kobal leaves home to tend an orchard in Slovenia.

Žarko picks me up at the Tübingen train station. His voice is deep, his German rich, flavored only slightly by his Slavic mother tongue. Lunch at the University Mensa. We talk about Handke, about the six

years since we last saw one another, about mutual friends. Žarko has
a plan: parallel diaries, he says, yours and mine as we read Handke's
Repetition, as we travel Filip Kobal's route in Slovenia, as we follow
Handke's biographical traces through Austria. Two separate yet simul-
taneous perspectives. Two foreigners writing about their experiences
with an Austrian writer's texts and contexts.

Žarko mentions that his brother Miloje has emigrated to Canada.
I tell him I haven't seen John since I stayed with him in Houston. We
have become strangers. Again.

12 MAY 1989, TÜBINGEN

I woke up to a room flooded with sunlight and to the sound of a
hundred birds. It reminds me of summer mornings at my grandparents' Colorado home. At *our* grandparents' home. John and I spent
those summers swimming in Windsor Lake, playing night games
with our cousins.

At lunch Zorica describes her relationship with Žarko: We have
divided up all necessary duties. I am responsible for theoretical physics,
money, the house, the car, shopping, health, cooking, politics, our
social life. And Žarko takes care of art. It's nice not to have to worry
about art.

I think she is hilarious. Žarko's not so sure. I'd like to hear your wife's
version of the tasks you share, he mutters. In the evening we go to a
party for a student celebrating his success on the state examination in
French. When he says he enjoyed my *Deutsche Vierteljahrsschrift* article
on Masonic ritual routes in Goethe's novel, I like him immediately. I
meet a junior editor for Metzler Verlag whose rigid bearing reminds
me of Henry Miller's description of a fellow train passenger, a young
man who describes his early training in art and more recent success
in real estate. He tells Miller that although he longs to return to his
artistic career, he can't leave the security of his business. Caught in the
bonds of security, Miller writes, and only twenty-two!

And I? Forty, a house, two cars, six children (six children!), tenure,
and an undisciplined longing to be an artist. The novel I started in
Tübingen is still a fragment.

12 JULY 1990, DIAMOND FORK, UTAH

After work yesterday I drove up the canyon to join my family at a church campout. A bull with a scrotum as big as an udder stalked along the middle of the highway, massive and powerful and sure of his right to be there.

Recovering from a restless night, I sit on a line between high-country desert and snow-fed river and wonder what I would see if I sat for days in this same spot. The smooth, cold rock I am sitting on, for example. It is rust brown with a thin white diagonal line cutting the middle. Patches of white-and-black lichen cling to the edges. Tiny white-bordered yellow seeds are scattered across the rock, stuck fast by a transparent adhesive. I sketch the rock and discover a second white line, faint across the top right corner. The rock's rough underside is caked with a white mineral crust. It has an acrid taste. The textures, the weight, the lines, the colors, and the taste are material forms to weigh against the paradoxes and abstractions of my life.

Aren't the paradoxes of your life largely the result of your jetting off to Europe every chance you get, leaving your wife and children at home? Or of your sitting alone on a rock while they are engaged with the other campers?

What can I say? While you're at it, you might as well quote church president McKay's assertion that "no success can compensate for failure in the home."

14 JULY 1990, OREM, UTAH

Last night I was thinking about a man whose stepdaughter attracted me more than a little during my high school days. I picked her up for a dance one night and found her mother sitting on his lap, an intimacy I had never seen at home. Another night a group of us were in their home for a church youth meeting. Dad was there, part of his assignment as the ward bishop. Somehow the discussion turned to alcoholic drinks. My friend's stepfather said that if his daughters were going to drink, he would rather they try it at home than experiment with it elsewhere. Dad spoke up, not in argument, but in solemn warning: You are wrong.

Dad's orthodoxy. The stepfather's unorthodoxy.

How would Dad and I have interacted had he lived longer?

My friend's stepfather was eventually excommunicated from the church for adultery.

For Christmas a few years ago Mom gave our children a colorful book called *The Body*. The pages about sexuality were carefully glued together.

Small thunderstorms sweep discretely through the valley. Benjamin struts by swinging a little plastic bucket filled with beetles. The horizon to the north is spectacularly drawn by the sharp, sure peaks and ridges of Mount Timpanogos.

* * *

Spurred by John's death to gather these fragments of history, these bits of photographic and syntactical memory marshaled like Maxwell's imaginary demon against entropy, my pen is drawn, I am drawn, into incalculable territory.

[John's Green and Tan Notebook #1]

The first was that no matter how great his loneliness, or how long the search for brothers and sisters in whom he might find some comfort.... And the other secret, which he kept from (his friends) for their sake, was simply the extent of his ever deepening despair.

That he craved nothing, cherished nothing, believed nothing finally, and took not one particle of pleasure in his ever increasing and awesome powers, and existed from moment to moment in a void broken once every night of his eternal life by the kill. *The Vampire Lestat*, Anne Rice

And I'm too much the slave of my own obsessions and fascination. Lestat

"I've been a rebel always," I said. "You've been the slave of everything that ever claimed you." Lestat

...felt a dark sense of myself as a hungry, vicious creature, who did a very good job of existing without reasons, a powerful (being) who always took exactly what he wanted, no matter who said what. I wondered if he knew how perfectly awful I was. Lestat

Well, it gave me a wondrous satisfaction to do it. And, after all, I had never been very good at obeying rules. Lestat

You have to suffer through this emptiness, and find what impels you to continue. Lestat

This is a page of glory in our history, which has never been written and is never to be written. We have the moral right, we have the duty to our people to destroy the sub-humans who want to destroy us. Only through the ruthless execution of our duty will we attain our rightful place as masters of the human race. Reichsführer Heinrich Himmler

acrostics for Larry, Doug, & Jay

liked young man,
arrestingly beautiful.
restlessnous subdued
reality gleaming brightly
yearnings still growing.

dandified jock,
omniscient youth
unending growth
goads libido.

jaded youth?
alluring man?
yesteryears remembered!!!!

Juxtaposition of time
Alluding to self
Yearns

Jockalar sage
Asshole persona
Yesterday's dreamer.

Laschivious entity
Anoulogaus past
Relatively honest
Randomly friendly
Youthful young man.

Craziness is the only sanity people respect.
I couldn't lie for your honesty.

I try to be myself
as well as

3

I Try to Be Myself
. . . as Well as

> Those who want to approach their own buried pasts
> must . . . not be afraid to return again and again to
> the same facts; to strew them about as one strews
> earth, to root around in them as one roots around in
> earth. . . . Broken loose from all earlier associations, the
> images stand as precious objects in . . . our later insight.
>
> —WALTER BENJAMIN

22 JULY 1991, AMERICAN FORK, UTAH

John died early this morning. Or maybe it was yesterday. A Boise coroner called Mom and asked if she was related to John Herbert Abbott.

23 JULY 1991, AMERICAN FORK TO BOISE

Driving west across southern Idaho, Jill's husband, Mike, points to the Snake River Canyon between Twin Falls and Jerome. A long time ago, he says, some cataclysm split it apart. See how the sides fit perfectly. Some say it happened at the time of the Crucifixion.

We eat breakfast at Mountain Home's Gear Jammer restaurant. Between bites I picture John lying on a coroner's table. The autopsy was scheduled for nine.

Two pink "Patient Copies" from the Physicians Immediate Care Center, each with the same preliminary information: "Sex: M. Date of Birth: 06/03/51. Age: 40. Home Phone: 345-4604. Address: 425 W. Jefferson #41. Employer: T&A Café."

The first is dated July 9, 1991, 9:23 a.m.

> A productive cough (yellow-gray), post nasal draining, chest tightness, very weak, S.O.B. X 2 wks. Arms and legs go numb, onset 1 month; last time he had pneumonia one side of body was numb. Exam: Ht: 6'2"; Wt: 150; B.P. 116/74; Pulse: 104; Temp: 100.4; Resp: 32 Current Medications: ASA; Allergies: NKMH; Other Observations: smokes 2 pack per day, pneumonia 3 X in last 3 or 4 years.
>
> Arm goes asleep if he lays on it. Legs will go numb if he sits too long in one position. Lasts for a few minutes until he shakes it out. Patient denies wheezing or asthma. Coarse breath sounds and prolonged expiratory phase. Given 2 puffs Alupent and clearing of coarse breath sounds. Bronchitis with possible bronchospasm. Amoxicillin 300 mg. Alupent Inhale 2 puffs. Recheck if any problem. Don't smoke. $37. Payment by the 19th.

The second was written nine days later, on July 18, 8:32 p.m.

> Lost 20 lbs in 12 wks, no energy, short of breath, headache, lost appetite, chills. B.P. 118/84; Pulse: 80; Temp:98.9; Resp: 28. Aspirin, Amoxicillin, and Alupent. Seen last Tues, given the Dx of Bronchitis, started on Amox. States he forgot to eat and lost 20 lbs. Hx heavy ETOH and heavy tobacco 2 ppd. Denies homosexual activity, o BRBPR.

The cost this time is $149: $45 for the exam, $104 for tests and a chest X-ray. Nearly two-weeks' salary. John wouldn't go to the doctor, his boss, Ted, said, until one of the waitresses insisted and went with him.

We find John's car a few blocks from his apartment. His keys open the door. I try to start the car. The battery is dead. A young man in a knit shirt and shorts comes out of the house. We explain we are family. I've been watching Jay's car for him, he says. I'm sorry about what happened. Would you like to sell the car? I could come up with maybe $500. He goes to get another car and jumper cables. By the time he returns, he has decided maybe $450 would be a better offer. The car starts right up. We agree to meet in an hour, when he will bring us $425 in cash. We buy cold sodas at a convenience store to combat the July heat. An hour later we add the $425 to the $210 in John's wallet. And John had a $5,000 life-insurance policy Grandpa Hilton gave him when he was born. Aren't we blessed? Mom says.

Used-car dealers in the face of death.

Decisions of style, syntax, vocabulary. Does this literate mourning draw me nearer to John or distance me from my brother? I look back at "Autopsy," at my first attempt to tell this story. When I described the visit to the T&A Café, I said that "we" went in, that "we" spoke with the owner. But the truth is: I remained in the car while Christy and Jill and Mom went inside. I didn't want to talk with anyone about John. I didn't want to talk period. *Caveat lector.*

25 JULY 1991, AMERICAN FORK

For John, for a man who put cardboard inserts in his shoes and borrowed money to buy flowers for waitresses, we buy a beautifully crafted casket of Carolina poplar.

I drive to a clothing store to buy underwear and socks for John, then drop them off at the mortuary. The mortician adds them to the shoes, black-and-white-checked pants, and starched chef's jacket and toque that were John's most formal clothes.

Now the question of a gravestone. John Herbert Abbott / June 3, 1951–July 21, 1991. Those are the facts. I wander around the American Fork cemetery where John will be buried. In the southeast corner next to three cedar trees stands a delicate sandstone obelisk from the late nineteenth century. Cut into it is a half sun below which two hands are joined in a curious grip. I decide to borrow the Masonic symbol adopted by Mormons. It will symbolize my fraternal hand of fellowship gripping John's.

Your use of the religious symbol is idiosyncratic, don't you think? I would see the hand of God reaching out to welcome your brother into the Celestial Kingdom.

Yes. But the image works for me as well. It's precisely the kind of multivalence that allows me to function in a church made up of members whose views I share only in part.

27 JULY 1991, 9:00 P.M., OREM, UTAH

Sitting alone in the window seat in Maren's room, feeling, for no specific reason, grateful to be a father. A canyon breeze through the window.

I'm a pinchy-assed anarchist, torn by contradictory desires. I shun disorder and invite chaos. I want to step into John's cracked shoes; I washed his clothes as soon as possible.

A gentle bishop conducted John's funeral. I loathed him. The funeral prayers were couched in the language of an orthodoxy that would have damned John. It felt good to hear the sincere words of faith spoken by my siblings.

We told family stories. We laughed. Some of us sobbed. I pictured John relaxed on his balcony as a hot July day began to cool and the mountains to the north lost their color. I pointed out that his modest salary scarcely covered his medical bills.

Six-year-old Benjamin walked straight up to the casket and pulled at one of the knotted-cloth buttons on John's coat, the white uniform that represented John's creative ability, his discipline. It also bore an unsettling resemblance to the ritual robe and hat that accompany temple-going Mormons into the grave.

Unlike the bishop's earnest promises of a reunion in an afterlife, my friend Alex Caldiero's "Funerary Instructions" are corporeal:

1. I came in naked, let me go naked
2. Wash me like a baby
3. It should be a simple rectangular box
4. Leave the eyes alone
5. Breathe on the face so I can hold fast to the wind
6. Imagine the beating of earth upon wood is yet another heart...

Another of Alex's poems comes to mind: "I enjoy reading the biographies of suicides. I start at the last page and read back to before the thought ever came up; back to the child with the big eyes who can't tell the difference between the cloud and his own head."

In the grass by Grandma Abbott's back steps, neither John nor I has yet identified himself as the image in a photo or as the Other in a mirror. Not yet inhabitants of the prison-house of language, the thought of suicide is still impossible for us.

John phoned Mom while he was still in Houston. He said he was in trouble, that he needed four hundred dollars or he would go to jail. She sent him a check immediately. Then she got a call from a man who said she had filled out the check improperly and that it couldn't be cashed. Would she send a new one? She did. Both checks were cashed.

How much I don't know about my brother.

How much he didn't know about me.

31 JULY 1991, OREM

In the afternoon sunshine, John's death certificate glows bright green on my desk.

> Never married.
> Sex: Male.
> Not a veteran.
> Autopsy: yes.

The sun transforms the books on the north wall into an ordered riot of colors.

In a radio interview, a Utah AIDS patient opines that "we all feel immortal for quite some time."

1 AUGUST 1991, OREM

I still have John's things in the garage. I decide to make a list.

Personal Effects

A large black plastic clock with red hands. The face displays a stylized eagle and the words *Miller Genuine Draft Light, Cold Filtered.* The second hand lurches in quartz-driven one-second segments around a brass post.

Greasy running shoes with cardboard inserts.

A pair of stiff, resoled, leather lace-up shoes. Black.

One small khaki-colored can: "Emergency Drinking Water."

A black-painted cardboard African mask.

A life-size bas-relief plaster bust of a Roman soldier. He wears a gold-plumed helmet and a black breastplate decorated with a lion's head.

Ashtrays: (1) stamped metal, round; (2) white-and-black porcelain shaped like the collar of a formal dress shirt with black tie; (3) heavy glass square with a line drawing of a grotesquely earnest smoker and the text: "Smoking Is Very Glamorous—Idaho Interagency Committee on Smoking and Health."

Two cooking pots.

A frying pan.

Two forks.

Three spoons.

Three wooden-handled cooking knives.

A stainless-steel butter knife with a red-brown substance burned onto both sides of the blade.

A metal box stuffed with yellowed recipe cards.

Kitchen Consultations, "Favorite Recipes of the University of California Doctors' Wives Association."

One set of car keys.

A heavy ten-speed bicycle, both tires flat.

An aluminum bicycle pump.

A dirty green backpack holding several bicycle parts.

A black-and-white TV encased in white plastic and a separate rabbit-ears antenna.

A small GE radio, missing its battery cover.

A Dylan Thomas poem, typed and taped to a cupboard: "Do not go gentle into that good night."

A framed quotation from Ayn Rand: "If I had one desire in this world, it would be to desire something."

One condom, still sealed in plastic: PRIME, Lubricated with SK-70.

Handwritten IOUs for the Cactus Bar, $5, $10, and $20 denominations.

1990 Pocket Pal, handwritten addresses and telephone numbers.

Newspaper and magazine clippings in an imitation leather briefcase.

A manila envelope containing legal papers.

PUPPIES, a 1990 calendar marked with several handwritten notes.

Three ballpoint pens and a blue plastic pencil sharpener.

A black nylon wallet. Inside, a photo of a woman in her sixties, a water-damaged photo of a red-faced infant, a Social Security card, a Boise Public Library Card, and $203 in bills.

$7.12 in coins.

A blue duffel bag.

Masking tape. Written on the fat roll with a black marker: "J. Abbott 1132 S. 4th #3."

Liquid Ivory soap.

A small bottle of Wella Balsam Conditioning Shampoo for Dry Hair.

Suave Shampoo Plus Conditioner for Normal to Dry Hair.

A small bottle of Listerine Antiseptic.

2 bars of Lux, the Pure Beauty Soap.

A large-toothed red plastic comb with handle and a matching red-handled brush with black nylon bristles.

A bottle of aspirin.

MAX FOR MEN hair drier.

A yellow toothbrush.

Curity, wet-pruf adhesive tape.

Four TELFA sterile pads and one Band-Aid.

Plastic sunglasses.

A one-edged razor blade.

A 100-tablet bottle of Advanced Formula Centrum, High Potency Multivitamin-Multimineral Formula. "From A to Zinc." Expiration Date Oct. 93. There are 115 tablets.

Twenty-six gray, green, red, or white matchbooks advertising the Interlude Bar & Grill in Boise. A stylized young woman kneels to consider her putt. Her left hand holds her putter, her right hand a martini.

A green matchbook advertises Free Cash Grants: "Call 1-900-USA-RICH. Valuable Money Making Information and the ABC's of Receiving FREE Money from the Government. Now the one dollar per minute two dollar first minute charge is the first step to RICHES."

Nine Kent III Ultra Light cigarettes.

A burlap-covered corkboard. Glued to the top of the burlap is a black paper cross. A hand points upward toward the cross. A pair of lightning bolts. At the bottom bold letters spell "ONE WAY." Four magazine photos have been thumbtacked over the Christian display. Two of them feature coyly posed electric-haired women, one white, one black, both topless. The other photos depict the shaved, blindfolded heads of two black women against a chain-link fence.

Two posters from the Monterey Jazz Festival, 1982 and 1983: Trumpets posed on chairs.

A poster of a fantasy landscape: castle and dragon and hero and princess.

A ten-by-fourteen-inch pencil drawing of a hooked trout.

A framed magazine photo of camels dark against firelit clouds.

A magazine photo of an eagle perched in front of a brilliant sunset.

A framed painting of a demure little girl with long red hair.

A spool of navy-blue thread.

A needle with a loop of purple thread.

An old pair of Levi's; five patches sewn on with meticulous stitches.

A worn satin comforter, rust colored on one side, tan on the other.

A blue quilt tied with red yarn. Splotches of white paint, cigarette burns, and grease spots.

Three pair of black-and-white-checked restaurant uniform pants.

Two heavily starched white chef's hats.

Two collarless chef's jackets. Starched, with tightly woven cloth buttons.

Eleven pastel-colored knit shirts advertising the 25th Interlude Open. A young woman kneels with putter and martini.

A pair of gray sweatpants and a gray sweatshirt.

T-shirt: "FALLIN' ANGELLS SPORTING CLUB, Angell's Bar & Grill, Boise, Idaho."

T&A CAFÉ T-shirt: "Where the 'ELITE' meet to 'EAT.'"

A wheeled brown vinyl bag with strap handles.

Three sweaters, colors faded, one unraveling at the left cuff.

A worn leather-and-canvas coat.

Two limp bedsheets.

Cassette tapes: *The Best of Judas Priest*; Guns and Roses, *Appetite for Destruction*; Anthrax, *State of Euphoria*; *Foghat Live*.

A plastic ruler with geometric formulas and the admonition: "Stay in School, Upon Graduation...Join the Aerospace Team, U.S. Air Force."

Twenty-six paperback novels, most of them missing the front cover. Eric Van Lustbader dominates the pile, but there are others as well:

Neon Mirage, by Max Allan Collins: "Another shotgun blast ate into the side of Ragen's once-proud Lincoln."

Vision of the Hunter, by John Tempest: "In his hands, his people's future. In her eyes, the promise of a love stronger than time."

Burt Hirshfeld's *Moment of Power*: "The savage new shocker."

Superconscious Meditation, by Panda Arya, PhD.

Self-Hypnosis: The Creative Use of Your Mind for Successful Living, by Charles Tebbetts.

Louis L'Amour's *Education of a Wandering Man*.

The Magnificent Century, by Thomas B. Costain.

Home as Found, by J. Fenimore Cooper.

Radclyffe Hall's *The Well of Loneliness*: "Banned in the U.S.... Foreword by Havelock Ellis."

Hoyle's Rules of Games, second revised edition.

Edith Hamilton's *Mythology*.

Reader's Digest: Secrets of Better Cooking.

Basic Documents Supplement to International Law: Cases and Materials.

ETCETERA: The Unpublished Poems of e. e. cummings.

Six spiral notebooks: two of them green and tan, one blue and tan, two yellow, one blue. Notes and drawings in John's hand throughout.

The dust jacket of a Modern Library edition: *The Philosophy of Kant*. The book itself is missing.

2 AUGUST 1991, OREM

I hang John's clock in my office. The moving hands connect me to a time when his heartbeat was a measure of life.

The tiny khaki-colored can of Emergency Drinking Water among John's things was for that horrible moment, perhaps, when there was nothing stronger in the house. During telephone conversations with Mom, John routinely promised he would quit drinking and get more education. His calls to me were often fortified by alcohol.

I don't get drunk. Nor did I call him.

3 AUGUST 1991, OREM

I've been reading John's missionary letters from Italy. Nearly one a week for two years. From what Mom told me when I asked about them, I expected requests for money, reports of trouble, and depressed silences. John communicated all of that, of course, but his letters are uplifting as well (or is it fraternal nostalgia I'm feeling?).

The first one to catch my interest is from Genoa, John's first assigned city after two months learning the Italian language and missionary techniques in Provo's Language Training Mission.

November 17, 1970

Dear Family,

We started teaching a young boy, 17, about a month ago. He came to every meeting, was reading the Book of Mormon, but didn't believe in God. I have gotten so I really love this guy, Michele. Last Sunday he came to church and was really upset, down etc. He finally told us he wasn't going to come anymore. He said he knew our church was the best church around but that he just couldn't believe in God. He doesn't know why but he's been sincere, he tried to believe, but he just can't. He tries to pray but how do you pray to someone who doesn't exist to you. I've never felt worse. I can't tell you how much I learned to love him. It hurt me so bad. I'd give anything if he could accept God, get an answer to his prayers. I never knew I could be hurt so bad. But then he told us he wasn't coming anymore, because he couldn't be part of us and not believe everything. He wanted, he wants to believe but he tried, and it didn't work for him. I don't know why; I almost started to cry. Well that's that. I just pray for him every time I pray. I can't see how God can let this happen to such a great guy. I don't know

John's pencil slashes down across the paper.

Desire works powerfully between a missionary and the persons he teaches. They are attracted to each other, pleased by reciprocal interest. They feed mutual longings for religious community, for order, for divine love. They join in fervent prayer. They sacrifice and serve. The missionary teaches truths calculated to enhance life, to bind families together, to give purpose. The investigator accepts the teachings as truths, changes lifelong habits, takes on the name of Christ, and becomes a new person. The remarkable transformation reinforces the missionary's sense for the truth of his message. The two years he spends on his mission become unforgettably beautiful.

Because the potential for intimate personal relationship is so high under these circumstances, missionaries are required to work in pairs at all times, and their mission president transfers them often from city to city. The rules of conduct are made explicit in a handbook every missionary is told to read daily. John's handbook, which I find in Mom's storage shed, is a black loose-leaf notebook similar to the one I had. It contains the church president's essay "The Calling and Obligation of a Missionary," a "Church Organization Chart" depicting the church's hierarchy, and an essay titled "The Conduct of a Missionary":

> Conduct yourself circumspectly. . . . Guard against familiarity with the opposite sex. There must be no courting, kissing or embracing. Your kisses should be for home consumption and be brought home (unused) to your loved ones where they belong.

Kissing and hugging aside from this lead to immorality....
[I]mmorality is the bane of missionary life.

John's notebook also contains a section called "Ordinances and Ceremonies," a list titled "Scriptural References on Tithing," and "Un Sistema Uniforme per Istruire gli Investigatori."

On blank pages at the end of the notebook John compiled several vocabulary lists, including Italian food words and a list of Italian idioms and these English equivalents:

damn
in the wolf's mouth
draw water for your own mule
he hasn't even discovered America yet
I lick my own mustache
he was born lucky
sleep with angels or have beautiful dreams

On one page he copied John Henry Newman's "Lead Kindly Light." On another he collected a hodgepodge of maxims drawn, I suppose, from talks given by church leaders in the Language Training Mission:

You set your personality for eternity during your mission
Turn my friends over to the Lord
Obedience, the first law of the universe
No sacrifice is too much for the Lord
Christ suffered for me, what do I owe him?
The priesthood is the power to act as if you were God
As soon as I open the window Satan is waiting to get in, and will if I'm not careful
Discouragement and depression are tools of Satan

I distinctly remember the feelings of commitment and faith that motivate a missionary to subsume himself completely to a system perfectly designed, as he supposes, to bring him salvation here and in the next life. The rewards are immediate and substantial. John's notes reveal that the system also breeds absolute rhetoric: for eternity, no limit, the first law of the universe, no sacrifice, as if you were God, Satan as the absolute antithesis. I wish John had embraced a gentler vocabulary, one far enough from the march of Christian soldiers to provide space as he found and developed desires this mostly productive system could not address.

The collection of thoughts I made as a nineteen-year-old missionary had such gems as

Be like a duck, unruffled on top, but paddle like hell underneath.

The ladder of life is full of splinters. Never slide down.

Atheist—a man without an invisible means of support.

From a book of quotations I copied uplifting phrases by Samuel Johnson, Emerson, John Kennedy, Lincoln, Thoreau, Longfellow, Edgar A. Guest, Benjamin Franklin, St. Francis of Assisi, Elizabeth Barrett Browning, Norman Cousins, W. C. Fields, Socrates, Dale Carnegie, William James, and Adolph Rupp. In most cases I didn't even know who the author was, much less the context of the quotation.

A nineteen-year-old, required to teach answers to questions he has never asked, grasps at straws.

25 January 1971, from Cagliari, Sardegna
Dear Family,

I was transferred from Genova this week to Cagliari Sardegna. I'm really sorry to leave because it's a great town and great people whom I love very much. Michele came to the apartment Thursday and I got to talk to him for a little while. He's a great guy, and I'm sure he'll accept God and the Gospel when the time is right. Then he, Elder Nolens and I went to the port in a taxi. I bought my ticket and paid for my bike. It cost me about $15.20 in all. It was raining so we waited inside till 5:00. Then we took my stuff on the ship (they got to come, too). They waited till 5:30 and then Elder Nolens left, but Michele waited. I was on the ship, he was on the dock. We couldn't talk because of the distance and the wind. We just looked at each

other. Finally at 6:30 he had to go. We said good-bye. I sure felt sad, and realized how good a friend he'd been. I'm sure I'll get to see him again though.
Love John

We just looked at each other. In contrast, I keep my distance. I keep myself out of trouble. I circumvent messy situations, personal entanglements, potential failures. I protect myself. The Great Stone Face, a girl in high school once called me. My wife complains, justifiably, about emotional distance.

I don't want to be that person. And so, in the wake of my brother's death, I write to reveal myself. I write to expose myself, to admit motivations, to reveal fears, to open myself to change.

I ask a friend to read my manuscript, apologizing for the exhibitionistic quality of my writing. Her reply after having read it: Yes, you're an exhibitionist, but you're wearing a full suit of clothes under the overcoat.

> 24 February 1971
> Dear Family,
> Thanks for sending my letter. It was from a guy I met when I went to the Junior Civitan Seminar 3 years ago.
> We had a party Saturday. We went out to the sea and had a weeny roast. It was kind of fun, but not really.
> Well I guess that's all. One of our contacts gave me a seahorse (dead) but it's really pretty.
> Love John

Mom thinks John was introduced to gay sex by a boy at the Junior Civitan retreat. Was the letter from him? It's so tenuous, this construction of a life out of memories, a few photos, and some letters. What if John were reading this manuscript looking for clues regarding my sexuality? He would certainly underestimate the love I once shared with my wife.

On the back of this envelope John wrote, "Send me Scott's address." Reading his note, decades old and in the third person, I feel the warmth of something approaching conversation.

> 25 February 1971
> Dear Mom & Dad,
>
> There's something I have wanted to tell you for many years now. I love you, and the example you've been to me, although you haven't seen me follow it, until now. I had more or less hypnotized myself into not seeing the real you. Looking at only your mistakes and enlarging them, making them into large oversized lies, and telling myself this was my parents. I fought, argued because it kind of pleased me for the moment to see you get angry etc, but I always felt really bad afterwards. There were so many times I wanted to accept you but I just didn't and couldn't change; I told myself the reason was because I didn't want you to be pleased or satisfied with me. I'm sorry I caused you much heart-break and sorrow. I always wanted to be close to Dad, like my friends were with their dads, but I wouldn't let myself. I was too proud to accept, what I called then, "defeat." There aren't any two lovelier or better people in the world. Two people who have sacrificed for and loved their family more. I love you, each.
> Love
> your son John

John is feeling remorse. He wants to be good. He is a missionary of the Lord Jesus Christ, and the Gospel of repentance is working powerfully within him. Confession eases his soul and makes progress possible. His desires, however, will continue to conflict with the system he has internalized.

How can you be so sure? Don't you, after all, believe in repentance, change, spiritual rebirth?

Not in the black-and-white sense of your question. Not in the sense of absolute or total or radical change. Not any longer. I am indeed the product of a Mormon worldview: Honor Society president in high school, mission in Germany, BYU graduation with honors, marriage to an intelligent and beautiful woman, graduate studies at Princeton, university professor, seven children. Yet in and through it all runs a web of desires and beliefs and hopes that conflict with the prescribed curriculum vitae as often as they conform to it. For me, at this point in my life, "spiritual rebirth" is a kind of magical thinking that grows out of belief in absolute goodness versus absolute evil. No. I don't believe in that, "after all."

> 2 April 1971
> Hi Family,
>
> This has really been a good week. We highlight it tomorrow when we baptize Sister Sicardi. She is the lady from Holland.
>
> The Giordanos are trying to make up their mind about tithing, 10%. They agree that it's right, but that they should only pay what they can afford. He's a teacher and makes 130 mille Lire a month.
>
> We got a telephone call a few minutes ago. Another one of our members died. He was in a car accident. He was inactive, and I have never seen him.
>
> Well, I'm out of things to say, so ciao.
> John
> p.s. I'm getting better at the organ

A really good week. John would have risen at six to read the scriptures, to work on Italian vocabulary and grammar, and to prepare for the day. He would have gone to bed at ten or ten thirty. He would have worn a suit, white shirt, and tie. He would have left his companion only to shower or use the toilet. He would have spent most of each day going door-to-door to offer a life-changing message to people whose lives were just fine, thank you. He would have visited Sister Sicardi, making final arrangements, teaching final concepts and commandments, disabusing her of anti-Mormon ideas well-meaning relatives had brought up at the last minute. He would have met with the Giordano family to bear testimony that the law of tithing came from God and that blessings would follow if they paid tithing first and worried about their bills later. The inexperienced nineteen-year-old could be confident about sacrifice and its attendant blessings because he had watched his parents donate 10 percent of a meager junior high school teacher's salary to the church, plus a monthly "fast offering" to provide assistance for the needy, plus periodic deep-cutting assessed donations to building funds. They expressed pride and pleasure at helping to build the "Kingdom of God on Earth."

15 April 1971
Dear Family,

It's Easter or *Pasqua* in Italian. It's really a big thing here, too. They have chocolate eggs, vacazion from school and horrible church services. Last night we went into one of the churches here and it's sickening to see the paganism. Apparently the Catholic church rakes in the $ this time of year. The incense, the statues of the madonna or Mary, of all the Saints, the Priests officiating over the communion or sacrament. It's really sad to see these people doing things like this. Well, that's the reason we're here.
Love John

17 April 1971
Dear Family,

Well, we had the funeral last Tuesday morning. It was sure a different experience for us all. I started thinking since I first heard that Pino was dead that this could happen to me sometime and if it did would I be ready to meet God with a clear conscience? I made a resolution to start living so that I could.

Ciao till next week
Love John

5 November 1971
Dear Family,

We had an experience Wed. that I want to share with you. We had taken our clothes into a laundry and I went back to get them. She had them all wrapped up and then told us the price, L7,500, over $10. She had ironed the shirts, washed my socks specially, because "they were wool." I got angry and we yelled at each other because I'm sure I told her not to iron my shirts. Well finally I just paid her and left. I told myself I wasn't even going to apologize for yelling at her. Well that night when I knelt down to pray nothing came out, no matter how hard I tried. I got in bed and started thinking of a scripture in the Bible, Matt. 6:14–15: "For if you forgive not men their trespasses, neither will your Father forgive your trespasses." I decided to go back and apologize and at that moment felt the peace I needed. I was able to pray.

Love, John

A mission works on you that way. You truly want to be a better person. You try to follow the example of Jesus Christ. You strive to be humble. You burn to be filled with saintly love. I am still grateful for the spaces those feelings opened inside me.

12 November 1971
Dear Family,

We have a sweet little old landlady. Everyday we talk a little. Her husband died about a year ago and she is all alone. She has lost all she had, money, trucks, etc. and cries when she thinks of the injustice, the sacrifice she's gone through. She was going to live with her sister in America but fell and broke her arm which hasn't completely healed yet. She is always trying to help us, dusting our room, shaking the rugs, and telling us to be a little more orderly.

Love John

The weeks passed, and John discovered his landlady was going to lose her apartment if she couldn't raise money. She had nineteenth-century furniture and crystal and dishes to sell, and John decided to help her. There were several quick notes home explaining her need, describing the furniture, and promising it would be a good investment. The three thousand dollars should be sent immediately.

Our parents indeed had money in the bank, although three thousand dollars was an enormous sum for them, saved over the course of a decade. They sent the money. The crated furniture sat in a US Customs' warehouse for months until another substantial sum was paid. An Albuquerque antiques dealer was finally found to take the furniture on consignment. Years later, long after Mom and Dad had resigned themselves to a total loss, someone bought the furniture for about the money already spent. Signora Sicardi saved her apartment. Mom ended up with a set of crystal. And John satisfied the workings of a generous heart.

Late in his mission, John was transferred to Milan as a zone leader, responsible for several districts of missionaries. He had a car he hated, a leadership position he disliked, periodic bouts of depression, and continued struggles to fit the missionary mold and to "perfect himself."

> 23 December 1971
> Dear Family,
>
> Until yesterday I still hadn't been able to get back into the spirit of missionary work. I lost a whole month here in Milano without accomplishing a thing. Yesterday however we started working. It is sure hard to keep a strong testimony if we don't use it. I have found out that each period of depression I let myself fall into it takes longer and is harder to pull myself back up. For that reason I have decided to "fall no more," to occupy my thoughts with the work and nothing else.
>
> Why isn't Scott getting married?
> John

What tensions were at work in John as he tried to be one possible version of a saint yet fell into depression and felt "unholy attractions"? What memories weighed on him? Did he lie to his stake president when he asked if he was sexually pure? How did those lies, if he did lie, work in him as he exhorted others to be honest and pure, as he sought the "guidance of the Holy Spirit"?

Firmly centered in a strictly defined theological and cultural system, John had no fulcrum outside that system. Once he broke away from what was eating him alive, he faced an equally difficult task: creating a self without the stories that had guided his life.

Why didn't I get married? Because the intimacy was too much for me, perhaps. I wanted space and time to grow. I wanted to be "clean." I was only twenty-one.

4 March 1972
Dear Family,

I am really sorry I haven't written more than I have lately, but there hasn't been much to say and I hate to send cruddy letters, also as you know it's very hard to write letters. I start, get about this much written, and then go all "bla" inside and can't write anymore. It's really hard to keep myself on a high spiritual plane.

I hate driving "Little Horse," our car. It's expensive but also nerve racking. This week we must have almost been hit 20 or 30 times, each time the car missed us by less than an inch. Our "guardian angel" must have really been helping us. Alma asks if we are ready to die in this moment, I have to say no, because there are so many things I have to do before I go meet my Lord. As I said, I hate to drive. It takes twice as long to get anywhere than if we used bikes and costs so much more.
Love, John

In a subsequent letter John returns to the car:

Well another interesting event happened Monday night. I just about totaled our little car. We hit another guy coming through the intersection but thanks to our Father in Heaven no one was hurt.

March 1972

Dear Family,

Well, I haven't been happy lately, largely because I'm not satisfied with myself to any degree. I have been very depressed and because of that haven't done the work, which makes me in turn feel worse about myself, becoming more depressed which I imagine is what made me make myself sick for the last two weeks. My temper has been bad, my emotions on the rampage etc. What I thought when I heard I was to be a Zone Leader was "Why?" I didn't want it, I was shocked because since I've been here in Milano I haven't done anything hardly at all. I realize what I have to do but it's so very hard for me to do it.

I got a real nice letter from Scott today. All of the Elders want to see Carol's picture. If you have one that is in color I'd like that. Well, I love all of you. Don't worry about me. I'll do fine from now on! Thanks for everything. I love you,

John.

What did I write him? Our sisters *are* beautiful. I carried a photo of Jill in my missionary wallet.

Zone leader. Second only to the assistant to the president in mission hierarchies. A position I never achieved, perhaps because of a sketch several of us did at a mission conference poking fun at a speech given by our excitable mission president and the response from his wife: "Use your common sense, elders! We've had several elders collapse this summer due to heat exhaustion. If you are out tracting and can't find something to drink, use your heads! Go into a bar and put a couple of beers under your belt!"..."Horace!"

For a European missionary, John had remarkable success, baptizing whole families and several single people. I helped teach only one woman who was baptized, and until the final hour it was nip and tuck whether she would choose us or the Jehovah's Witnesses. It's no wonder then that my strongest mission memories are of chance encounters while knocking on doors: the energetic old woman who ushered us into a pack rat's claustrophobic apartment and claimed to be Max Weber's daughter whom the world had forgotten, the publisher who regaled us with stories of American authors he knew and sent us away with armloads of his books, the students who prayed with us and then taught us songs protesting our country's war, the Freemason who recounted Lessing's parable of the rings to teach us that religions are true only as they make their adherents good people, the beer-bellied behemoth who bumped me down three flights of stairs while shouting down the anti-Christ.

One memory stands out. I find the details in my missionary journal:

> The Sievers weren't in church today, the Wuppertal Branch President tells us on the Sunday before Christmas. Could you visit them and see how they are doing? He hands us an address. Brother Siever fell from a scaffold, as you know, and broke his back. Little Sonja is in the same hospital with twitching legs, possibly from malnutrition.
>
> We set out the next morning. It's cold! First the *Schwebebahn*, the hanging train that snakes along the steep Wupper River valley. Then a bus to the city limit. Another bus over icy country roads to a windswept stop in front of a house surrounded by white fields. The Sievers, it turns out, live in the low cinderblock shed across the yard from the house. Sister Siever opens the door slowly, looks at us with dull eyes. Two of her children huddle under a blanket on a bare mattress in a corner. Food wrappers litter the floor. The stove is cold.
>
> We try to clean up. We build a fire with the few sticks of wood we find out in the entryway. The stove belches smoke. We put

the fire out and open a little window to clear the air.

There's a knock at the door. A Catholic priest enters with a box of food, speaks softly, leaves the food. We leave as well. And never return.

Teaching the gospel of Jesus Christ is our task. We have no training, no resources, no place on our weekly report for time spent getting firewood or food for the Sievers. Hours tracting + hours teaching + hours traveling. If they add up to 60, it is a good week.

In one letter John writes about interviewing a man for baptism. As zone leader John would have had a list of questions to help ascertain the man's worthiness: Do you believe in Jesus Christ? Do you believe that Christ's Gospel was restored through Joseph Smith? Do you believe the Book of Mormon to be the word of God? Do you believe the church today is led by a prophet, seer, and revelator? Will you donate 10 percent of your income to the church? Do you have sexual relations with anyone besides your wife? Are you honest in your dealings with your fellow man?

March 19, 1972
Dear Family,

Friday night we went out for baptismal interviews with the Bellincioni family. Brother Bellincioni and I went into the kitchen. We talked for a while, started the interview, read from the scriptures and were periodically interrupted. First the plates on the refrigerator started rattling, he moved them, then a stack of clothes fell for no reason at all. Other things like that, that shouldn't have happened. He told me it was Satan trying to interrupt us and I fully agreed. We spent about one and a half hours talking, clearing up problems and questions and then we knelt in prayer. He offered a very sincere beautiful prayer, pleading with the Lord to help him know the truth. Then I offered a prayer. It was one of the most beautiful experiences I have ever had in my life. We both felt the Spirit of the Lord, which was very very strong. Oh, it was beautiful. The next day they got baptized and it was so very beautiful, so very very beautiful. They asked me to confirm the father, was I ever grateful, I love them as much as any family I ever baptized. Brother Bellincioni paid me a very high compliment. He said that I really helped him during the interview to make up his mind. They say each missionary can touch the heart of certain people and I believe it.

Love, John

So do I, even as I attribute the rattling plates to the refrigerator's compressor. John loved them, and they loved him. And then he was transferred again.

6 AUGUST 1991, OREM

Done with John's letters, I keep searching. For John? For myself?

John kept a photo that probably comes from this time, although I'm not entirely sure about that. He is dressed like a missionary, and his hair is shorter than he will keep it after he returns home. The size of the photo indicates a photo booth, and I imagine three other photos originally attached to this one. Was John equally responsive in the other shots? The earlier photo with Michele shows John with a more careful face, constrained, perhaps, by the angels surrounding him in the missionary display, although he does have his arm around Michele. This later young man, in a jean jacket rather than a suit, a cross dangling from his neck, has his arm around John in the intimacy of the photo booth. Innocence characterizes the first photo. Flirtation this later photo.

I contrast the "very, very beautiful" spiritual experience John had with Brother Bellincioni with the intimacy of the pose in the photo booth. Can they coexist? Doesn't the one cancel out the other? Not in my experience. In fact, intimacy and spirituality may be siblings.

John stands next to helmet-coifed Grandma Abbott in another photo I can't quite place, stylish in his early 1970s fat tie and white-bib shirt. He is holding what I take to be a set of Mormon scriptures. Is this the Denver airport? Has he stopped to see Grandma on his way back from Italy the second time? I so eagerly settled into college after returning from Germany that it's hard to imagine why John wanted to go back. In fact, I have semiannual nightmares in which I am required to go on another mission despite fervent protestations that I have already done my duty. At least I'll speak good Bulgarian after two years, I console myself in a typical dream.

21 AUGUST 1991, AMERICAN FORK

23 AUGUST 1991, OREM

One of the medical forms from the clinic said that John denies homosexual activity. Who asked him the question? How would the doctor have reacted if John had asked him in return: How many times did you fuck your wife last week?

Was his lie an act of aggression directed at the health workers who might have used the information to protect themselves? Was there still enough Mormon puritanism in him that he felt guilty when confronted with what had infected him? Or was he simply what Nietzsche's Zarathustra called an "awful counterfeiter, you have no choice! You would use cosmetics on your illness when showing yourself naked to your doctor"?

A brilliant orange sunset across the western horizon. Slowly, it flames pink. A lawnmower goes silent. The light fades. I throw Honey's dumbbell again and again, and she brings it back to me, her tail wagging.

25 SEPTEMBER 1991, OREM

A colleague at Vanderbilt ate countless carrot sticks while he worked on his translation of Dostoyevsky's letters. He was gay and sexually active, and the news of AIDS terrified him. He welcomed a new report that touted raw vegetables, especially carrots, as anticancer agents. Maybe what was good for cancer was good for AIDS.

The irony of the condom among John's things. How soon did he start using them? When I visited him in Houston during that watershed year for AIDS, prophylactics were primarily for heterosexuals. Without a sense for the dangers, John was defenseless.

Defenseless? The abstinence the church teaches would have protected him.

And it would have left him indescribably lonely.

I recall bad decisions of my own that didn't lead to complications only because of dumb luck. We lean on accepted wisdom, trust to instinct, and hope for a little good fortune.

22 SEPTEMBER 1991, OREM

I frame the cardboard we found in John's Boise apartment and back the holes with Miroslav Mandić's drawings of feathery, grassy, and pebbly feet, traces of his poetic pilgrimage from Yugoslavia to Hölderlin's grave in Tübingen.

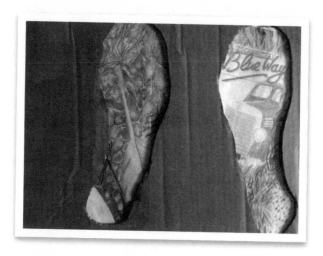

26 SEPTEMBER 1991, OREM

The *New York Times* this morning: "To date, 120,000 people are estimated to have died of AIDS and about 1,000,000 people are infected. In the next three years, another 230,000 people will die and 200,000 to 600,000 new infections will occur."

17 OCTOBER 1991, OREM

What's that? Samuel asked yesterday, pointing up at the sharply defined half-moon in the late-afternoon sky.

The moon, I answered.

I didn't know the moon could only be a half, he said.

18 OCTOBER 1991, TEMPE, ARIZONA

I sit in a hotel room finishing my paper for a session of the Rocky Mountain Modern Language Association convention. Last night I wrote in fits and starts, flipping through TV channels and then turning back to the table where books by Žarko Radaković, Peter Handke, and Julia Kristeva lay next to my notebook. The final playoff game between the Braves and Pirates came on, and with that as background I was finally able to concentrate. By the end of the game I had a lecture on living as a foreigner, every sentence colored by thoughts of John's decision to leave his family and religious tradition for another life. A couple of excerpts:

> Near the end of July I received a postcard from my friend Žarko Radaković: Lieber Scott, aus der Welt, die es vielleicht nicht mehr gibt. Dein Freund, Žarko (Dear Scott, from the world that perhaps no longer exists, your friend, Žarko).
>
> He was referring, of course, to Yugoslavia's civil war. But the postmark was Cologne. Just two months earlier I had visited him there. One night we saw Amos Poe's 1977 film *The Foreigner*. A German comes to New York for some indeterminate business. He is attacked in front of the United Nations building, then shot in Battery Park with the Statue of Liberty looming in the background.
>
> Julia Kristeva argues in *Strangers to Ourselves* that natives will fear the foreigner as an anarchist. The foreigner has left the origin or "arche" behind and is apt to disturb the ruling social order. In its root sense, the German word for misery, *Elend* (*eli-lenti*), means "out, away from one's country."

23 OCTOBER 1991, OREM

I find notes I wrote on a legal pad the summer of 1973. I was home from college, working for a drilling company in and out of southern Colorado. John, who had been back from his mission for about a year, had left home to live across town. (I never went to his apartment. Why the hell didn't I ever go to his apartment?)

> Tonight we celebrated Mom and Dad's 25th wedding anniversary with a family dinner. After dinner we listened while they

reminisced about the early years of their marriage, and then we looked at slides of the family. Although it was a pleasant evening, the thought of John (why wasn't he with us?) kept creeping in. No one spoke of him.

John's friend Calvin called twice last night and finally rode his bike the fifteen miles from Aztec to Farmington. He showed up just as we were getting ready for bed. I talked with him for a minute and left him with Jill in front of the TV. I rescued Jill a little later, leaving Calvin with Dad, who finally shooed him out the door. On the way home Marvin was hit and killed by a car.

Why doesn't someone help the Johns and Calvin of the world? Mom sobbed.

Christy took this blurred photo of John and Calvin in our backyard. Jeff looks on in his BYU shirt. The embrace feels indescribably daring, absolutely transgressive. Our backyard!

2 DECEMBER 1991, PROVO, UTAH

Eight in the morning. A fine corn snow falling outside. My office dark except for the half-light coming through the window.

Yesterday in church, after Brother D. bore testimony to the abundant blessings and perfections of his life, I surprised myself by standing and speaking about the question my brother Paul asked the night before while he helped me put up drywall in the basement: Why wasn't John successful? The question makes sense in the secure and satisfied world Brother D. described. John had few possessions, a distant family, and an uncertain career. But he made savory soups and tasty sauces. He enjoyed the warmth of spring sunshine. He made people laugh. He had lovers. He wrote in his notebook: "I try to be myself / as well as."

You call him "Brother D." Does that still mean anything to you?

Less and less as I realize there is no place in the church for my gay brother. But some ideas and feelings linger, charity, for instance, love, and yes, brother and sister.

18 DECEMBER 1991, OREM

Dream: I was trying to get into an apartment, but the front door was locked. I swung myself up through a window, then up through another one. I found an aged woman lying on the floor. She seemed immobile, but alert. She was wearing a turban. While we talked I looked out her window. Policemen with rifles were chasing a man who didn't seem overly concerned. The police were not going to shoot, nor would they use force of any kind. I entered the scene and raced after the fugitive. I tackled him and held him down until the police could arrive. It was John.

31 DECEMBER 1991, OREM

Mom's birthday today. I take her out for lunch, after which she helps me look through some of the belongings John stored with her. I find a handwritten page of notes, an application, perhaps, for a scholarship.

> I was born in Greeley Colorado on June 3, 1951. My family moved to Montpelier Idaho in 1955. In 1959 we moved again to Farmington New Mexico where we are presently living.
>
> At the age of 8 I began piano lessons which I continued for 7½ years. I have had a paper route for 5 years of my life and am now engaged in distributing papers to stores, paper boys, etc. one morning a week.
>
> I have held offices in church groups. They were Senior Patrol Leader in a church sponsored Boy Scout Troop, vice-President of an Explorer Ship (I hold this office at this time), and have twice been President of Quorums in our church (I hold this office now also). I have participated in all church activities such as softball, basketball, volleyball, etc.
>
> At school I have been a member of the band, am now a member of the National Junior Honor Society. I am a member

of the tennis team, Latin Club, and am serving on the Student Council.

I have gained many honors. Some of these are: I am an Eagle Scout, I have won first place in an Industrial Art Fair, I have entered Science fairs and have won two top awards in the County Fair and an honorable mention and a second place in the Regional Fairs.

These are my main extra-curricular activities since I have lived in Farmington.

Like John, I was born in Greeley, but in 1949. I would have substituted German Club for Latin Club. And I'd give my eyeteeth to compare résumés written under the rubric: Things We Would Never Tell Our Parents.

I just read an article about Amasa Lyman, a seventy-two-year-old church leader who was excommunicated after two fellow apostles and a policeman caught him in bed with his seventy-year-old mistress. Ten years later he was rebaptized, eligible now because at the age of eighty-two he was impotent.

I've also been reading sections of John Cheever's journals published in the *New Yorker*. Perhaps like the Mormon apostle, Cheever longed for (longed for—all this deep, clichéd emotion!)—perhaps Cheever longed for love in his emotionally sterile marriage:

> Are we, lying in our separate beds and our separate rooms, only two of millions or billions who wake a little before dawn each morning thinking hopefully that surely there is some man or woman who would be happy to lie at our sides? Happy for cheerful kissing, fucking, jokes, the day to come? I suppose we outnumber the felicitous by millions, and I must say that had I been given a loving and uncomplicated woman I might very well have run.

Like Cheever, I number among the infelicitous. My new sentences, engendered by the sight of my brother's violated body, where will they take me? I know where one part of me wants to end this story: comfortably close to the end of my previous stories. I can bend my narrative to that end. I am the author; I have the authority. But what if I allow my sentences their own will?

Are you saying you've got homosexual inclinations you will now explore?

No. I've always been drawn to women, excited by women—a thrill I don't feel around men. I'm disappointed, however, that my upbringing has infected me with disgust at the thought of homosexuals. I'm no longer willing to accept that.

[John's Yellow Notebook #1]

Mormons' hierarchy not knowing when lied. Stake President, General Authority more impressed with number of baptisms, President Harold B. Lee, ecc

Friends: ??? Who's fault? Mine!!! You've got to be a friend to have a friend. Either too much of a friend or not enough. Meeting people, making friends when drunk or loaded but diminishes when they see me time after time the same way.

Life, an enigma
Many are lost.
Yet existing
is paramount.
Why?
Day after day
Life continues.
few smiles,
Less content.
Why?

Oct. 10, 1988 – goal*: Afford to, and go, visit Carol before 6 months are up, or preferably before the end of the year. Jay
*At least it's a goal!!! and one I could make come true!!!

Seeing Dad, his Aura, kinetic energy, whatever in Houston – early 20's – standing in door. Loaded, but seeing what had to be him
Write script for comedian showelbow grease

You can gain experience, if you are careful to avoid empty redundancy. Do not fall into the error of the artisan who boasts of twenty years experience in his craft while in fact he has had only one year of experience — twenty times. Shibumi, Trevanian

    1. Hero: Thorn Garner Age: 38
        A) Incarnation
            1. Babylon
            2. Christ/Leper
            3. Midevil   Century City LA
    B) Appearance
            1. Age: 38
            2. Good health — body of 25 year old
            3. Successful — Junior partner law firm
            4. Married
                A) Wife works, age 30
                B) heiress
                C) house wife
                D) paints
                E) Kerri

This Saturday, like every Saturday morning Thorn Garner indulged in his second love. Since childhood, his obsession with fine expensive cars helped

    1-800-453-1500

A modest proposal, Jonathan Swift

1. stretch	1st rep	2nd rep	3rd rep	4th rep	5th rep
2. sit ups	4	4	4	4	4
3. push ups	4	4	4	4	4
4. stretch					

Physicians Mutual Health Ins.

24 Sept.

about owning own restaurant no reason to own Renaissance take 3 or 4 days to reflect on future think about financial opportunities think about wisdom of John Clark ideas dreams / dreams ambitions of youth

4

Variations on Desire

There is never a single approach to something
remembered. The remembered is not like the terminus
at the end of a line. Numerous approaches or stimuli
converge upon it and lead to it. Words, comparisons,
signs need to create a context for a printed photograph
in a comparable way; that is to say, they must mark and
leave open diverse approaches.

—JOHN BERGER

I cannot even attempt to reconstruct his life. Every
biography is as futile at laying claim to truth as is an
autobiography. One witness is not enough, and the
statements of two witnesses are never identical.

—DAVID ALBAHARI

2 JANUARY 1992, OREM, UTAH

His feet are livid, I wrote. Uneven teeth. My teeth.

13 JANUARY 1992, OREM

Because John was gay, am I at more risk than men without gay
brothers?

At risk?

I've been reading about human sexuality, theories about why some
of us are homosexual, some heterosexual. Sexuality seems to be a place
on a continuum—the irreducibly heterosexual cluster at one pole, the

absolutely homosexual at the other. Between those secure places, most of us are predisposed to more ambiguous positions.

Last night I told my children about characters in Ann Tyler's novel *Saint Maybe*, about responsibility for children, about sex. When I said the word sex, ten-year-old Nathan jumped. What's wrong? I asked. It's gross, two people naked together. People in the novel have a baby they don't want, I said. What should they do? They could sell it, four-year-old Samuel suggested.

15 JANUARY 1992, OREM

"Seeing Dad, his Aura, kinetic energy, whatever ... standing in the door. Loaded, but seeing what had to be him." Loaded or not, the experience John recorded in his yellow notebook must have been powerful. Did he feel loved? Judged?

Christy heard Dad's voice in the hospital minutes after he died. Jeff spoke with Dad while praying. Jill had a very real dream in which Dad taught her a lesson in forgiveness.

Dream: I open Dad's coffin. No longer held prone by the long, low box, his partially mummified body begins to curl up. I straddle it and fight to restore its horizontal order. When I push on one part of the body, another part curls up.

In his notebook John contemplates writing a comedy routine that would include Dad's trademark "elbow grease." I imagine a routine built on another of Dad's nuggets of wisdom: "Have an open mind for new things, but not so open that your brain falls out."

17 JANUARY 1992, HOBBLECREEK CANYON, CENTRAL UTAH

High on a ridge overlooking thousands of acres of snow-packed backcountry, still gasping for oxygen after our climb, I tell a friend and colleague about the fraternal tangles I'm trying to unravel. He replies with a description of his older brother:

> Allen went to BYU to study math and then struck out on his own, working obsessively to square the circle. After a breakdown, our parents committed him to an institution in Sheridan, Wyoming.

I hitchhiked from Nebraska to Sheridan to visit him. He pointed to birds out the window and said they were angels who talked to him. Whenever two burly attendants appeared and said in sweet voices that they wanted to take him for a walk, he knew he was in trouble. One day he broke away and ran down the hall to the treatment room. Before they caught up to him he had shattered the shock-therapy machine.

You seem fascinated by people with mental illness. Are you implying that John was troubled in that way?

If I were, that would reveal more about me than about John. I'm feeling a connection of a different sort, I think. My friend is concerned for his brother because of his marked difference. My thoughts slip from there to my own brother and his experiences in a predominantly heterosexual and largely homophobic world.

John Nash had the respect and resources of Princeton University to support him while he battled his demons. So did I when my father died during my first year of graduate school. I flew quickly to Denver and then to Farmington and then back to Princeton, the ticket and my expenses paid for by the dean of the graduate school and by generous members of the Princeton Ward. What did John fall back on when he was too sick to work or when he was between jobs? He had no insurance, no institutional connections, no church support. His family was distant.

One could argue that John's choices put him in that situation.

Isn't our free agency constrained by many factors? Why can't we construct a world in which the choice to work full-time in a café doesn't preclude a living wage with health insurance?

1 FEBRUARY 1992, OREM
I dial a number from John's notebook: 1-800-453-1500.
Hello. This is Victoria. How may I help you?

I'm not sure.

What product are you calling about?

What sorts of products do you have?

We have thousands of them.

Who have I reached?

We are a telemarketing agency.

Can't you tell me more about what you do?

Not really, not if you don't know what you want.

Dream: I was working feverishly on a puzzle, matching one set of colored squares with another. I left for a minute. When I returned, I found that John had rearranged them. I beat him up.

2 FEBRUARY 1992, OREM

At church we sing "Let Us All Press On," a boisterous favorite. Today the military metaphors sound threatening, the divisions between us and them ("though the wicked revile") immense. After the hymn, a balding man prays for the Lord to lead and guide us, protect and defend us, bless and sanctify us, give us knowledge and assurance.

I fashion my own prayer: Many of us gathered here, Lord, are sure of ourselves, secure in the knowledge that this is Thy Church and that we are Thy People. Some of us, however, are not so sure. We pray today, Lord, for the sure and unsure.

The closing hymn is a vigorous evocation of shared duty:

> Put your shoulder to the wheel, push along,
> Do your duty with a heart full of song,
> We all have work, let no one shirk,
> Put your shoulder to the wheel.

In *Howl, and Other Poems,* a book that isn't quoted much in church, Allen Ginsberg offers (threatens) to do his duty: "America I'm putting my queer shoulder to the wheel."

I think that the homosexual scene in American life, and particularly in the Mormon Church, is so poignant. Families drive out one of their own for a slight difference in orientation and style. In so many ways we honor the differences in our children, but not in this way. I am sensitive to this because of my left-handedness, which I think is very much like homosexuality—just a slight difference in wiring that puts me in another world. Although we still have the word "sinister," at least they don't stone lefties anymore.

3 FEBRUARY 1992, OREM

Church leaders suggest many ways to keep from thinking about sex, hetero or homo, methods to restrict and rechannel desires. The visiting authority who spoke in church yesterday recounted a fantasy he uses when "bad thoughts" enter his mind: he parachutes onto a mountain peak and skis down through powder snow. Or, he said, I hum a church hymn.

Virtuous experts at redirecting thoughts, these same church leaders are supposed to be "prophets, seers, and revelators." According to John's notebook, he deceived them in interviews as a missionary. Alex tells a story of religious disillusionment John might have understood:

> The priest told us that if we touched the container holding a holy relic we would be struck dead. One day when the priest was in the next room I couldn't help myself and sneaked over to the container. I hesitated, calculated the risk, then reached out a shaking finger. It felt cool. I jerked around and raced blindly down the aisle, through village streets, out to an orchard. Breathless, terrified, curious, I leaned weakly against a tree and waited for God to strike me dead. Nothing happened. I never went back to the altar.

4 FEBRUARY 1992, SALT LAKE CITY

Alex and I drive to Salt Lake to see *Naked Lunch*, David Cronenberg's film of William Burroughs's novel.

The brown-suited exterminator eats his own bug powder so he can think like Kafka. Trussed-up authors, their heads dimpled by multiple penises, provide seminal fluids for thirsty readers. The married man kills his wife for inspiration. The straight man samples homosexuality to enhance his writing. The American writer enters the Interzone in search of material. The relatively sane but boring man becomes an insane and gifted writer. In short: drug addiction, violence, and sexual obsession are the impetus and the stuff of art.

John had no cinematic brown wool suit. Nor do I.

7 FEBRUARY 1992, OREM

On a September 1987 application for employment, John wrote: "I am a qualified cook, in all fields, with 16 years of experience. Previous Employment: Sept 85–Sept 87, The Renaissance Restaurant, Night Cook, $1,100/mth; Feb. 82–July 85, Van Winkle House, Santee, California, Day and Night Cook, $1,200/mth. Educational History: BYU and New Mexico State, not graduated, Pre-Dentistry."

I too wanted to be a dentist. Where did we get that idea?

13 FEBRUARY 1992, OREM

Did John grow up with the same childish misunderstanding I had of our mother's word bee-em, unaware that it was an abbreviation for bowel movement? We heard the word long before we could spell.

In his French Alpine village, John Berger refuses to abstract: "A week ago I cleared out and buried the year's shit. The shit of my family and of friends who visit us." On the same topic, Milan Kundera argues that "kitsch is the absolute denial of shit."

Steven Epperson, graduated from Temple University and now a curator for the Church Museum of Art and History, is working on an exhibit of documents related to the Salt Lake Temple. He and his colleagues want to display the blueprints used to construct the sacred building. Church authorities have granted permission only on the condition that all toilets and plumbing be whited out.

*Why don't you just line all of us up, all the mothers, all the church
leaders, and shoot us? Don't you have any positive feelings for your
religion, for the culture that informs even your sentence structure?*

**I hope my text is more dialectical than you think. If it isn't, then I
haven't done justice to the influences, both positive and negative,
that have shaped my identity, that continue to make me who I am.**

The tragic-heroic trajectory for this story would be (1) obedient
child raised by religious parents, (2) mission, (3) education (BYU), (4)
marriage (temple), (5) family (in the LDS mold), (6) growing doubts,
(7) shock at the death of an errant brother, (8) brilliant recognition
that the religion is deeply flawed and harmful to its adherents, (9)
courageous breakaway. That simply won't do. Even Ed Abbey does
better than that: "Mormonism: nothing so hilarious could possibly
be true. Or all bad."

14 FEBRUARY 1992, PROVO, UTAH

After lunch I often lay down on my office floor to take a nap and
use a pile of books for a pillow. I daydream about an effortless transfer
between book and brain and sometimes choose the top book with this
in mind. Just in case. Today the book is John Ashbery's *Flow Chart*,
and as I fall asleep I think about what he calls today's "unprincipled
mire" in which even "white slavery" can be condoned, "but /
then again / nobody is forcing you to save yourself either." I have grown
up in a principled mire, warned insistently of perils to my soul, saved
at every turn.

With my head at floor level, I see the husk of a dead fly. A metal
screw on the carpet portends the fate of a second screw dangling
from the desk bottom, drawn by gravity but obedient still to the
press of metal.

Apprehending lines of poetry while asleep would be like sleeping
through sex.

2 MARCH 1992, SALT LAKE CITY AIRPORT

I have a semester's research leave to work on a book I'll call "On Standing," subtitled, I tell friends, "Human Erections through the Ages." Freud wrote that "civilization begins (fatefully) with the adoption of an erect posture." I'm hoping to tease out some of the implications.

In prehistoric times humans erected enormous stone structures that still stand thousands of years later. Some of them seem to mark the point in time and space when the sun stands still—the sol-stice. Others mark burial sites at which the standing stone staves off the forgetting that follows death. John's headstone squats rather than stands; it stands for him nonetheless. In May I'll travel to Great Britain to study standing stones. Today I'm leaving for Vienna to examine Bruegel's paintings in the Kunsthistorisches Museum, most specifically his *Peasant Wedding*. I'll discuss it as a document of religious and political revolution—the phallic bagpipes and knives of the standing musicians as opposed to the passively seated lord of the manor and the priest hunched beside him.

The airport buzzes with dark-suited Mormon missionaries ready to "preach the Gospel unto the ends of the earth." Identical plastic badges proclaim their new identities as representatives of the Church of Jesus Christ of Latter-day Saints. I boarded this plane to New York in 1968. John boarded it a year and a half later. We too had new identities, although mercifully the plastic name tags came with later generations.

Across the aisle from me a young woman grins up at the man next to her. Her lips are moist, her teeth strong and untamed by orthodontic science. Her hair shines in the morning sunlight. A voice behind me says, "The dog has got new medicine, so it won't be leaking all over." The two missionaries sitting next to me have Soeur stamped in front of their names. The woman with the no-longer-leaking dog leans over the seat and asks where they are going. To France. Too bad, a male voice says. A little farther east, and you could be in Romania.

The non sequitur irritates me while the plane takes off. When the engine noise abates, the couple behind us tell the sisters that they have just returned from an eighteen-month mission to Poland. Only forty-eight hours at home! And now, because church leaders are facing a crisis, they are headed to Romania. Her hair is dyed two complementary colors. She wears red designer glasses and bright lipstick. Her husband is bald, gray, and stout. He will run the mission. She will be his lovely wife.

I turn to Bruce Chatwin's *The Songlines*—a European among Australian aborigines. The sister next to me asks where I'm going. To Vienna, I answer, and turn back to my book. She volunteers that she is going to France. Staring at the book, I wonder why I don't want to talk with her. How good are the instincts I have always trusted? Have the years ripened my soul or soured it? My fingers smell of the lime wedge I have squeezed into mineral water.

On Sunday I taught a class of ten-year-old girls and boys. The stories in the official church manual were about dissenters from apostate churches: Wycliff, Huss, Luther, the Puritans, Anne Hutchinson—all persecuted by established churches. The children were shocked by the idea of coercion in the name of Jesus.

Bruce Chatwin writes about his most treasured possession as a child, a conch shell: "I would ram my face against her sheeny pink vulva and listen to the sound of the surf."

Waiting for a plane at Kennedy Airport, I watch a young woman with legs. She enters a Bloomingdale's outlet. She moves from sequined T-shirts to sunshades to purses. She shakes a bikini bottom out of a little plastic sack and measures it against her hips. I catch my breath. I am hungry for the brush of skin against skin. For hungry eyes that look into mine. For the smell of more than lime on my fingers.

You realize that some readers will take offense at this and other revelations of your desire. They will, in fact, see this as the root cause of your increasing disaffection.

Yes, I am intensely aware of that predictive link between affection and disaffection. It has inhibited me throughout my life. As a result, I have been quick to confess transgressions that may not have been transgressions. This text, however, is a confession of a different sort. I can hardly write about John's desires, about the pleasures and consequences of his choices and needs, without revealing and exploring my own desires, my longing for the rich tangles of interaction between loving human beings.

A monk died and went to heaven. Saint Peter welcomed him with open arms: You have been a faithful servant; let me reward you. The monk's fondest wish was to see original manuscripts. At the end of the day he emerged from the library crestfallen. What's wrong? asked Saint Peter. Some son-of-an-ascetic-bitch miscopied it! the monk replied. The original doesn't say "celibate"; it says "celebrate."

3 MARCH 1992, VIENNA

A poster on a kiosk announces performances and literary readings on the subject of being a foreigner: (N)irgendwo zu Hause (At home somewhere and nowhere). I've already missed the Wolf Biermann concert, but tonight in the Messepalast there's a reading by Irene Dische.

I arrive to find an aggressively intellectual crowd, cigarettes the indispensable accessory, Memphis the brand of choice. We sit on backless risers. Hallo mein Schatz, says one young woman to another. A bank of TV cameras stands ready.

Pianist Anatol Ugorski appears. Thick hair over his ears. Slightly bald. He has to wait while the soundmen try to hook things up. May I begin? he asks impatiently. He plays Beethoven's "33 Variations on a Waltz by Diabelli"—Dische's inspiration for what she will read. His fingers are spiders on the gleaming keyboard. Hyperbolic shadows of his jointed arms dance on the white wall to his left. The variations build and fall. Twenty minutes of music. Then ten more. The crowd grows restless. Another variation. Then another. And another. A slight woman with shaved head and red boots gets up and leaves. Loudly. A tall woman in black rises and stilts her way down the risers. She pauses in front to look at her watch. Mine reads 21:25.

A film of sweat burns on Ugorski's high forehead.

Four men leave together, tiptoeing down the squeaky risers. Another variation. The woman next to me begins to snicker. She guffaws each time Ugorski begins a new variation. She unwraps a stick of gum, crinkles the paper noisily, sends a sharp mint scent through the room. The measured tones of one variation give way to the cascading notes of the next. People leave now in a constant stream. The tall woman wanders back in, cuts through the spotlight, climbs the risers, reaches over a woman to retrieve her purse, and makes a second exit.

It's 21:42. The pianist rises. Someone applauds. Then others. Bravo, bravo, shouts a male voice. We do our best to make up for our absent compatriots. Ugorski bows. He mops his forehead with a handkerchief and stalks short-legged from the room.

Rising from her seat in the front row, a woman approaches the table. She puts down a folder and arranges herself in the chair. She wears a blue jacket. Her black shirt is tucked into black jeans. Leaning toward the microphone, she says, in German: I can't read with those lights. You must do something about those lights. She waits until they dim. I'm going to ask a lot of you, she announces. I'm going to read in English, and I'll read for a long time. One piece for each variation.

Hasso Something Something von Wallerwallerstein is the protagonist. His tiny chin is threatened by plump folds. His nose describes a huge arc. He wears a silk shirt under a silk jacket.

A fine gold chain caresses Dische's neck. Her hair curls around the sharp features of her face. The low, liquid vibrations of her voice arouse me. I will write her into my own story. Dische's story—our story—where will it lead us?

Ten minutes and three variations into the narrative, she quits reading. This isn't working, is it? she says. I can't read thirty-three of these. Shall I read something else, something in German? No one answers. Belatedly, breathlessly, I say *Ja, bitte.* My neighbors turn their heads.

Dische reads a funny little story about a can of deodorant. There is thin applause when she finishes. She shrugs and backs away from the table. She signs a few books, then flees to an interview room. She answers questions for a TV camera. Her German is beautiful.

She will look up and see me standing here, I think. I speak the same two languages she does. We are writers. I will tell her about my own set of variations on a fraternal theme, and she will ask me to join her and the pianist for dinner. Or perhaps the pianist has other plans. I remember how her long fingers held her manuscript, the warm sound of air moving precisely yet laxly through her mouth, the brilliance of her metaphors.

She finishes her interview. She walks toward me. Excuse me, she says, and looks past me with tired eyes. The pianist and the writer leave the building.

I chant a line of Alex's poetry: "I read in her eyes the obituary of my desire. I read in her eyes...I read..."

This is an old story. I know the next lines by heart. I'll describe the whole thing in a wry narrative. I'll begin with the sentence: Her uncertain smile sent me, alone, back to my room. Or better: Her smile sent me, uncertain, back to my lonely room.

I walk past dark-haired street sweepers in reflective orange jackets. I sit on my double bed and fill pages of my notebook. From the courtyard below my open window I hear the percussion of light rain. "The percussion of light rain." I look out at a clear sky and a single dull star.

4 MARCH 1992, VIENNA

Dream: A tour through the chaotic rooms of a huge house. I'm with a woman in search of a place to make love. Every room is taken, many by children.

Another dream: A poster announces a lecture: Muhammad Adjani Describes His Favorite Wives by Means of the Following Theorem:

$$L = MS(SX\sqrt{43}) \, .$$

5 APRIL 1992, HIGHWAY 6, CENTRAL UTAH

We're on the way home from Goblin Valley, a wild place dotted with wind- and rain-carved Entrada sandstone hoodoos balanced on softer, crumbling pedestals. I didn't sleep well. Stars burned apocalyptically in the moonless night. Orion slipped beyond the horizon. The Big Dipper rotated across the sky. Always constant. Always changing. Night wind sifted soft red sand into my sleeping bag. By morning

I was a small dune. Beside me, not stirring yet, our seven children formed an uneven row of smaller dunes. My wife a dune at the far end.

22 APRIL 1992, 8:00 A.M., PROVO

Robert Hass, who will speak here today, writes that

> two beings...
> connected at the belly in an unbelievably sweet
> lubricious glue, stare at each other,
> and the angels are desolate. They hate it.

I've been reading in my office for nearly two hours, dozing off and on. I dream I am in an auditorium with my wife. She gets up and goes out. A woman waves to me from a seat across the way. She comes to sit next to me. We talk. She puts her hand on my leg. She shifts the hand closer to my crotch. I suggest we go somewhere more private.

I wake up and think about my desire, open like a sweet wound, responsive to any touch. I'm no angel.

23 MAY 1992, LONDON

I've been looking at standing stones from Land's End to the Orkney Islands. I visited, for instance, the Welsh burial site Leslie Norris describes in "The Twelve Stones of Pentre Ifan":

> Points of adjusted rock, taller
> Than any
> Man who will ever
> Stand where I stand, lifting their hope.

And now, after two solitary weeks among ancient stones standing like Leslie's stanzas, lifting up their adjusted hope for immortality, I'm in London for a couple of days. I make a beeline for the National Gallery.

Crowded rooms, long lines, famous paintings. I stand for a long time before Rembrandt's *The Anatomy Lesson of Dr. Deyman.* A former thief lies on his back, his feet toward the viewer, his body foreshortened, a cavity opened just below his chest, his head forced forward. Skin and hair are peeled back to expose his brain, a piece of which the good doctor is drawing out with a pair of forceps. The coroner in Boise cut John open from stem to stern. His hands registered the vibrations of a scalpel pulled through resisting flesh. He knew John's body more intimately than any lover, and those lovers, those sweet and deadly lovers, knew him more intimately than did his brother.

Neither lover nor coroner, I continue to write, to measure and probe with the instruments I have at hand.

26 MAY 1992, LONDON

Sitting in a small park just off the Thames. A cool breeze teases the hair of a man and a woman and a five- or six-year-old boy. He plays with a plastic bat. His parents (I suppose at least one is his parent) sit together on a park bench. The man wears red Converse tennis shoes, faded blue denim pants, no shirt, and an open jean jacket with the head of an Indian chief embroidered on the back. The woman wears sandals, black denim pants, and a white shirt. They can't keep their hands off one another.

I don't remember my own parents embracing. Our children will have gaping holes in their experience as well.

He caresses her neck. Her hand moves on his thigh. The boy wanders over. He stands in front of them. He waves his bat and jumps up and down.

5:30 P.M., TRAFALGAR SQUARE

I've been reading Derek Jarman's *Modern Nature*, a journal written in 1989 and 1990 after the filmmaker discovered he was HIV positive. The passage in which Jarman describes boarding-school officials catching him in bed with a boy named Johnny echoes my anger during John's funeral: "'Christ! What are you doing?' 'You'll go blind!' Then the blows rained down, millennia of frustrated Christian hatred behind the cane.... We were shoved into the wilderness they had created, and commanded to punish ourselves for all time. So that at last we would be able to enter their heaven truly dead in spirit."

Angels in America, a new play by Tony Kushner, an American writer I've not heard of. Under the heading "Real-Life Characters in the Play," the program features pictures of Roy Cohn and Ethel Rosenberg. I turn the page and stare at a portrait of Joseph Smith. The program quotes Kushner: "I wanted to write about three things: Roy Cohn, who had just died; AIDS; and Mormons. I had no idea what Mormons might have to do with Roy Cohn or AIDS, but I wanted to find out." The play's primary angel is described as the angel Joseph Smith incorrectly identified as Moroni.

What have I stumbled into?

During the intermission I stand among women and men with whom I have just shared the brutality and humor of the first act. The play is about Louis, a gay Jew, and his drag-queen lover who is dying of AIDS. Joe, an ambitious Mormon lawyer who protests when Cohn takes the Lord's name in vain and whose neglected wife compensates with Valium, fights to kill his homosexual urges. Joe's wife tells the drag queen that "my church doesn't believe in homosexuals." "My church doesn't believe in Mormons," the drag queen replies. Louis explains the Jewish view of the next life to his dying lover.

Did John have any chance or inclination for such conversation?

End of act 2. The Mormon admits he is queer. The philosophic Jew leaves his dying lover. Roy Cohn has AIDS, is about to be disbarred, and needs the Mormon to cover for him in the Reagan Justice Department. There is violence. Self-destruction. Blood dripping from the dying man's ass. Betrayal. Self-loathing. Beauty.

Act 3. One of the characters speaks of "the monolith of White America. White Straight Male America. Which is not unimpressive, even among monoliths." Joe makes several moral choices: he tells Roy Cohn he can't be dishonest, he won't take the Washington job, and he decides to spend the night with Louis and go to Mormon hell.

I'm brimming with compassion, burning with ideas as I come out (I'd better say—as I leave the theater). I wish I could have seen the play with John. Did he even like plays?

27 MAY 1992

I've flown over Greenland before, but today, for the first time, it reveals itself through scattered clouds. Sheer, sharp mountains thrust like shards of black glass through the frozen flesh of ancient snow, snow unmarked, untracked, unbroken except where sheer verticality ruptures the pristine blanket. Lascivious liquid tongues lick between peaks and snowfields, mountains of ice random in the dark water.

Flight is always precarious. Today the airplane feels precarious above the threatening mountains of Greenland. Yet the natural forces down there, terrible as they are, are extraordinarily beautiful from this perspective. Kant's sublime.

I wake up as the plane eases over the Wasatch Mountains. Foothills glow in the setting sun like the tawny hide of a deer in perfect health. The familiar mountains are crumpled together in north-south convolutions. Like brain tissue, not like glass shards. Tawny, not black-and-white.

No snow left on the mountains. That's an ominous sign in the high desert.

3 JUNE 1992, OREM

John's birthday. He would have been forty-one.

A couple of years ago I sent John an essay by Wayne Schow, an LDS father responding to his son's homosexuality and to the tragedy that ensued. Schow delineates the LDS Church's stand on homosexuality:

> 1) The practice of homosexuality is held to be unnatural because it is biologically unfruitful; 2) only within heterosexual marriage may sexual desires be expressed with full intimacy; 3) homosexual inclination, therefore, must be suppressed, either through celibacy or through reorientation of sexual feelings within heterosexual marriage; 4) this suppression or reorientation is possible because homosexual inclination and practice are learned behaviors and lie within the control of righteous choice.

He goes on to present a wide range of arguments that call these assumptions into question, including recent scientific studies that suggest there are genetic predisposing factors. He reports that his son "prayed fervently over a long period that God would help him to reorient his feelings toward heterosexuality." To no avail.

Did John read the essay? He was using the manila envelope I sent it in for things listed by hand on the outside: "Life Insurance, drilling papers, P.I.N.#, Birth Certificate, I.R.S. crap, Receipts."

5 JUNE 1992, BENSON, ARIZONA

I squat on a low-slung mesquite branch in a grove of the desert-adapted trees. Late morning. Gathering heat. When I walked into this shaded place, I disturbed two neon-bright hummingbirds.

Last night Benjamin, Samuel, and I slept on top of their grand-parents' gazebo. A spectacular falling star just after sunset thrilled the boys, and later a satellite hurtling from south to north caught their fancy. Long minutes later Samuel asked, quietly: Dad, when do we get to go to sleep? Right now, I answered. I love you. He slept immediately. Gripped by less simple questions, I lay awake. The Milky Way rose from the east and flooded the sky with pale light. Cassiopeia's W wheeled up from the Northeast, and the Big Dipper finally sank in the West.

A breeze caresses the mesquite leaves. Birds call. Insects fly past. A fat quail bobs across the wash toward me, springs into the air. This morning I found two desert wrens frantic in the car, too excited, too confused by the solid transparency surrounding them to find their way back out through the open window that had given them access. I hear a call from the tree where the quail now roosts. Black-and-yellow swallowtail butterflies wobble past. Black ants are busy among the gray and tan mesquite leaves that curl in on themselves in the sand.

Dad? Nathan calls me from the house. Dad! Where are you?

6 JUNE 1992, 1:00 P.M., AMERICAN FORK, UTAH

My grandfather Clement P. Hilton was one of eight brothers who ran the Hilton Brothers' Motor Company near Delta, Utah. Today I'm at a reunion of what has become a large number of Hilton descendants. Someone hands out a packet that contains the following: "Dream

of Eugene Hilton in 1974 in which his ancestor appeared to him: It
was then that I went to the authorities in Heaven and asked them to
lengthen your life so that you could go to the St. George Temple and
submit my personal records. After some delay they approved."

A bureaucratic, time-bound heaven!

5 JULY 1992, NEHEMAS BEACH, OREGON

The children play in the sand. Maren, holding her youngest brother,
Timothy, in her arms, is a vertical line standing knee-deep in the horizontal lines of surf. The sun glows soft and red on the humid western
horizon. Maren makes her way to my side and says quietly: It's paradise.
Footprints gather darkness. The shadows stretch eastward forever.

13 JULY 1992, PROVO

John and I smile in our Sunday suits. Or we don't smile.

My brother Jeff named and blessed his and Carol's baby yesterday in
Salt Lake's Emerson Ward.
Eight men in a circle, the
baby perched on the hub
of the wheel of our right
arms. A mural on the front
wall depicts a handsome
family in a stand of aspens
overlooking a prosperous

valley. Harvested grain, vegetables, and fruit surround them. The man stands tall with one arm outstretched, his gaze on the horizon. The woman kneels at his side, her hands clasped, her eyes closed, her head bowed. The rewards of righteousness: dominion over the earth, a bounteous life, fertility, family, distinct gender roles.

After the church service, Mom and Jill and I discussed John's homosexuality.

It's evil, Mom stated flatly.

Why?

Because it's evil.

Why was John gay? Jill asked.

It happened when he went to Colorado for a week for some sort of camp, Mom explained. He was a junior in high school and roomed with someone who turned him into a homosexual.

Maybe he was born that way, I said.

God does not make us evil.

Exactly. Some people are born that way. God does not make us evil. It is not evil to be gay. Syllogism. I had her there.

Why are you so angry, Scott? Jill asked. Why can't you discuss this without being angry?

Mom described the letter from the roommate telling John how to recruit other boys into homosexuality. The trick was expensive gifts. And soon after that, he wanted to give someone an expensive gift for Christmas. She mentioned letters he had written home about a mission companion. He then had an interview with a general authority of the church, an interview that resulted in a series of lies. His mission was over at that point. He wrecked a mission car. Because another missionary agreed to be his companion, the mission president let him stay the last two months. But they didn't do any work.

There are no letters like that in the packet you gave me, I said. And in fact, the car was wrecked before John wrote several of his most spiritual letters.

Jill remembered the family reunion at which John's general truculence turned nasty: He told the little children who got close to get out of his face. He complained about how we didn't discipline our children. He wouldn't eat with us. He took his tent to the other side of the campground. He attacked me as the poorest mother he had ever seen. I went out to where he was and told him I wasn't judging him and that I resented his judging me. I was doing the best I could, and I thought I had pretty good kids. He went in and laid down on the couch. Later I was feeling bad about my outburst, so I got John a book and brought it in to him where he was still lying on the couch. I knelt down beside him and put my hand on his arm and told him I was sorry. He looked at me with a gaze that scared me to death and said that from that time on, I was dead. I had nightmares that he would drive down from Boise, head up our driveway, and kill me.

I know that look, Mom said. Soon after he moved out of our house in Farmington, I went to visit him in his apartment. He stood at the door and looked at me with a gaze that was satanic. I was seeing Satan.

27 JULY 1992, OREM

Reading the history of the word gay in the Oxford English Dictionary, my obsessed mind interprets one entry as a nineteenth-century prophecy of the AIDS epidemic: "The gay parade grew thin—all the fair crowd Vanish'd. Hoop, 1845." I turn from the dictionary and find, among John's things, intimations of death in a letter from a California friend: "Dear Jay, Well, I have some time off work. I have bronchitis and pneumonia. Not as bad as yours, thank goodness. I only have a small amount of fluid in my left lung."

30 AUGUST 1992, SALT LAKE CITY

At the Sunstone Symposium this week I presented a paper called "One Lord, One Faith, Two Universities: Tensions between Religion and Thought at BYU." The audience was responsive, I think, to thoughts like these:

> Influential talks over the last decade by Elder Boyd Packer, a member of the university's Board of Trustees and an LDS apostle, have served to denigrate reason and to undermine the work we do at the university. . . .
>
> At its worst, academia is indeed sterile, mind-numbing, and spiritually destructive. So is religion at its worst. But we don't choose to be academics or practitioners of a faith because of how bad they can be, we do so because of the power they give us to live good and productive lives. . . .
>
> The word "Mormon" can and does evoke thoughts of bigotry, exclusion, narrowness, and sectarianism. In John Gardner's 1982 novel *Mickelsson's Ghosts*, for example, Mormons are described as a "sea of drab faces, dutiful, bent-backed, hurrying obediently, meekly across an endless murky plain." In Tony Kushner's *Angels in America* a Mormon woman describes Salt Lake City as a hard place, "baked dry. Abundant energy; not much intelligence. That's a combination that can wear a body out."
>
> It doesn't have to be that way. In our recent history we have many examples of the kind of vision that would make us whole.

Hugh B. Brown's 1969 talk at BYU, for example: "Preserve, then, the freedom of your mind in education and in religion, and be unafraid to express your thoughts and to insist upon your right to examine every proposition. We are not so much concerned with whether your thoughts are orthodox or heterodox as we are that you shall have thoughts."

How did we move from Brown's robust confidence, I asked, to Packer's pinched pronouncements?

Your thoughts directly critical of this powerful man put you in an awkward position as an employee of BYU. No good will come of this.

19 SEPTEMBER 1992, SALT LAKE CITY

In Salt Lake for the John Cage memorial event at the Salt Lake Art Center, I stop at a Burger King for something to eat. Strike one, the woman tells her Chicano employee. What? he asks. Improperly made sandwich. You put the onions on the lettuce, not the lettuce on the onions. We will make sandwiches properly, or we will not make sandwiches at all. John would have told her to shove the properly made sandwich up her ass and would have been out of work again. That's precisely my own response to authority.

Nearly a full house at the art center. A man stands in front to deliver a monologue. I am an echo of a ghost of a whisper of a memory, he says. White tennis shoes, white pants gathered at the ankles, white turtleneck bulging at his butt and waist, sagging breasts. He rubs his hands. He dances awkwardly in what he calls his tenny runners. Liver spots mark his head under thinning hair. He worked in the New York Public Library and saw Cage come in every morning at exactly eleven o'clock. He bends over, snakes his hands to his crotch. We are not Homo sapiens but MAMMALS! he says. Bosom buddies with Duchamps, he says, real bosoms!

Nam June Paik's 1976 *A Tribute to John Cage* is next on the program. After the film, Alex reads his poem to the memory of Cage, a series of questions and answers that end brutally:

Q: When will we see each other again?

A: (he slaps his face hard).

25 SEPTEMBER 1992, PROVO

Late Friday afternoon. Sunlight slants through the window. I've just read a story called "Intensive Care" that describes a man who flies in to be with his younger brother dying of AIDS. The familiar guilt of being older, "successful," emotionally distant. The minutes slip by. I'm grateful for the quiet light and the scratch of my pen on the paper. The mountain will flush with color as I ride toward it on my bike.

22 OCTOBER 1992, PROVO

Moisture in a desert loosens knotted muscles. Outside my office window, even in the gray light of an overcast morning, the leaves of the locust tree glow golden against rain-blackened limbs. I can hear John's Miller Genuine Draft clock ticking off the seconds.

4 NOVEMBER 1992, OREM

Two dreams.

In the first I attend a church service, perhaps Greek, and perhaps in Salt Lake. I am very happy to be there, surrounded by long tables of cakes and pies and other delicacies.

In the second dream I decide to make some architectural changes to a church front. Someone describes for me how the round forms repeating themselves across the front have a kind of aesthetic integrity I had not noticed.

I had these dreams the week after my stake president, the man who decides each year whether I am worthy to take part in the ordinances of the temple, reprimanded me for statements in my *Sunstone* paper he found critical of "the Brethren." He demanded that I write letters of apology and publish a retraction.

I am anxious, the dreams suggest, at finding myself in conflict with the church. The second dream could be interpreted as suggesting that there is much good in the church that I am missing. The Greek dream seems to offer other, less restrictive, more productive, traditions. I suppose the dreams are most interesting in dialectical tandem.

Last night when I started home the ginkgo tree outside the building was still holding on to most of its double-lobed leaves. This morning about half of them had fallen. I stood and watched leaves fall in handfuls. Each puff of wind brought golden cascades. By noon the tree was bare. One moment the leaves are integral parts of the tree. Then, suddenly, the connection is severed.

10 NOVEMBER 1992, OREM

I've been doubting my creative abilities, questioning my future, worrying about my judgment. And this morning I received a letter from my mother calculated to raise more questions. She wasn't happy about my public critique of how "the Lord's University" is being run:

> I'm sure you know that the first step to apostasy is criticizing the leadership of the church. If they make mistakes they are answerable to the Lord, not me. More than anything else, I want you and your family to be happy. You will be if you are humble, have love in your family and don't criticize the beautiful leaders God has given us. They will do His will. These are men I sustain and love with all my heart, men who have given their entire lives in the service of our Savior. My son, what have you given that qualifies you to criticize them? Happiness and joy and peace come from obedience.

I grew up her child. My sense of self is intimately linked to her support and censure. How was John marked by her? Did her sure belief gnaw at him? Did the lethal consequences of his "immoral" life prove the goodness of her morality? The Mormon ethic, an offshoot of Weber's Protestant version, works. Daring to leave it behind, you court ruin. The risk is great. The benefits of separation are more tenuous.

I remember a story Dad used to tell, a moral tale I have told my own children:

A man comes to a town and asks a man on the street if it would be a good place to live.

What is the town like you are coming from?

It's an awful place.

This town will be awful as well.

Another man comes along and says he has just left a wonderful place.

Our town is equally fine, answers the wise native. Why don't you stay with us?

I've always taken the story to be about the benefits of a positive attitude and the consequences of a sour disposition. But maybe there was something wrong with the previous town. Maybe it was impossible for the person to survive there. And maybe the next town will be just as bad.

12 NOVEMBER 1992, OREM

Browsing in Atticus Bookstore, I find an eye-catching dust jacket: JOHN ABBOTT IS THE PSEUDONYM OF A WORLD-FAMOUS AUTHOR.

7 DECEMBER 1992, OREM

Žarko Radaković arrived Friday to lecture about his response to multiethnic Yugoslavia's split into nationalist factions. This morning we skied up Hobblecreek Canyon, breaking trail through a foot of new snow. Snow-laden branches hung over us, and thin clouds veiled and then revealed the mountains. Wearing borrowed clothing—my stocking cap, my sweater, my jacket, my gloves, my wool pants, my wool socks, my boots, holding my ski poles—Žarko looked like my doppelgänger.

Yesterday Žarko came to church with us. The ten-year-old children I teach asked him questions. What kind of work do you do? I'm a writer. Are you married? Yes. Do you have any children? Yes. What did you do yesterday? I rode in an airplane for fifteen hours. Did they give you food? Yes. Where are you from? I live in Cologne, Germany, and I'm from Yugoslavia.

Then he asked them what they wanted to be when they grew up. A dermatologist, Carlos said. Brandon said president of the United States and a scientist. Karen wants to be an anesthesiologist, a radiologist, or a hair stylist. A carpenter, Brian said. Erika corrected him: No, he wants to be the teacher's pet. The other Brian wants to be an engineer. Lydia and Erika aren't sure they know what they want to be. Maybe mothers.

I asked the children to tell stories about their ancestors.

Carlos: My grandfather was asked by leaders of the church to buy the land for BYU and donate it to the church. He's now in the BYU Hall of Fame. It's really hard to get into that.

Karen: My grandma died, and my grandpa was feeling depressed. We went to visit him to cheer him up. My cousin and I went down into the cellar. On the steps we heard something loud—whoosh!—and ran up to my grandpa. He said it was just the furnace.

Brian W.: The prophet asked my grandpa to run a ferry across the Colorado River at Lees Ferry. He went down there and ran the ferry, and they forgot him. All four children from one of his wives died of some disease. After ten years some apostles were going through, and they were surprised to find him still there. We've got to get you out of here, they said. It's too hot.

Lydia: There were a lot more women in the church than men, so my great-grandfather had to marry a second wife after my great-grandmother had already had a lot of children. Later he died and then his other wife died, and my great-grandmother had to take all eighteen children and be a pioneer and go on foot from Mexico to Utah.

Brian S.: My great-great-great-great-grandfather was Hyrum Smith, Joseph Smith's brother.

Brandon: My grandfather was in Salt Lake when they laid the cornerstone for the temple. He and a friend took a stone and laid it on the other corner.

10 DECEMBER 1992, OREM

Žarko read his essay on emigration yesterday at the Kennedy Center for International Studies, three or four German sentences at a time, after which I read my translation. His voice. My voice. It was strange to feel his "I" resonate in my own head and chest.

> Approximately fifteen years ago I left my country. Back then, in 1978, it called itself the Socialist Federal Republic of Yugoslavia. . . . I didn't have the least suspicion that in fifteen years, that is, now, my country would no longer exist. . . .

Haven't I always had something of the nomadic spirit of my ancestors in me? Haven't I shunned every uniformity and every emphasis on a center? To be Serbian and not simultaneously some second or third thing on this always complex (unintelligible) Balkan peninsula—that seems to me today an impossible thought....

15 DECEMBER 1992, MOAB, UTAH

Žarko and I have driven south. I'm anxious to show him more of the Great Basin landscape that is my home, to show him I am a Mormon in the western United States and simultaneously some second and third thing.

We're waiting for breakfast in Moab's Westerner Grill. Country music on the radio, the clatter of thick porcelain, grease popping on a grill, and animated conversations all around us:

> ...The water in my well is so full of minerals that if someone would come out and do a full analysis, they would freak out. But the human body, if it is normally healthy, just takes care of that naturally.
>
> ...a buck-naked guy...
>
> ...great to be ambidextrious.
>
> ...then they raise your taxes; all they want is more regulation.
>
> ...There better be some pretty good mathematical brains to figure all that crap out.
>
> ...It was my birthday yesterday. Happy birthday. Is that all you're going to do? Not buy me breakfast or something? I'm so poor I can't pay attention. I've been thirty the whole time you've known me. Now I'm thirty-one.
>
> ...Lookee there! My ex-mother-in-law, walkin' right down the street. He and me lived together for six months, got married, and it lasted for seven weeks. The bills came due, and he left. He said he couldn't deal with my past. Seven years ago I was in a wet-T-shirt contest, and he can't handle that? Get the hell out of my life!
>
> ...Is Valium a natural plant?

16 DECEMBER 1992, FARMINGTON, NEW MEXICO

In the night after I return to my hometown for the first time in more than a decade, I dream about the smartest girl in our school. None of the girls I found attractive make an entrance. Žarko and I have spent the night with the Moellers, dear friends since high school. I wake to strains of Mozart. It is Doug and Tyra's son practicing the piano. On my way to the bathroom I see him hunched on the piano bench, wrapped in a green blanket, his sparsely bearded face concentrated on the music. By the time I return, he is playing Van Halen.

We drive through the growing town, tour Doug's law office, and say good-bye near the now-abandoned A&W root-beer stand where John got his first lessons in short-order cooking. Tyra worked there too, she says: John was so much fun to work with!

12:00 P.M., KAYENTA, ARIZONA

I pull into a muddy field next to the post office where an open-air market is under way. We stroll among long tables spread with car parts, home-cooked food, silver-and-turquoise jewelry, woven wool blankets. An ancient woman sits on the tailgate of a pickup next to an arthritic man, before them a table piled with hand-labeled cellophane bags containing herbs for five or six dollars a bag: Injury Medicine, Mountain Smoke, Lose Weight, Toh' Kok for Words, Red Ant Medicine, Vomiting Medicine, Itching and Sore, Spider Medicine, Your Hair Fall Out, Surgery Medicine, Kidney, Arthritis Herb Medicine, Rain Lightning, Evilway Medicine, Cancer Medicine, Hair Grow Medicine.

Žarko wants to take a picture of the couple.

No, the man says.

I buy juniper beads strung into a ghost-bead necklace.

The answer is still no.

MONUMENT VALLEY, EARLY AFTERNOON

Žarko and I stand on the overlook from which John Ford directed scenes for *Cheyenne Autumn*. The Navajo man in Kayenta was afraid the camera would capture his spirit, Žarko ventures. He wasn't afraid of anything, I claim. Without the continuity of his life, the photo would have only the context we give it. He wanted none of that.

ZION NATIONAL PARK, MIDAFTERNOON

Clouds are moving in, but the high canyon walls still glow with sunlight. It's bitter cold in the shade. A woodpecker's percussion. Two ducks skim our heads and skid into the river. NARROWS' TRAIL CLOSED. NO ENTRY. We bypass the sign. Around a bend an over-hanging rock face bristles with hanging ice. The glassy crash of a massive icicle on the trail ahead sends us scurrying back to the car and on up the road to Bryce Canyon.

17 DECEMBER 1992, MANTI, UTAH

Žarko sees this part of America through the lenses of his heroes: Monument Valley as framed by John Ford, the cheap motel in Moab a staple of Wim Wenders's road movies, Hurricane and Durango names he knows from Bob Dylan's lyrics. A different hurricane, I explain, and Dylan's Durango is in Mexico. I stop the car in front of the Manti Temple, which Žarko recognizes from the Ansel Adams photo.

I was married here, I tell him. The man performing the ceremony twice asked us to quit looking at each other, to pay attention to him. A Mormon temple, I explain, is a representation of a higher reality. The star, moon, and sunstones on three levels stand for three degrees of eternal glory. Volunteer actors present a mystery play drawn in part from Masonic ritual during which the audience accepts the players as authorized stand-ins for God and Jesus and Satan. That God would speak with a Danish-tinged rural accent makes perfect sense in this building built by immigrants.

We press a Frank Zappa tape into the cassette player and feel our way north through a fierce blizzard.

19 DECEMBER 1992, OREM

I dream I am in Farmington, approaching the high school. In place of the school stands a temple. I scramble up the hill, worried that I might miss something. Inside the building all sense of tardiness vanishes. I feel comforted, timelessly sheltered.

Waiting to enter the main room, I see Žarko and Zorica. Žarko holds a bottle of wine in his hand and a long loaf of bread under his arm. I am surprised and delighted to see them in a Mormon temple. Zorica drinks deeply from the bottle and smiles at me. My last name, she says, means "son of a priest."

Inside a lofty room a performance is under way. One of the actors once insulted me, but now he reaches over and gives me a peculiar and warm handshake. Children are singing a happy song and clapping in unison. From another room I can hear a quiet, cerebral jazz improvisation on piano. Cans of paint line the base of a white wall, and I paint enormous brilliant poppies on the wall. Wearing his starched white jacket and toque, John populates another wall with mythical Eastern figures. People are engaged in animated conversations all around me. I walk among them until I find my family in the center of the room. Thomas is tired, but when I lift him to my shoulder and show him the paints, the drama, and all the happy people, his spirits lift.

20 DECEMBER 1992, SALT LAKE CITY

After the official version of Mormon history we just experienced at the Church Museum of Art and History (not a single reference to polygamy), arko and I wander around the Museum of the Daughters of the Utah Pioneers.

A photo of Porter Rockwell bears a caption that identifies him as the "feared bodyguard to Joseph Smith and Brigham Young: History states that Porter Rockwell cut his hair to make a wig for the widow of a friend. She had lost her hair after a bout with Typhoid Fever. He went into seclusion until his hair grew out. This is a rare photo."

Behind a detailed model of a two-masted ship is a photo of a bearded man with a cane. The caption reads: "Claus Johnson, Pioneer 1863. Ship carved while in State Penn, for Polygamy in 1887."

"Stuffed two-headed lamb: Born in 1919 on the J. E. Sorenson Ranch."

"'Meat'—Dried horse meat, bits that saved the lives of Carson Valley Mission while crossing the desert. It was found in lunch box of OLIVER HUNTINGTON by his wife and preserved in this tin box."

"Raspberries :: Which grew in cave where Melissa Jane was born."

"Quail Feathers taken from a Quail when Miraculous Droves Saved the Pioneers From Starvation After Leaving Nauvoo, Illinois 1846."

These are for pulling teeth, aren't they, Žarko says. I look at a pair of fierce-looking pliers in a case with shoemaking tools. For shoemaking, I tell him. But they can also be used for pulling teeth, he says with a grin.

22 DECEMBER 1992, SALT LAKE CITY

I sit in a bagel shop, sip coffee, and read an article in the *Salt Lake Tribune*: "Militant Serbian Leader Claims Big Victory in Disputed Election." This morning I dialed Žarko's mother's number in Belgrade and handed him the phone. Leaving my office so he could be alone, I heard him say "Mama." When I got back he was sitting on the floor against the wall. He said his mother thought the borders were going to be closed. And after Christmas, he said, his brother Miloje was going to bring Žarko's daughter to visit him in Cologne.

25 DECEMBER 1992, OREM

The excitement of Christmas morning. While the older children help the younger ones with their presents, we exchange wan smiles across the room, proud, at least, of the children we share.

[John's Blue Notebook]

Nietzsche—Ultimately one loves one's desire, not the desired object
   …"strategies of narratizing", his theory that human beings impose
a more or less arbitrary narrative framework upon their more or less
formless lives in order to tell their lives to themselves and others,
presenting their actions in the best possible light— usually as heroes
but sometimes, surprisingly as victims. *Lives of the Twins*, Rosamond
Smith

      insouciance
      paroxysms
   Lisa's Cinnamon Rolls
   3 qts H2O (warm)
   12 oz yeast
   18 eggs
   3# butter
   3# sugar
   4# cake flour
   12# gluten
      rise
   roll out, butter, raisin, cinnamon sugar

A man, particularly a servant, was entitled to his small recalcitrant
bolsterings of self respect.
The Skull beneath the Skin, P. D. James

   ie. schools (institutions)…were designed as much to discourage
too personal a commitment as to promote a corporate identity.
      Ibid.

(re drugs?)
"…And deep down there was the knowledge, unfrightening and
almost comforting, that he only had to let himself go, to give himself

up to the power and gentleness of the sea, and there need never
again be guilt or anxiety or failure. He knew that he wouldn't do it;
the thought was a small self-indulgence which like a drug, could be
safely experimented with as long as the doses were small and one
stayed in control. And he was in control."

learned how to cook at Hotel Utah
3 ⅓ years Van Winkles   cooked, order ecc
3 ½ years Renaissancecooked, ordered, ecc.
6 mths Village Inn

      up to Junior High School Farmington. Remember summers in
Greeley, driving back from Las Cruces. Grand Canyon trip with Scott
Rhein—trailer coming off. Getting caught stealing licorice candy by
Dad and having to go into store and pay for it. guess my mouth was
black. Stealing from paper. Comic books, ecc, cheating on tests. Too
lazy to study.

We being, not each other without love

      Life
absurdity in fullness

Beckoning, begging —-
around shadowed corners

diamonds sparkling
liquor flowing

Damn drugs! yet —-
co-existence
time fabric

Dissimulate
Disincorporate

Flow
IS

How can you be a good citizen when the basic strains of the society
run against your strongest ideas and feelings.
American Mischief, Alan Lelchuk

So when this Pop (art) came along, I thought, Jesus, this is the
stuff for me. So fucking cheerful, you know—going down but going
down with a smile.
The Witches of Eastwick, Updike

What you do is not a sin, unless you think it so. And then it is. For
who can say they do anything wrong by giving joy to another? And
is it less noble to ask money for joy than ask money for material possessions?...For the sweetness comes from the soul, which no act of
the body ever can, at the last, corrupt.
Delirium's Mistress, Tanith Lee

The body's love will teach the spirit how to love. The spasms of the
body's carnal pleasure, forgetting all things but ecstasy itself, teaches
the body to remember the ecstasy of the soul, forgetting all but itself,
the moments of oneness, and freedom. Ibid

5

Horror Vacui

> The true picture of the past flits by. The past can be
> seized only as an image which flashes up at the instant
> when it can be recognized and is never seen again.
>
> —WALTER BENJAMIN

1 JANUARY 1993, OREM, UTAH

His feet are livid, I wrote. His face is drawn; an open eye leers
upward. My own leering eye hunts images from the past and when
they flash up delivers them to my inadequate pen.

6 JANUARY 1993, OREM

Dream: I was beating up John. I was on top of him, pounding him,
blind with rage. Then pain! My testicles! John had grabbed my balls.
He controlled me. The turnabout was inconceivable.

In a second dream I searched for John in downtown Farmington. I
found him working in a small pizza place, and we talked for a minute
before he had to return to his dough. I walked through town looking
for Dad. I found him sitting at the counter of a café drinking a cup of
coffee. He looked like a derelict, his shirt torn, thin stubble scattered
across his drawn face. He was embarrassed to be seen with coffee.

7 JANUARY 1993, PROVO, UTAH

Nearly a foot of snow during the night. I'm in the cave of my office,
a single light burning, snow falling softly outside.

"A boy he picked up in his Alfa Romeo sports car ran him over with it and left him helpless in the dust.... Pasolini spent so much time in the lower depths because he found them ethically preferable to the heights." So writes Clive James in the *New Yorker*. I'm afraid I have been seeing John as the victim of a sordid accident, in some romantic way more moral than the rest of us. Ten years ago Žarko and I argued about Pasolini. In response to what he called my moralizing, Žarko maintained that an artist can't restrict himself. As soon as you refuse to experience everything, he told me, you close yourself to the sources of art. Pasolini is profoundly subversive, as is art. If you can't stomach Pasolini, you'll end up a repressed, reactionary, unfulfilled, narrow-minded, bitter, bourgeois shell of a man. I responded that his string of adjectives exemplified moralizing.

A wall always separated me from John. I have been distant from other siblings as well, from my parents, from my wife. From myself. The wall metaphor is misleading, I think. There is no wall. I am the wall. To reach my brother I must destroy myself, must risk obliteration as the self I have become. And what will rise from the rubble? It won't be a wall.

Getting a little carried away, aren't you?

It's awkward for a wall to confront its own rigid structure.

15 JANUARY 1993, OREM

Today's mottled clouds remind me of a Magritte painting. Blotches of sunlight and shadow alternate on the snowy mountainside. Yesterday afternoon, when a sudden sunbeam lit up the books on my shelves, I realized I hadn't seen the sun for days.

The current *Spiegel* magazine displays a photo of a skeleton, an archaeologist's measuring stick, some pots and tools. The caption reads: *Skelett eines Syphilitikers* (Skeleton of a syphilitic). The singular definition turns my stomach. This man or woman was certainly more than that—an artisan, perhaps, a tender lover, a cruel despot, a bumbling idiot. John Abbott: AIDS victim. It's not enough.

I take out a letter to John from Bonnie, his concerned and psychologizing friend from Santee, California. John lived and worked there for several years until some set of events, including a fire that burned part of the restaurant, sent him on his way.

Dear Jay,

People aren't letting you go so easily this time are they? Someday you might try staying put somewhere and letting people care about you. A lot of people really caring is a hell of a responsibility, but it does have its rewards.

You were the only person I could ever really relax and be me with. You made me feel good about myself. I wonder about whatever it is you keep hidden away. What you don't let anyone close enough to know? Not wanting anything is just about the best way in the world to keep yourself from being given things you don't think you deserve.

You are the first person I ever cared about who wasn't absolutely safe. You weren't safe at all.

Always, Bonnie

Always. In all ways. Forever. Never changing. It's what we all hope for, what we most fear. Some of us move on, prefer to move on, flourish when we move on. What did you mean, Bonnie, about John not being safe at all? Was he unpredictable? Erratic? Wild? Other than you expected? I wish I could talk with you about him.

18 JANUARY 1993, PROVO

It's snowing steadily outside my office window, partially obscuring the bare-limbed locust tree. A single crow flaps heavily through the fat flakes. Yesterday Joseph, Thomas, and I skied up to a quiet meadow above Hobblecreek Canyon. On the way down Joseph barreled over a ridge with seventeen-year-old abandon and plummeted down a steep slope until he threw himself backward to disappear in a flurry of powder right next to where my sweeping turn had run me into some scrub oak. Thomas crashed just below us, and we lay there, the three of us, gasping for air at first, smiling and gasping, and finally whooping deliriously. We got up and sliced down through stands of aspens, powder snow hissing around our knees. Wool-scented warmth in the car on the way home.

19 JANUARY 1993, OREM

Dream last night: A short, muscular, bullet-headed man held me hostage. He was going to rape me.

20 JANUARY 1993, OREM

Just after dawn this morning I dropped Joseph and Maren off at the high school. I love you, I called after them. Clouds hung ragged across the mountains. The city's lights were still bright, the temple on the foothill still floodlit. A bank's sign flashed the time and temperature: 7:30 a.m., 34°. The world's in good order, I thought.

Except in Bosnia. Except in Somalia. Except in the homophobic heart of the columnist in yesterday's *Provo Daily Herald*. I tightened my grip on the wheel and tailgated the car in front of me so the driver to the left couldn't get into my lane.

28 JANUARY 1993, OREM

A story told twice during Neil Jordan's film *The Crying Game* claims that a scorpion stings because that is its nature. Fergus, a member of the Irish Republican Army, is nice to the captured black British soldier because that is his nature. It is also his nature to be heterosexual, and when he discovers that the beautiful young black woman he has fallen for is a transvestite, he hits her. Violence is unnatural to him, and he regrets the angry blow.

The actor playing him/her is named Jaye.

31 JANUARY 1993, OREM

Dreams:

I beat John viciously. In response, he hired an accountant who will investigate every aspect of my financial life. I'll have to provide endless detailed documentation.

A man wearing a bulging codpiece like one of Bruegel's peasants dances with a sexy woman. A giant penis rises out of the codpiece. He pulls out the whole dark apparatus, prick and balls, and throws it at me.

4 FEBRUARY 1993, PROVO

Naturalist Terry Tempest Williams was on campus today to read from her book *Refuge*. Cancer fells her mother, as it has other women in the family. Fluctuations in the water level of the Great Salt Lake bring destruction and then renewal of the bird refuge on its northeastern flank. She prays to the birds. She describes the morning her mother called her to tell her she had found a new tumor. They shop for a robe in Nordstrom. Dazzling, she tells her mother. She remembers their trip to New York and the makeovers they had between the art museum and the theater. Dazzling.

John and I shared nothing during the month he died. Nor during the previous year while he skirted death. Nothing. Not a word. I wish it had been otherwise. After the nurse in the clinic asked him about homosexual activity, for example, we could have had dinner together. Dazzling.

I have lost one son, Mom warned me, and I don't want to lose another. She meant death, perhaps. She also meant that she had lost John eternally, that he couldn't be in God's Celestial Kingdom where she planned to be. Didn't she lose him earlier, as she is losing me, when she no longer found room for him in the corner of the world she calls good?

Williams reads from "Winter Solstice at the Moab Slue." Wetlands again, birds, and human beings: "How cautious I have become with love...to withhold emotion just to appease our fears...lack of intimacy with ourselves...lack of intimacy with the land...terror of loss...the knives of our priests are bloody."

John's death ferments in my soul. His death is undermining the *arche* that has controlled my life. Perhaps I can risk a cautious anarchy (that's all the anarchy I can muster); I want to live more freely in the here and now.

It's not that easy. You're fond of quoting Nietzsche. Don't forget Zara-
thustra's demand that you declare what you are free for and not what
you are free from.

11 FEBRUARY 1993, PROVO

John's "COLD FILTERED" clock is still ticking. I heard it this
morning in the silence before I turned on my computer. To see it,
however, I had to move a potted plant and two mailing tubes. A clock
advertising Miller Genuine Draft Light in a BYU office! I feel like a
rogue professor. A predictably juvenile rogue professor wracked by
laughter at his own insouciance. The word *insouciance* makes me smile.
It was written above the word *paroxysms* in John's blue notebook.

22 FEBRUARY 1993, OREM

"All the turtles on this beach have some kind of tumor." I've forgotten where I read this now random sentence, but I copied it in my
notebook next to Tolstoy's "All happy families resemble one another,
but each unhappy family is unhappy in its own way." I look up the
sentence to make sure I have it right and notice the epigraph Tolstoy
placed above it: "Vengeance is mine; I will repay." Anna Karenina
didn't have a chance.

Taped to the cabinet of John's kitchen in Boise was a poem typed
on an eight-and-a-half-by-eleven sheet of water-stained paper: "Do
not go gentle into that good night. / Rage, rage against the dying of
the light." Dylan Thomas's dying father. Rhyme stacks up sensuously
beyond meaning. Wrinkled, watermarked incantations taped to the
side of a pine cupboard.

2 MARCH 1993, OREM

I've been reading travel narratives, most recently Kenneth White's
The Book of the Golden Root and Bruce Chatwin's *In Patagonia*. "Let it
begin," White writes, "with the young American member of the Peace
Corps, reading Rimbaud there in the harbour at Marseille, and the talk
we had about 'wild mystics.' Or better, with the young girl, lovely to
look at, standing at the ship's rail, her blue dress blowing in the wind."

The mind and the body. The body. Travel to blow the mind.

Paul Theroux writes that "when [Chatwin] fell deathly ill soon after his China trip, the word spread that he had been bitten by a fruit bat in Yunnan and contracted a rare blood disease. Only two other people in the entire world had ever had it, so the story went, and both had died.... What kind of bat was this exactly? Bruce was vague, and he became very ill."

17 MARCH 1993, OREM

Last night I went upstairs to where Nathan and Thomas were watching a movie on TV. Charles Bronson races through a snowy wilderness. Lee Marvin and friends chase him relentlessly. At night the four pursuers sit around a campfire. One of them grabs the youngest man and kisses him hard. The young man beats the assaulter viciously. I silently cheer the violence. Blow after brutal blow.

This is very disturbing. Why do men act and feel this way? What kind of society constructs such anxious and violent creatures?

Good question.

19 MARCH 1993, OREM

This evening I found an official letter among John's things:

> August 5, 1965
> Dear John:
>   Congratulations on becoming an Eagle Scout! I am personally proud of young men who attain the rank of Eagle in the Boy Scouts of America because I believe they will be better equipped to meet the challenges which America faces today. More than ever before we need men of courage and judgment and of understanding in the things they believe to stand up and be counted. **STRENGTHEN AMERICA—SCOUTING CAN MAKE THE DIFFERENCE**

I too became an Eagle Scout. The author of my letter was even more sure America was in dire straits. He wrote that Eagle Scouts were needed to stand up against "the forces that threaten America" (free-love hippies and communists?).

The next step for a young man who had been equipped by the Boy Scouts to stand up for America was my military obligation. The mimeographed pamphlet we received at Brigham Young University was called *A Guide to Opportunities Open to the Young Men Faced with the Obligation (Opportunity) to Serve in One of the Armed Services: Prepared by Detachment 855 Air Force ROTC BYU for Bishops' and Stake Presidents' Day.*

We gathered in the DeJong Concert Hall where an elder of the church, Hartman Rector, spoke to us about duty, obedience, and patriotism. He reminded us that "the members of the church have always felt under obligation to come to the defense of their country when a call to arms was made." He described the war that liberated Japan as a war used by God to introduce the Gospel of Jesus Christ to the Japanese. Ditto the Korean War. And "exactly the same thing will happen in Vietnam. When we pull out the U.S. troops . . . we will move the mission president and the missionaries right in behind them. We will build up the kingdom of God there. Yes, it took some of the best of this nation to do it, but these nations must be redeemed by blood. It's in the economy of God. . . . Yes, this is God's nation, and the Stars and Stripes is God's flag."

In mid-December, when it looked like my lottery number for the draft might in fact be called, I dutifully took a bus to Salt Lake City for a preinduction physical. I passed the physical, and, well schooled by church and state, I would have gone if the draft for the year had not ended a number or two lower.

What was John's experience with the draft? We never talked about the war.

I have a dozen photos of me in uniform. Family, church, Little League, Boy Scouts, school. Molds to shape a growing boy. "Uniform." One form. All the same.

Please. These are simply ways to achieve a healthy socialization. You look handsome and proud next to your father.

I am proud to be Dad's son. I did enjoy church, where I had lively interactions with friends and caring adults. Camping with the Boy Scouts was fun. I liked sports. I was pleased to be named president of our chapter of the Honor Society. But I look back at the uniforms and awards and certifications and feel like an especially well-trained product of a kennel club, of a set of clubs rife with downplayed but powerful prejudices that have colored my judgments ever since.

John was similarly trained. In his Boy Scout uniform he stands a little awkwardly, his uncertain fingers and turned-out foot contrasting with the solid mass of our little dog Sox. Has Dad (who took most of our family pictures) said something to make him smile?

29 MARCH 1993, OREM

Nathan's birthday. Twelve years old. This morning he dodged my birthday spanking and hugged me when the threat was past.

Yesterday I threw away the cardboard neo-African mask we found hanging on John's wall. Where did John get it? What made him want to keep it? Was the artist his lover? Did he make it himself? I now have one fewer physical link to him. I replace it with words.

3 APRIL 1993, OREM

My stake president wants me to recant criticism voiced in the *Sunstone* essay, to apologize to the apostles of the church I took issue with, and then to be silent on university issues "better left to God's anointed." Last night I entered his office in the Stake Center to find him waiting with both his counselors and my ward bishop. All four men wore black suits, white shirts, and dark ties. We shook hands all around. The stake president asked one of his counselors, an eighty-year-old orchard owner, to pray. We knelt on the office floor. The counselor prayed that God would "soften Brother Abbott's heart so he would listen to council."

Curses ricocheted behind my dutifully closed eyes.

You put yourself in grave danger, the stake president began, when you criticize leaders of the church.

We're in grave danger as a people, I answered, when we can't discuss policies and doctrines.

You are willfully rejecting my council, he said. Do you have your temple recommend with you?

I pulled the certificate of worthiness from my wallet and handed it to him.

I'll keep this until you've met my conditions, he said. He will report the disciplinary action to BYU administrators, who might, if they so wish, use it as a reason to fire me. Were any of my children to marry in the temple, I would not be able to attend.

I go home and draft a letter to the church leaders mentioned in the essay. Perhaps one of the apostles will see my stake president's actions as something Joseph Smith predicted: "We have learned by sad experience that it is the nature and disposition of all men, as soon as they get a little authority, as they suppose, they will immediately begin to exercise unrighteous dominion." Smith continued the thought with an admonition: "No power or influence can or ought to be maintained by virtue of the priesthood, only by persuasion, by long-suffering, by gentleness and meekness, and by love unfeigned."

> Elder Boyd Packer, Elder James Faust, Elder Dallin Oaks,
>   Church Administration Building
>   Salt Lake City, Utah
>   Yesterday a member of the Religious Education faculty at BYU and president of the Orem Stake in which I reside, asked me to talk with him about my recent *Sunstone* article, "One Lord, One Faith, Two Universities: Tensions Between 'Religion' and 'Thought' at BYU." He expressed his feeling that I had "spoken evil of the Lord's anointed" and that I had offended you. He took my temple recommend and said there would be further disciplinary action if I did not apologize. He also wants me to publish a public statement of retraction.
>   I won't retract what I believe to be true, but I told him that if I had offended you I would welcome the chance to apologize and to explain that was not my intent. As part of my duties as a BYU faculty member, I wanted to raise productive questions about the university. To the extent that I failed to achieve this, I beg your forgiveness.

What I didn't write was my own question: Who really ought to be begging forgiveness here? In a talk to the men of the church in October 1976, Elder Packer spoke disparagingly about homosexuals and praised a missionary who had beaten up his homosexual companion. He said he would have done so himself, but as a general authority of the church he had to practice restraint.

4 APRIL 1993, OREM

One of John's Farmington friends called me the other day. He had heard I was writing about John. He had a friend, he said, who worked at the A&W with John and who claimed that John had propositioned him.

And why shouldn't he have? I asked. Isn't a proposition a form of flattery?

9 APRIL 1993, OREM

For his English class, Joseph is supposed to discuss William Carlos Williams's poem about Bruegel's *Peasant Dance*. I show him a copy of the painting and tell him about the paintings in Vienna. Together we scan the poem and find the basic dactylic meter that suggests a kind of waltz. Then we look at the breaks in the meter where Williams makes fun of the dancers' butts and shanks. Joseph is surprised and delighted, I think, to see meaning flow out of the form.

He has a second assignment to look at Dylan Thomas's villanelle "Do not go gentle into that good night." We trace the form. I tell Joseph that John had the poem taped on his cabinet when he died. Words to live by. *Night* rhymes with *light*.

10 APRIL 1993, OREM

A note to all BYU faculty members last week reminded us that "Unlawful Sexual Harassment is contrary to the principles of the Church." Lawful harassment, however...

Mom said she couldn't afford to lose another son. One son "lost" to his sexual inclinations. Another to a shifting set of beliefs. John couldn't afford to lose his mother, yet he did. And so am I. The loss, I think, is not related to eternal kingdoms. It happens when change is unacceptable.

Or when those who don't change are looked down on.

John, Mom once told me, read Hesse's *Steppenwolf* sometime after his mission. It changed him, she said. Suddenly, the commandments no longer applied to him. I wish he'd never read that.

I heard Wayne Booth lecture at Princeton about the ethical pitfalls awaiting readers of *Huckleberry Finn*. Let me begin with a personal story, he said. It took place in American Fork, Utah. One Sunday I was sitting on my grandparents' front porch reading *Huck Finn*. I heard the screen door open and slid the book under my chair. I figured it was my grandfather. It was Sunday. And although he didn't subscribe strictly to Brigham Young's belief that novels undermine character, he was a strong believer that there were better things to read on Sunday than a novel like *Huck Finn*.

Like Booth's grandfather, Mom read church books on Sunday and books of many kinds on the other days of the week. She loved for us to read as well. A fat new paperback appeared in our Christmas stockings every year. What did she think she was doing when she encouraged us to read? Which books did she think we would read? Did she suppose we wouldn't be attracted to descriptions of men who abandon ordered lives for the thrill of creative chaos? To books about women who flee stultifying marriages for love? Didn't she know that Harry Haller and Madame Bovary were out there waiting for us? And that we might be grateful?

13 APRIL 1993, OREM

What's he doing to her?

He's putting a sperm in her. So she can have a baby.

What's a sperm?

It's a thing that she needs to have a baby. There, they've just had sex. That's what that is; they had sex.

It's Benjamin and Samuel and Timothy, I finally ascertain, watching elephants on PBS.

I begin to explain to Ben how the sperm and the egg unite. Thomas comes in, then Nathan. I tell them about the eighteenth-century theory that there was a little man or woman or elephant or mouse in the sperm that just needed a female's womb to begin growing. The older boys know enough biology to find the theory wonderfully grotesque.

Timothy has a measuring tape. He rolls out six or eight inches and waves it at me. It's a sword, he says. It's a tape measure, I say. It's a sword, he says scornfully, and waves it threateningly. Later I hear him say to Benjamin: How tall are you? So he knows my truth too.

I read to Nathan and Benjamin from *The Lord of the Rings*. Maren works on her Civil War history assignment. Timothy smiles when I slip his stuffed rabbit into bed with him. Benjamin gives me a hug goodnight and doesn't let go; I think I'll just go to sleep hugging you, he says. Thomas is asleep in his room with jazz playing on the radio. Joseph is at the church playing basketball. Samuel fell asleep in Maren's bed some time ago. I move his warm body into his own bed. I sit in the quiet night and read Berger and Mohr's *Another Way of Telling*.

15 APRIL 1993, OREM

John's notebook musings about his desire to desire has me thinking about an anxiety Immanuel Kant called "*horror vacui*: A lack of feelings, perceived in oneself, which gives rise to a terror and to the presentiment of a lingering death which is held to be more painful than when destiny cuts life's thread suddenly." My own lingering lack of feeling, perceived most acutely after John's death, disquiets me. I write to feel.

20 APRIL 1993, PROVO

In the men's room down the hall from my BYU office, halfway up the corner between two walls, hangs a pale spider. I blow at it, wondering if it is dead. It shifts position. How does it sustain itself in this sterile environment?

21 APRIL 1993, OREM

Jill sent me the notes she wrote for her talk at John's funeral:

> He made a really nice desk for Carol and me in shop. He was always good at making things. Posters, art work, science projects. I remember his fruit flies all over the house. He was always a big tease.
> Senior class picture: very striking, handsome.
> At BYU he worked for some campus fund-raising drive. He was so charming that he raised a lot of money.

He said he didn't like kids, but more times than not I saw him teasing and enjoying them. He looked forward to being with Carol and her boys and talked about feeding the ducks with them.

He admired Mom. I know he got mad and intolerant of her at times, but that was just his way. One time we went to the Jerome County Fair and he was mad at her for some reason. He grabbed her and put her behind bars in the Cancer Society Jail. It took her quite some time to earn her way out. After that he enjoyed the rest of the fair with all of us.

He told me one time he just didn't believe the same as we did.

"That was just his way." Jill's deflection of John's anger is her own good-hearted way.

22 APRIL 1993, OREM

Tucked in a zippered vinyl pouch stamped "Property of U.S. Government," John had a collection of recipes clipped out of newspapers and magazines. I leaf through the colorful "Weekly Guide to Food, Home and Family" section from the *Oregonian*, Tuesday, April 3, 1990: "Sarah Bixby fine-tunes dinner for gourmets on the go.... Author Rosalind Creasy says if you get pleasure and glory from something, it isn't work."

In the same envelope are John's handwritten menus du jour for the T&A Café. November 12, 1990, for example:

Soup—Chicken noodle ($1.00), chili ($1.40)
Braized Swiss Stk, Tossed Salad, Veg, R&B $3.90
Pork Chow Mein over Rice, Tossed Salad or Soup, R&B $3.70
Chicken Rice Casserole, Tossed Salad, Veg, R&B $3.60
Grilled Meat Loaf Sandwich on Sour Dough, Cheddar Cheese, Onion, FF $3.45

A printed card falls from a folded menu: "I Won't Fart If You Won't Smoke."

24 APRIL 1993, OREM

I drove out to John's grave in American Fork yesterday. The stone is marked with the formal name his parents gave him: JOHN HERBERT ABBOTT. John hated the "Herbert," and he didn't like it when Dad called him "Hannes," a nickname for Johannes picked up from German immigrants in Windsor, Colorado. And while John never disavowed the family name, he changed John to Jay. Dad also called us Snickelfritz.

25 APRIL 1993, OREM

Combing my hair after a shower, I finger a thick scar on my forehead and remember a summer's night on a drilling site between cotton fields outside Eloy, Arizona. A pump had lost pressure because of worn gaskets, and we were replacing them. Sweat burned my eyes and dripped off my nose and chin as I wielded a thirty-six-inch pipe wrench to back out a heavy steel shaft. The third time my hard hat slid off, I threw it aside, grateful for the slight breeze in my hair. An hour later, the gaskets replaced, the shafts screwed back into place, Rudy signaled for Howard to switch the pump back on line.

Scott! I heard someone say. Are you all right? I was lying on the ground with three faces hanging over me in the floodlit night. When I tried to sit up, my brain threatened another shutdown. Where's your goddamned hard hat? Howard muttered. I put my hand to my head. It came away slick with blood.

On the way to the Casa Grande hospital, holding a wet rag to my head, I asked what happened. A brass fitting broke when I kicked in the compressed air, Howard said. It swung around on its hose and knocked you on your ass. The only time you've had your hat off in two months. With that kind of luck, if you fell into a bucket of tits you'd come up sucking your thumb.

A doctor cleaned me up, stitched the wound, and said he wanted to keep me there for observation. Howard asked to talk with me for a minute, and the doctor left. In two and a half more weeks, Howard explained, I'll have enough accident-free hours with my crew to get a paid Caribbean vacation. If you check into the hospital or if you don't show up to work tomorrow night, I'll lose that.

The doctor returned, and I said I just wanted to go home. I can't allow that, he said. You have a concussion. I asked if I could stay without checking in. The doctor spoke with a nurse, and she made a bed for me on a lobby couch. At the rig the next day, my hard hat teetered precariously on a fat bandage.

27 APRIL 1993, OREM

Bob Walter **Abbott** and Janice Hilton, Roy Leslie **Abbott** and Dorothy Arvilla Boreing, John Herbert **Abbott** and Harriet Belle Elliott, Benjamin **Abbott** and Arie Elizabeth Beals...

Janice **Hilton** and Bob Walter Abbott, Clement **Hilton** and Evelyn Louise Schank, John Hugh **Hilton** and Maria Parker, Hugh **Hilton** and Isabella Pilkington...

While the male names march a straight line between future and past, in this pedigreed system women's lines follow a series of right-angled digressions. Homosexuals without children fall right off the map as the chart moves into the future. One blip. Roots, but no branches. Malachi's curse. The Lord promised Abraham progeny like the dust of the earth, a promise Mormons believe is theirs as well. If my seven children procreate like I did, I'll be "as Abraham" soon enough, in contrast to the wicked Sodomites whose land God promised to Abraham's descendants.

My friend Sam Rushforth has a digital counter in his botany lab that displays the current world population. The number grows relentlessly while you stand in front of it. And while you are asleep at home. Six billion and counting.

28 APRIL 1993, OREM

I woke up this morning thinking of early sexual attractions.

As a second or third grader I had a crush on a dark-haired classmate, her bangs cut straight across. I remember her patent-leather shoes flashing as she swung into the southern Idaho sunlight.

In the seventh grade, inspired by the Beatles' "I Wanna Hold Your Hand," I wanted to hold Patsy Simmons's hand. I walked her home one afternoon after school. Retracing my steps to the school and then toward home, I sang with all the adolescent emotion I could muster: "P.S. I Love You."

A year later I arranged to meet Bonnie Gardner at the movie theater. In the dark I touched her hand. She responded. We clenched sweaty hands for the rest of the movie. When I got home, Dad and Mom were sitting at the kitchen table, home after a night out. Dad had a smile on his face: Who was the girl you were holding hands with?

After I could drive I began taking a girl home from youth activities at church. There were kisses, and I remember her lying with her head on my lap next to my erection while we sat in the car and talked. One night an icy corner near her house threw the car into a spin, and nothing but dumb luck left us backed neatly into a driveway instead of wrapped around a tree.

Standing at Debby Whalen's door after a movie, I kissed her lightly. Then we kissed again. Driving home, my lips felt sweetly branded.

Pleasant memories all. The first whispers of sexuality linked body and mind in new ways. But there was guilt, even with these rather chaste pleasures. Late one night, a week before I left on my mission, I made a tortured call to my priesthood leader to confess that April Jorgensen and I had kissed our way through long evenings at college. I wanted to be clean and worthy. The theologically aroused guilt could be assuaged only by a church authority. He graciously obliged.

How different would it have been had my "sin" been defined by biblical fulminations against sodomy? Death to the sodomites! Fags, queers, buggers, sods, pansies: AIDS IS YOUR PUNISHMENT! Concluding backward from the act or event to the will of God is an old practice. Cromwell argued that although Charles I had ruled by the grace of God, his severed head was proof that that grace had been withdrawn.

Among John's things stored in Mom's shed, I find a play called *The Tender Age*, published for the Mutual Improvement Association of the church. "Sparky" is handwritten on the cover. There are only four lines for Sparky, of which this is my favorite: "Personally, I guess I'll pass the strange redhead by and ask good old Donna again."

29 APRIL 1993, PROVO

When asked what he thinks about his BYU students, a visiting Polish theater director opines that they are honestly, sincerely, humbly, and earnestly trying to appear better than they really are.

30 APRIL 1993, PROVO

John and I shared a room until I left for college. Bunk beds. Sometimes he on the top bunk, sometimes I. At night he often wanted to sleep while I wanted to read. Or vice versa. One of us would turn off the light. The other would turn it back on. I remember my furious leaps down or up to beat him into submission. He always, finally, cried. And then turned the light back on, or off.

Late one summer our room began to stink. Dirty socks were not a sufficient cause. Getting a shirt out of the closet one day, I noticed something odd about the white dinner jacket a family friend had given me for junior prom. One shoulder of the jacket was mottled with reddish-pink stains. Above the jacket, wrapped in newspaper at the back of the highest shelf, I found half a watermelon. What had been a rigid botanical structure had collapsed into a gently fizzing mass. John's secret pleasure. Necessarily secret because his five siblings would have inhaled the watermelon had we known.

3 MAY 1993, OREM

In 1970, at the end of my missionary service in the thick black air of Germany's industrial *Ruhrgebiet*, I sent John a package of things I wanted to get rid of. Perhaps the new missionary in northern Italy could use the indestructible suit, slightly shiny in the seat? I included some shirts, a tie or two, and the football I had carried around for a year.

John and I were assiduously prepared for those missions. In 1964, for example, I received a birthday letter from Grandpa Hilton. With his third wife, "Aunt" Joie, he was working in New York City as a volunteer guide at the LDS World's Fair pavilion:

> Dear Scott,
> August 14th marks another important milestone in your life.

You and your life are <u>very</u> important to us. We are proud of you and our love for you goes deep. You are a clean, handsome young man and we can look upon you with joy—grateful that we are a part of your life. We are anxious for you to always be clean and handsome and to always be a stalwart for those things which bring joy—the true meaningful kind.

We look ahead about four years and see Elder Scott Abbott—a missionary called of God with authority to preach, to baptize, and to bestow the Gift of the Holy Ghost by the laying on of hands—we see this and our hearts swell with pride because we have confidence in Scott and know he has the ability to become not an average or mediocre missionary but a great one. We have confidence in you to prepare yourself diligently in the next four years—to make Seminary count; to study the scriptures and to learn to love them and make them real in your life; to give joyous and full measure of service in the Church and to your family, your school, and this choice land of freedom. We have confidence in you to keep yourself clean, virtuous and unspotted from the sins of the world.

We challenge you to honor the priesthood you hold and to prepare to be worthy and ready to hold the higher priesthood—even that same priesthood by which The Son of God created the worlds. We challenge you to ever be true to yourself, to your family and to <u>The</u> Church. We challenge you to use your great gift of free agency to make the right choices. We challenge you to live so someday you might take a choice young woman to the House of the Lord for an Eternal Marriage. We challenge you to become the man you will one day want your sons to be.

You are a grandson to truly be proud of. We love you. Happy Birthday, Scott
Grandpa and Aunt Joie
The "Fair" Hiltons

I was fourteen when I received this letter. I don't remember any specific feelings, but the fact that I kept the letter and the similar one that arrived from the Mormon Pavilion a year later indicates the importance they held for me. It could have been the official envelope and stationery, proof of Grandpa's standing in the church, or maybe it was the fervor with which Grandpa "bore his testimony," or perhaps it was simply the rarity of the letter. I was proud to be his grandson, proud to be a Hilton, and the letter was tangible proof that he was proud of me as well.

Thirty years later I recognize the contingency of his pride. He is proud as I continue to be true to The Church, proud as I fit his mold and become his kind of man, proud as I pass on his formula of steadfastness and uprightness to my sons.

But isn't pride always, by its nature, contingent? How can you argue, after all, with the principles of living your grandfather sketches out: faith, industry, honesty, concern for others, learning?

The letter's sentiments, constantly reinforced by parents and friends and church leaders, became the stuff of my moral structure. For that I am, for the most part, grateful.

5 MAY 1993, OREM

In *Modern Nature* Jarman pays attention to flowers and gardens. To the weather. He's also gay, and that is why I am reading his journal. How else to get into a mind "bent" like John's? But when Jarman invites me into a secret garden of violets to watch him and another schoolboy take off their uniforms to share "that lovely feeling," I quit reading.

Does a homosexual feel that way about depictions of heterosexual experience? Only, I suppose, if he or she shares my intolerant naïveté.

10 MAY 1993, OREM

After a week of rain, snow, and gray skies, the morning dawned bright blue and warm. A big gibbous moon. A calf sucking its mother's teat. A mountain of steaming, composting manure. They all remind me as I spin along on my bike that life renews itself, that nature is a constant, that there is serenity beyond the daily annoyances that keep me tied up in knots.

11 MAY 1993, AMERICAN FORK, UTAH

We had dinner with Mom today, joined as usual by Grandma Hilton (with the passage of decades no longer Aunt Joie). Washing dishes with her after dinner, I mentioned I had reread the two birthday letters sent from the World's Fair. They were important to me, I said. Grandpa didn't send me many letters.

Were the letters handwritten? Grandma asked. You know Grandpa had that strong left-handed scrawl.

I thanked Grandma for her letters, and while we finished the dishes I smiled at the memory of the talk she gave at a church youth meeting when I was sixteen or seventeen. Her topic was modesty in dress. Girls should not wear miniskirts, she argued, because they expose the knees. Have you ever looked at the backs of your knees in a mirror? she asked the girls. They form an ugly X. You are much prettier if you keep them covered. She made a strong impression on me. The backs of those lovely knees!

12 MAY 1993, OREM

I'm reading Susan Griffin's *A Chorus of Stones: The Private Life of War.* What makes us silent and secretive and violent? she asks. She looks at the work of Daniel Gottlieb Moritz Schreber, a nineteenth-century German child-rearing expert (and champion of the *Schreber-garten*) and finds pictures that "recall images of torture . . . pictures of children whose posture or behavior is being corrected." Schreber tells parents: "Crush the will. Establish dominance. Permit no disobedience. Suppress everything in the child."

"I am not free of the condition described here," Griffin writes at the book's onset. Nor am I, goddammit. Nor am I.

19 MAY 1993, OREM

Just after midnight I picked up Joseph from his new job at Wendy's. For hours he had stood at the grill cooking hamburgers. The odor rising from his clothes transported me back to the day in July when

I put John's clothing in a bag in his Boise apartment. The whole lot, even the clean clothes from his drawers, smelled of cooking oil.

Mom thinks John said something unguarded to a companion who reported it to the mission president who banished him to a village near the Yugoslav border. Ronald, the president's assistant who was from our hometown, was sent along as his companion. This morning I called Ronald, a physician now practicing in Farmington, and asked him about the six weeks he spent with John in San Giovanni al Natisone. I expected something about a homosexual advance, an ugly scene with the mission president, a gallant friend who agreed to spend the last couple of months with the morose young man. Ronald said they had worked very hard. John, he remembered, had enjoyed the six weeks as much as he had. They had no success in finding someone who wanted to join the church, but they helped Mormon immigrants from Uruguay set up their new upholstery business. When I asked about something John might have done to disgrace himself, Ronald could think of nothing. He remembered periods of depression near the end of John's mission, that he had withdrawn some. In San Giovanni al Natisone, however, that was not the case.

I asked Ronald about his friendship with John in high school. Something changed during our junior year, he said. John distanced himself from me and from others as well. I don't think he had anyone he was really close to. He said once he wasn't getting along with his parents, that they didn't understand him. He said he had to do his own laundry. That made him feel like a visitor in his own home.

27 MAY 1993, OREM

Our son John graduated from high school last night. I meant Joseph—I've made this mistake a dozen times when speaking. Both names begin with *J*. Both are in my thoughts a lot lately. I have tried, in the past, to force both of them into submission. I love them both.

Yesterday the editor of *Sunstone* sent me a letter written by a man in Heber, Utah. "I was enjoying Abbott's article about BYU," he wrote, "until I came to the section about how outsiders see Mormons. I don't give a rat's ass what Tony Kushner thinks about us."

30 MAY 1993, OREM

Boyd Packer recently spoke to the heads of several church departments. He warned that members of the church are being "caught up and led away by three groups that on the surface seem so reasonable and right: gays and lesbians, feminists, and so-called scholars or intellectuals." "That young man with gender disorientation," he said, "needs to know that gender was not assigned at mortal birth, that we were sons and daughters of God in the premortal state."

Utah Jazz basketball player Karl Malone spoke at BYU a few years ago as a member of a panel on the origins of racism. We all need "escape goats," he concluded.

1 JUNE 1993, OREM

Yesterday was Memorial Day. I thought of taking the children to American Fork to see John's grave, but decided not to. I didn't want to give the impression that I was mourning unduly. We are a moderate, balanced people.

Mom and I recently continued our conversation about John:

> One time we were visiting Carol in Boise for Thanksgiving, she said. I don't know what he was thinking, but John brought tortellini and alcohol.
>
> Alcohol? I asked.
>
> Yes.
>
> Cooked with the tortellini or in a bottle?
>
> In a bottle; then he cooked the tortellini in the wine. We all said we didn't want any, and he got angry.
>
> You didn't object to the meat and vegetables I stir-fried in sherry a few weeks ago.
>
> I didn't notice, Mom said, looking grievously hurt. I wish you hadn't.
>
> John stayed with me for almost a month, Mom remembered. He helped me paint the house. He didn't sand where we had filled. I told him to, but he didn't. I would have done it myself

if I had known. But then he might have blown up. I took him to the movies while he was here. He went crazy with all the kids running up and down the aisles. He was so full of anger and bitterness.

I asked Mom if she remembers the food-poisoning John, Grandma Hilton, and I got while cutting up chickens at the family reunion.

That wasn't Grandma Hilton, she said. That was me.

Memory is a slippery medium. Slippery and malleable. The paucity of sources allows me wide latitude as I write my brother's story. John is in no position to contradict. Not so with my mother or my wife. I write with the constant knowledge that they will read what I write. They will take issue. And they should.

John's eyes were brown like Mom's. None of us inherited her left-handedness. John stands proud in the white dinner jacket (how did they get the watermelon stains out?). I don't recognize the girl. Mom can't identify her either.

John's clock is beginning to lose time. This morning I had to add more than thirty minutes.

2 JUNE 1993, OREM

The pack of IOUs dated June 19, 20, 21, 22, and 26 included nine notes amounting to exactly one hundred dollars. In the envelope holding the IOUs, a "Payroll Deduction Receipt" records "74 Hrs. at Basic Rate $7.43—$550.00." Minus taxes, $439.22.

3 JUNE 1993, JOHN'S BIRTHDAY, OREM

Driving rain in the night. This morning delicate clouds veiling the mountains remind me of Tao Yuanming's poem "Return Home"—"The clouds rise aimlessly out of the mountains, / The birds, tired of flight, contemplate their return home"—and of Li Zai's fifteenth-century drawing after those lines. Old and foreign and familiar ways of seeing the world.

My colleague Bill Davis stops by my office, and we talk about images and texts. We turn to mountain biking, depression, chaos theory, real estate, Lacan's symbolic order, Bill's new article on Goethe's *The Sorrows of Young Werther*. I show him what I have just written about John, and he tells me about his uncle Allen, another story to go with the one his father told me. Allen was mathematically gifted, Bill says. He served in the navy but at some point lost contact with reality. Besides his mathematical calculations, he had a thick book he used for notes for a screenplay. It'll be the biggest movie hit since *Gone with the Wind*, he would say.

Does Bill's anecdote describe me with my bloated journals and authorial delusions? And while I'm doubting: Where is my story going? I know the standard plotlines, the ones that move from desire to fulfillment, or from desire to fulfillment to tragedy. As this story follows its meanders, I don't find myself to be a satisfied, fulfilled husband or a faithful member of my church, but neither is mine the story of a brave individual triumphantly separating himself from a disastrous marriage and an abusive religion. I live chapters of each of these stories, but always intermediary chapters, never the climactic ones. Absent is the single seductive strand that engages and satisfies readers. "A delicate slowness," Nietzsche wrote, "is the tempo of these conversations."

4 JUNE 1993, OREM

John's clock has been running fine for the last two days. Can I finish this before the battery gives up the ghost?

What will it mean to finish? To finish what? To finish writing about my brother? To finish thinking about him? To abandon him again? To jettison this means of access to my own past and present experience?

Closure would be the ultimate distortion. Better the small, progressive, self-canceling, and self-correcting distortions of an arbitrary dialectic. Let the clock determine the moment when I stop writing.

7 JUNE 1993, OREM

Over the weekend I opened another of the boxes John had stored at Mom's. There were old textbooks, several copies of *La Stella* (the church magazine from Italy), student manuals from BYU's Book of Mormon and Church History courses, Monarch Notes for high school Latin, and two wood-and-brass plaques announcing John as the winner of divisions of the San Juan County Science Fair: 1965 in earth science, 1967 in animal biology.

9 JUNE 1993, OREM

I sort through the bags of John's things from Boise, setting aside the best clothing for a thrift store. John's soap and shampoo I put in the bathroom. Shampooing my hair with his Wella Balsam, I feel connected to him two years after his death. My hair feels luxurious, smells beautiful.

Alex recently explained his theory about talking with the dead. He walks into the house, smells a sauce Setenay is cooking, and hears his dead mother's voice intoning a Sicilian proverb comparing life to a good sauce. She lives on because his memory retains her vocabulary, her syntax, her inflections, the scent of her sauces.

11 JUNE 1993, OREM

The thick, watermarked letterhead reads: The Church of Jesus Christ of Latter-day Saints, The Council of the Twelve. The envelope is stamped PERSONAL & CONFIDENTIAL.

> Dear Brother Abbott:
> You wrote extending something of an apology for statements you made in your recent *Sunstone* article....
> ... [T]he entire spirit of your article causes us very serious concern. You acknowledge that you are familiar with the statement counseling members concerning certain symposiums and

organizations. You then proceed to misinterpret the statement and continue in a tone which projects a spirit of bitterness, even defiance.

For one to do so who has made sacred covenants and, in addition, is under contract represents a fundamental breach of integrity; particularly when one's livelihood is drawn from the tithes and offerings of the Latter-day Saints.
Sincerely yours,
Boyd K. Packer

You receive your salary from the church. You have made sacred covenants in the temple. Therefore, your criticism is a fundamental breach of integrity. Sit down and shut up. And by the way, the points of your argument are irrelevant. Are rebukes of this type effective with some kinds of people?

Although I have been your critic, I'd like to suggest that you take this patriarch's admonitions with a grain of salt. God rest Elder Packer's male soul.

15 JUNE 1993, PROVO
Directed by the BYU Board of Trustees, of which Boyd Packer is an influential member, the administration has fired three outspoken members of the faculty. Inadequate scholarship is the putative issue. Our ad hoc faculty committee quickly published information that shows their scholarship to be better than or equal to fifteen other professors whose third-year reviews resulted in positive outcomes this year. Gail Houston, of the English Department, was fired, we suggest, because she admitted in print that she sometimes prays to her mother in heaven. Cecilia Konchar Farr, also of the English Department, was fired for her prochoice views. David Knowlton, an anthropologist, had the temerity to publish an article suggesting fewer missionaries would be killed and fewer chapels bombed in Latin America if the church would downplay its colonizing, corporate CIA image. In passing, Knowlton noted that the new church office building—a tower

with globes on either side at the base—is an unfortunate symbol of phallic power.

University administrators don't want to admit limits on academic freedom and have tried to shift the question in these cases to what amounts to a lie. And now they've gotten themselves and us in an awkward place.

Do you think university administrators are liars? a TV journalist asked members of our committee last night. Bill Davis looked straight into the camera and said YES! Today he has a different story: Didn't he ask if I thought they were lawyers?

I'm more sure every day that I don't belong here.

Why do you so easily accept their definition? You and John. Humans, especially powerful humans, are fallible. The church is larger than its troubled leaders.

My *Sunstone* essay made a reasonable and faithful argument: in a healthy religion there should be no conflict between reason and faith. I was told that we don't "steady the ark." We don't question prophets, seers, and revelators. We submit ourselves to authority. Somehow, somewhere, I developed a taste for questioning authority. More than a taste—it has become a moral stance. Or maybe it's an inherited bullheadedness, a self-destructive gene John and I share. His unwillingness to submit cost him community among fellow Mormons and within his own family. As a "so-called intellectual," I have already found myself shouldered to the margin of the university and the church. If this text I'm writing about my homosexual brother finds its way into print, I'll be looking for a new job.

I tape a sign to my office door: "Religion is being destroyed by the Inquisition, for to see a man burned because he believes he has acted rightly is painful to people, it exasperates them."—William of Orange

18 JUNE 1993, OREM

During the Second World War, enlisted days after he graduated from high school, Dad was trained and double-rated as a navigator and pilot of a B-29. It's impossible for me to visualize what that meant for him. I can read about the 325 B-29s that first firebombed Tokyo, igniting conflagrations so fierce that the big bombers were tossed like toys on the updraft, fires that killed close to one hundred thousand civilians. Was he there that day? What were his thoughts while droning home after bombing raids?

Among Dad's things, companion to circular slide rules and colorful silk maps, is a large paper map titled

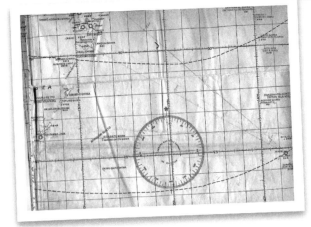

"U.S. Army Air Forces Special Air Navigation Chart: Caroline Islands to Japan (S-115) **Restricted**." A single straight pencil line slices across the blue of the North Pacific Ocean, connecting the islands of Tinian and Iô-Jima. Ruled pencil lines radiate from Iô-Jima to southern islands of Japan, punctuated by compass holes and cut through by penciled arcs labeled 1300, 1400, 1500. Miles, kilometers, times? A square of the map stands in relief above the rest of the map—raised, I suppose, by a small table mounted in front of the navigator with a band of some sort to hold the square fast.

This map on whose accuracy the soldiers bet their lives is remarkably clear about its contingencies:

First Edition, subject to correction. August 1944.

Warning: Due to war conditions, lights, radio facilities and other aids to navigation may be changed or discontinued without notice.

Caution: Streams or coastlines shown on this chart by broken lines indicate that the exact position or shape of the charted feature is doubtful.

Note: Officers using this chart will mark hereon corrections and additions which come to their attention and mail direct to the Aeronautical Chart Service, Headquarters, Army Air Forces, Washington, D.C.

The map, like all maps, tells an incomplete story. Because of the consequences of obfuscation, it does so as honestly as possible. Despite its deficiencies, the military map is encyclopedic compared with Dad's account of the war. The following is the only personal record we have:

In 1945, on my way to the Pacific Area as a member of a B-29 crew, we stopped over night in Honolulu. The next morning as we were taking off, an oil leak developed in number three engine. As we made an emergency landing we had some damage to the tail section of the airplane. Since it was going to take all day to repair the plane, I went to look up a service man whose name and address I had.

As I found this serviceman, I found that he was a recent convert to the Church of Jesus Christ of Latter-day Saints. He spent all day telling me about his new church. As we were ready to depart, he offered me a serviceman's copy of the Book of Mormon and *The Principles of the Gospel*. I indicated that I didn't care for them, but he insisted. I threw them in the top of my barrack's bag. As we went on overseas, they fell into the bottom of the bag where they remained. We were flying 20- and 24-hour missions over Japan. Because of the length of the flights, we had considerable free time before and after each flight. Because of this free time, I soon ran out of reading material. Finally I dug out the Book of Mormon and became interested until getting into the Isaiah quotations in II Nephi. Then back in the barrack's bag for the Book of Mormon. Finally, in desperation for reading material (and by the promptings of the Spirit), I dug the Book of Mormon out again and caught the spirit of it.

Finally I asked the Protestant Chaplin if there were any LDS Chaplains in the area. He said that he didn't know, but that his choir leader was a Mormon. He gave me Preston Bushman's address. Preston started taking me to church meetings.

About this time World War II was over. My outfit was scheduled to return to the States; however, a few of us were kept to fill out the complement of a group that had just come overseas. This was a great blessing because of the missionary minded brethren that I found in this group.

Later, on a Sunday morning, as we returned from Sunday School, they asked me to meet them that afternoon. I told them that I had already made other plans that afternoon. As they were driving away, I was impressed to call to them and accept their offer. That afternoon I was told that an LDS Chaplin would be at our Sacrament Meeting that night, and they would like to present me for baptism. That evening I was interviewed. The next Tuesday I was baptized in the Pacific Ocean and then confirmed the following Sunday.

My father's lifetime of silence about the war was broken only by this spare conversion account, written by assignment for a class at BYU. In his text the unspeakable uncertainties and horrors of war give way to the speakable companionships and certainties of a new religion. "The most correct of any book on earth," Joseph Smith said of the Book of Mormon. Not subject to correction.

19 JUNE 1993, OREM

I wrote that Dad's service in the war left few traces. This morning, however, I found myself singing the Army Air Corps song he and Mom sang with gusto on long car trips: "Here they come, zooming

to meet our thunder /
At 'em boys, give 'em the
gun!"

21 JUNE 1993,
OREM

We are free, a new
policy on academic
freedom at BYU states,
"to teach and research
without interference, to
ask hard questions, to subject answers to rigorous examination." Unless,
it turns out, someone objects to our questions and examinations.

A long mountain-bike ride up the Great Western Trail on the
south flank of Mount Timpanogos shifts my focus. What if Utah had
a culture to match its landscapes?

Saturday morning I attended the funeral of a church leader and
hard-nosed BYU administrator obliquely related to me. The ac-
complishments expounded during the service were hierarchal and
impersonal. Then one of his sons spoke of how distant he had felt
from his father while growing up. He gave his life to the church, he
lamented. Not until his father fell into serious physical decline were
they finally able to speak intimately with one another.

I will not give my life to an institution.

Then what will you give it to? Don't institutions enable as well as
inhibit? Where is your much-heralded dialectic?

I took this week's *New Yorker* to lunch with me, anxious to read
whatever it was that Harold Brodkey had written under the rubric
"To My Readers." "I have AIDS" is Brodkey's first sentence. "I am
surprised that I do." He describes his own experience with the cause
of John's death: "*Pneumocystis carinii* pneumonia, which almost killed
me. . . . From the moment my oxygen intake fell to about fifty per cent
and the ambulance drivers arrived in our apartment . . . I have not had

even one moment of physical stability." Brodkey lived to write about that attack. He had a wife to call the ambulance.

1 JULY 1993, PROVO

In a faculty seminar this morning, Claudia Bushman argued that Mormons believe in resurrection but not in death. While she spoke I stared at my ankle, uncharacteristically bare because of the sandals I was wearing. Between the ankle and heel I watched the pulse of a short section of artery. Fifty-nine times a minute. That pulsing means life to me. And it foretells my death.

5 JULY 1993, OREM

Last night I read Bushman's 1981 essay "Light and Dark Thoughts on Death" in *Dialogue: A Journal of Mormon Thought*. She and her sisters make a new temple dress for their dead mother. After overcoming an initial shock and aversion to the body, they dress her in temple robes and green apron and slippers. Their loving acts, Bushman writes, are therapeutic.

This book is my own therapeutic attempt to dress John's body, to feel the rasp of his cold flesh.

Bushman's mother left a detailed list: a white coffin, organ music, song titles, temple robes. Her children had only to perform her script. I am left to ad-lib.

7 JULY 1993, PROVO

We're in the thick of a tense fight over academic freedom. Our colleagues fired under false pretenses are at the heart of the battle, but underlying it all are limitations on our work in sociology and psychology and anthropology and philosophy and literary criticism and the sciences. I got an e-mail the other day from an unidentified student who said I should shut up about academic freedom. He came to BYU, he wrote, not to be subjected to my apostate opinions but to learn what he already knows to be true.

Monday morning I escaped it all (this is becoming a pattern) and rode my mountain bike up Provo Canyon, up the dirt road that crosses under the green snake of an aqueduct and on up the foothills of Mount Timpanogos. It's a gut-wrenching climb to where the road finally dead-ends directly across the canyon from Bridal Veil Falls. And that's what I wanted, to tax my lungs and heart and muscles until there was nothing in my mind except the trail and my bike and my body. I hid the bike in some brush and scrambled up over shale, past blue-limestone outcroppings, through sage, scrub oak, cottonwoods, and elderberry, to a small waterfall. On a cliff two hundred feet above the waterfall, I inched to the edge, fighting a delicious sense of vertigo to hang my legs over the rock like a Chinese poet.

Swallows dipped and rose around me. Cars crept along the road below like the beetles that make up one quarter of all animal species on earth. (Was John aware of that quirk of nature?) Winds tugged at me fitfully. Geological history was on display across the canyon: massive folds of blue limestone thrust up and pressed down into liquid curves by continental forces over eons of time.

I lay back on the rock ledge and closed my eyes. The grand spaces of the canyon vanished, and I was left with the feel of rock against my back, solar heat on my skin, the occasional sounds of birdsong and of wind in the brush, glimmers of red-orange light burning through my eyelids—a sensation more like touch than vision. Opening my eyes, I became a small part of a vast scene. Closing them brought me back to the physical immediacy of sun and rocks and sound and flesh.

My mind returned finally to the troubled state of the university. I am not careful in the face of coercion or injustice. I cannot hold my tongue or pen. BYU's attempt to rid itself of critics by brute force reminds me of earlier (I hope they are earlier) shock-aversion treatments to "cure" BYU faculty members and students of their homosexuality. A BYU librarian whom I see now and then on campus has blank eyes, shuffling feet, shaking hands, and an inability to sleep except when dead drunk. He was "healed" at the hands of men rigid with certainty.

John had two handwritten versions of a quotation from a *Penthouse* interview: "In Aldous Huxley's book *Brave New World* he warned about every human being conditioned to accept his lot so that the bosses arrive at a nice smooth situation where nobody questions anything and everything is supposedly 'taken care of.'"—Roger Waters

9 JULY 1993, PROVO

Yesterday "the University" decided to deny my promotion to full professor. Not enough scholarship during my five years here. That was the official word. BYU's president, Rex Lee, called to apologize and to explain that in the charged political climate, he simply couldn't forward a recommendation for my promotion to the board of trustees. A member of the university advancement committee told me later in the day that their discussion had focused on my writing for *Sunstone* and on my involvement with the ad hoc academic-freedom committee.

I find it remarkable that Rex Lee called. His personal gesture was risky, don't you think? But I'm troubled by adherents of a religion who so pragmatically say one thing and do another. There's a long history of the end justifying the means in Mormonism, starting with Joseph Smith's denial of the polygamy he was practicing.

10 JULY 1993, OREM

Mom sent me another admonitory letter this week:

> John became a liar, a thief, a drunkard, and finally died as a result of his <u>choice</u>. He was <u>not</u> born that way. This I know. This is one of the Church teachings you are fighting against. I watched this choice destroy a son whom I loved with all my heart. He always believed that the rules didn't apply to him. I see this same thing in you. They do apply. What we sow we also reap. Happiness and joy and peace come from obedience. What do you want at the end of your life? I want a righteous posterity who love the Lord.

She doesn't mince words. I respect her for that. But it won't be easy to speak with her again.

I wait a few days, then reply: Conformity above all else? Joy from obedience? You ask what I want at the end of my life. I want the sight and scent of cliffrose blooming in the spring, intimate relationships, good friends, the strengths and frailties of my body, as much honesty as I can bear, and maybe the chance to do a little good in this world.

You feel so superior to your mother, don't you? You vowed to tell multiple stories, but you don't have a clue. Your mother has given up things you would never, under any circumstance, think of giving up: talents, desires, goals, identity. And why? To foster and preserve family. There may be other ways to do that, but in her culture and generation that was the option. How hard is it, given those deep and abiding and productive choices, to see another way, to suppose, retroactively, that those sacrifices weren't absolutely necessary? You, on the other hand, fearful that your mother and wife are standing in the way of personal growth and expanded identity, are willing to bulldoze them aside. Where is your commitment to family?

3 AUGUST 1993, PARIS

As if to prove the point about my commitment to family, once again I'm in Europe to work on the "Standing" book.

I sketch the backside of the immortal *Victoire de Samothrace*, fascinated by the metal braces bolted to her wings and stuck into her butt to keep the graceful statue upright. Their presence testifies that she too will succumb to entropy.

Rigaud's *Sun King* shows off his legs in a ballet position, muscles defined by red high heels, tights, and garters. Those strong and fashionable underpinnings demonstrate his stability and strength and potency. Strap on the phallic sword, add the gold scepter he leans on, and you've got a royal stud.

I compare King Louis to Sam Levin's 1954 photo of Brigitte Bardot. High heels again. Artfully revealing clothing. These too are powerfully defined legs. But because Bardot lacks all the trappings of political power, because she has no phallic accouterments, because she herself lifts the dress to draw in the viewer, because she stands on a floor rather than on a raised platform, because her hips face the viewer rather than turn away, because she is woman and not a man, the effect is invitation as opposed to displayed power.

My experience tells me the nude figures in Jean Delville's 1898 *L'Ecole de Platon* should be naked women, bathers à la Cezanne, for example. I look for breasts. I try to ignore penises. But they are all men, beautiful men. How would John have responded to this painting? What would it have been like to spend a day with him in an art museum given his sense for line and color, his experience with watercolors and pastels?

Why do I feel uncomfortable looking at beautiful men? Because of the conventions I have grown up with? Because I connect beauty with sexuality? Must I do that? I can't imagine walking through an art museum without the tug of sex. Or through nature, for that matter. Is it an obsession? Or a common human experience?

I guess I'd answer that obsession is a common human experience. A male culture has given us plenty of female nudes, and I've learned as a female to regard them as exercises in form. But they're more than that, aren't they?

7 AUGUST 1993, BASEL, SWITZERLAND

I've come here to view a single painting, an antithesis to the vertical works I've been studying. The title character in Dostoyevsky's novel *The Idiot* remarks that Hans Holbein's painting of the dead Christ "might make some people lose their faith." I can empathize with that. This absolutely prostrate and claustrophobically framed figure, despite the bones and muscles and tendons characteristic of a biped, will never stand upright again. I'm not prepared, however, for how the emaciated, brutalized corpse stretched out on a slab reminds me of John's body after the autopsy.

14 AUGUST 1993, OREM

On Saturday I read part of this manuscript at the *Sunstone* Symposium in Salt Lake City, anxious to get responses but also nervous that my thoughts might be offensive, condescending, or simply uninteresting. It was a full room, people standing in the back and sitting around me on the floor. When I finished, they applauded until I blushed. That has never happened to me before. Not the blushing, but that kind of sustained response to something I've written.

17 AUGUST 1993, PROVO

Our Abbott family reunion was last week. Four days in the pure air of the mountains. An apocalyptic meteor shower. Good food. Rowing and horseback riding. Twenty-eight children to entertain. And a lot of talk about John.

He was a good man. He always brought presents for me. I didn't need them, but he thought I should have them. He always did things for my kids.

He was a thief, a drunkard, and he killed himself with his homosexuality.

He was a human being.

I was afraid of him.

I heard that someone John knew in San Diego died while they were living together. It devastated him. That was also about the time that a fire destroyed all John's possessions.

John had a bad crash on his motorcycle that put him in the hospital and left a big scar on his leg.

A bill collector came to Utah looking for three hundred dollars. I was listed as his mother. I paid.

John invested money with his boss in San Diego who cheated him out of it.

While John was working in the kitchen at the Hotel Utah and living with Grandpa and Grandma Hilton, I told him that if he was going to smoke, he couldn't live there. He moved out.

We didn't even know he was coming home from his mission. Dad and I had given permission for John to stay in Italy a few months longer. Ronald's parents went to pick Ronald up at the airport, and John was there too. John called home, and we went to the airport. We knew something was wrong. He wasn't overjoyed to see us or to be back. A church leader in Farmington told John that he couldn't use the other half of his round-trip ticket to go back to Italy. John went anyway. He couldn't work for the Mormon upholsterers he had helped, it turned out, but he still stayed for a month. I wish I had torn up the ticket. Other missionaries sent word that John's return visit was hurting the missionary work, that he had apostatized.

When John moved to Boise, he had sores that wouldn't heal, and there were several bouts of pneumonia.

18 AUGUST 1993, OREM

For most of my adult life, I have weighed exactly 150 pounds, John's weight when he died. Now I weigh 170. The extra pounds are on display when I sit down and lean to the front, a roll of fat completely foreign to my experience of self. At the reunion, Jill and Carol and Christy and I were sitting around talking about how we are changing as we age. Sensing an opportunity to make myself feel better, I mentioned the fat. Let's see it, Carol said. I rolled up my shirt and bent over to display what I figured they would declare an insignificant roll of flesh. That's gross! Jill and Christy said simultaneously. And that mole looks cancerous.

20 AUGUST 1993, OREM

Still thinking about the family reunion. We are a good family. We care for one another. And we share a sometimes troubled history, as in the story Carol told me for the first time.

At the end of a difficult summer, Carol crawled through her bedroom window at three in the morning to find Dad sitting in her room. There was shouting. An ultimatum. More shouting. Dad emptied Carol's purse on the bed. Marijuana! He grabbed her arm and threw her against a wall. He ordered her to pack her things, and before dawn they were on the road to Ricks College, a Mormon junior college in windswept Rexburg, Idaho. Carol swears she didn't say a word during the fourteen-hour trip. It was Christmas before they next spoke.

24 AUGUST 1993, OREM

The Miller Light clock still ticking—the arbitrary measure of this book.

28 AUGUST 1993, OREM

A Polaroid photo from John's briefcase. The black eyes look directly at me: strong, friendly, unsure, lost, humorous, insane, grandmother-ly—I obviously don't have a clue. How do you read eyes? The woman

has written on the photo:
LOVE! / Your drinking
buddy / Your pool buddy
/ Eight ball's mine / Beth.

Who was she?

*2 SEPTEMBER 1993,
PROVO*

It's 8:20 a.m. I listen
to a message on the an-
swering machine left by
a student in my Rilke
seminar. My brother
killed himself this morning, she says
tearfully, and I've got to go home. I don't know how long I'll be gone.

I didn't cry when I learned John had died. I haven't cried since.

She'll be gone for a long time.

3 SEPTEMBER 1993, PROVO

In my survey of German literature, we discussed Büchner's story
"Lenz," a harrowing account of a man fighting for sanity, desperate
for order as his life bleeds into chaos. Above all else he fears a life
without desire. Our discussion was more intense than usual. One
student spoke of his sister-in-law who had committed suicide just
weeks earlier. I mentioned Kant's *horror vacui* and John's fears to that
effect. What was Büchner's point? another student asked, his voice
as taut as the muscles bunched across his face. Why would he write
a stupid story like this?

4 SEPTEMBER 1993, PROVO

Several years ago, a BYU professor wrote a book about J. Golden
Kimball, a wiry general authority of the church whose high-pitched
profanities and alkali wit made him into a mythical figure. Kimball, the
book recounts, was on an irrigation board that included a more senior
general authority. A discussion ensued about a possible bridge over
the Jordan River. For God's sake, Kimball interjected, we don't need

a bridge over the Jordan River. I can piss halfway across the Jordan River. You are out of order, warned the senior authority. I know I am, admitted Kimball. When I was *in* order, I could piss all the way across.

There were complaints about the story, and the president of BYU had the book recalled and pulped. While I am president of this university, he is reported to have said, we will not have general authorities of the church pissing on the pages of our books.

6 SEPTEMBER 1993, OREM

Our golden retriever, Honey, escaped from the backyard this morning and gleefully followed me down the street. She refused to come to me despite repeated commands. If I could have caught her, I would have dragged her home. It was the same knot of anger that used to choke me while I pounded on John.

I stopped by Joseph's dorm last night. I told him he ought to tidy up his half of the room, gave him directions on when and how to work on his English essay, and after I left him in a boisterous crowd of fellow students worried about their inevitably bad influence on him.

Last night I had another in what has become a series of compulsory confrontations with my stake president.

Why do you think we are so concerned about your obedience to church authority? he asked.

I would rather not say.

Why not?

It will make you angry.

No, please tell me.

I think this all stems from your disapproval of what I wrote about your department's policy to base hiring decisions on church service and obedience rather than on academic credentials in religious studies.

My only motive is love for you, he asserted; my only motive is love. And for that you call me a liar. You can't know my motives, he shouted. You are claiming to know what I'm thinking, and you're calling me a liar. You are calling me a liar!

I'm sorry, I said. I knew I shouldn't have mentioned it.

My motives are pure, he said more quietly.

I have more complicated motives, I replied, and not all of them are pure. But I'm trying as well as I can to do what I think is right.

What do you think about BYU's academic-freedom policy?

What do you mean?

It was approved by the board of trustees. Do you disagree with them?

Are you suggesting I have to accept every university policy as scripture?

I wouldn't dare argue with what the Lord tells the brethren, he said.

7 SEPTEMBER 1993, OREM

On a trail high in the canyon lies a mouse. Its skin, stretched taut with the gasses of putrescence, shines with a healthy gray luster. The tail is a thin pole. The two hind legs poke out stiffly to finish the tripod. There are no front legs. No head. Where there must have been a bloody wound as big as the mouse, the skin has contracted. Sucking on that tight pucker are a swarm of yellow jackets, dangerously quick, ominously thirsty.

10 SEPTEMBER 1993, OREM

I just discovered that the pissing story was in fact published in the book in question. I was right, however, on a more general level. The story I recounted was put in to replace several other pissing stories that displeased authorities even more.

Dad, Tim told me yesterday, I know what you get when you mix yellow and green. What? I asked. Blue, he answered. When I was at the swimming pool the water was green, and when I peed in it, it turned blue.

It was months after I left home for college that I first felt comfortable using the words *piss* and *pee*. *Wet* was the proper word in our family.

11 SEPTEMBER 1993, OREM

Still going through John's things. A couple of newspaper clippings catch my eye today. The first announces that **TWO BOYS, ONE GIRL WIN $1000 SCHOLARSHIPS.** John, it says, will attend BYU as a predental student.

The second clipping reports that "the winners of an essay contest sponsored by the San Juan Mental Health and Counseling Service were announced at the annual meeting Tuesday night at City Hall. The contest topic was 'Important Factors in Teen-Age Mental Health.' First place winners received checks for $25. Senior Division: 1st, John Abbott, son of Mr. and Mrs. Bob Abbott."

I received a similar award (albeit third place) for a patriotic speech given in a contest sponsored by the Farmington Optimists Club. My ideas were bursting with Ayn Randian rectitude palatable to the conservative Optimists—"I believe that there is too much concern for the common man in this country. Unfortunately, the common or mediocre man is the center of attention. He *must* be guaranteed an income; he *must* receive free medical care."

I can't find John's mental-health essay, but I do uncover a typewritten speech called "Freedom's Challenge" with John's name in the top right corner. "Freedom challenges you to stand up and be counted," it begins. The first step is to be informed. Then, he exhorts, "Stand up and live your life as it should be lived, in its fullest glory.... [S]tand up and open your heart, your soul, your mind to the world. Let only good seep out of your heart into the world we know so well. Imprison the bad within the walls of your body." And finally, "Stand up and speak out, don't leave unsaid thoughts entwined around your soul.... Remember, your voice is the voice of democracy!... Speak out and use this freedom of speaking freely to rid our country of any undesirable elements." Vintage 1960s Farmington, New Mexico. The language of the time and the place speaking us both. And there's my potent standing metaphor!

14 SEPTEMBER 1993, OREM

A series of John's school photos:

Glasses and no glasses. Is it the same pair over all those years? A recurring curl. John's part switches from his left to his right. An orthodontist reopens his smile. Slight changes in the direction of his gaze speak volumes. I wish I had a photo for every day of John's life. For every hour of every day.

22 SEPTEMBER 1993, OREM

Christy called last night and said she had listened to a tape of my *Sunstone* reading. She liked the essay, she said, but pointed out that I had forgotten to list the ceramic hippopotamus bank she had kept from the things in his Boise apartment.

This morning I found a couple of John's stories in Mom's shed, written for a high school English class.

They Disappeared into Nothingness

Everything grew gray, then black, and then even a blacker black as it drew nearer. Soon everything was enveloped in such a darkness that, that, that … The blackness could not be described it was so black. Babies were crying, mothers screaming, fathers yelling on that dreadful black day.…

Suddenly a lonely bright disc appeared in that inky black sky.... What was it? Husbands clasped their husbands, husbands hugged their wives.... The disc rose, in the still quiet air of that black black day, just as slowly and stately as it had descended.... Where were the people? Where were the people?

A red *A* marks the first page of the handwritten story. The narrator almost gleefully disposes of everyone on the planet and (subconsciously?) features same-sex marriages.

There is a follow-up story, also marked with an *A*:

I Was the Last Person Alive in the World

Where was I? Where are all the people? Every building was intact. Then I remembered. The world's population, except me, had been killed by the "epidemic." What should I do? I thought about suicide. Wait, I told myself, I can go on living quite easily. I decided I would try it for a while.

When I got to New York I found a car dealer and got in the newest model and drove off. Speed, speed, speed was all I could think about. I drove far and fast, stopping only to get gas and to eat. When I got to the Utah Salt Flats I found the car with the world's record waiting to go. I got in and ZOOM! I was off. Soon I found out I didn't know how to stop it. 500 miles an hour and a house right in front of me. Crash! Bang! I hit it. And I was killed instantly.

23 SEPTEMBER 1993, PROVO

At lunch today my friend Sam mentioned he had a homosexual dream last night. He identified it as part of a series of events related to growing insecurities.

I had a strange dream last night as well. I was in bed with a very attractive woman. Noise from the other side of the door worried me, so she stuck a knife in the lock to ensure our privacy. We started to make love. When I discovered she had a small penis, I pulled back.

I explained very clearly that I wasn't interested in a homosexual relationship; I had thought she was a woman. She said she was in fact a woman and that the penis was vestigial. Convinced, I turned back to our lovemaking.

24 SEPTEMBER 1993, PROVO

Yesterday I asked my student whose brother committed suicide how she was doing. What, she asked through tears, what do you think will happen to him now? He's done all those things. Won't God judge him harshly? What about our eternal family?

Damn a religion that makes it even harder to lose a loved one. Goddamn it.

7 OCTOBER 1993, WASHINGTON, DC

In a Hot Shoppes restaurant for breakfast, I work on my paper for the German-studies conference. A thin-faced black woman in a blue overcoat sits across from me over a cup of coffee. Beside her stands a four-legged aluminum cane. She waves her hand at my papers and tells me I should have done my homework last night. I sure should have, I say. She has a story for me: A little boy came up to his mother. Mama, he says, I drank eight Cokes. Oh, sugar! she said. It's okay, he said. I burped Seven-Up. I laugh. She looks into my face to see if I really get it. Have a nice day, she says, and shuffles off.

The National Gallery features an exhibit of original Audubon watercolors. His obsession with birds was incredibly fruitful. The culture I grew up in works against such obsessions unless the focus is the family. "No success can compensate for failure in the home." Why must the family be the only measure? Audubon killed a lot of birds in his quest for a complete and exact catalog. His portrait of himself over a chasm with a dead eagle on his back reminds me of my own double-edged enterprise.

At the Hirshhorn: Francis Bacon's *Triptych Inspired by T. S. Eliot's Poem "Sweeney Agonistes"*—"Birth, and copulation, and death. / That's all the facts when you come to brass tacks: / Birth, and copulation, and death." And family.

Shampooing and conditioning my hair this morning with the Hyatt Hotel's "specially bottled products," I remembered the shampoo we used at home. Penny conscious as she had to be with seven children and Dad's junior high school salary, Mom gave us laundry detergent for shampoo. I can still feel the granules that bit into my scalp. Mom insists that people wondered how she got our hair so shiny.

It's a good allegory for the astringent religion she taught us. John with an open scalp wound.

9 OCTOBER 1993, WASHINGTON, DC

Corcoran Museum of Art: "I Remember... Thirty Years after the March on Washington: Images of the Civil Rights Movement, 1963–93." I remember too. Our years in high school and at BYU during the sixties and early seventies were flavored by an unrelenting political conservatism. The civil rights movement was a communist front. So was abstract painting. B. F. Larsen, chair of the Art Department at BYU, thought it prudent to warn abstract painter George Dibble about the dangers of abstraction: You are flirting with apostasy and are on the brink of communism!

23 OCTOBER 1993, SALT LAKE ART CENTER

Alex is scheduled to perform his "For the House." I'm early, and the auditorium is mostly empty. A man comes in and starts to sit in the empty row in front of me, then changes his mind and sits in the chair right next to mine. I don't much like the proximity and hope he's not a faggot.

My colleague Linda Rugg, visiting this year from Ohio State, said she asked students to speak in Swedish about something they didn't like. One of the students asked how to say "faggot" in Swedish. We don't say that in Swedish, she answered, nor do we say it in English.

Alex chants and sings and shouts:

> Don't worry about the sun, it won't happen in your lifetime....
>   Always and always and always and alwaysotherwiseotherways
>   and all....

Then there is the bird, then there is the bird, then there is the bird:
It flies for your eyes.

2 NOVEMBER 1993, OREM

John's clock is still ticking, although when I set it back for the end of daylight savings time, I only had to fall back fifty-one minutes.

The day before Halloween I drove Maren and two other girls to their ballet class. I'm going to dress up like a man, one of them said, with a suit and a tie. I said I thought that would be cute. After the class, Maren and I walked into our kitchen and found a girl sitting at the kitchen table. On second glance it turned out to be Benjamin, wearing a wig and dress. He said he was going to wear it to school the next day. I told him the other children would make fun of him. He looked at me like I was from another planet.

4 NOVEMBER 1993, OREM

J. Edgar Hoover, certain that left turns were dangerous, instructed his driver to make only right turns. J. Edgar Hoover, certain that homosexuals were security risks, instructed his men to flush out the faggots. J. Edgar Hoover, when driving alone, was said to have made secret left turns.

11 NOVEMBER 1993, OREM

I heard Adrienne Rich read poetry and essays last night at A Women's Place Bookstore in Salt Lake. She is a small woman with short gray hair and a stiff leg. The poems were as beautiful as they were enlightening. And shocking. One poem described a man who killed two lesbians on the Appalachian Trail, "his defense they had teased his loathing / of what they were."

She spoke about the drive to connect and about the dream of a common language, and I watched a translucent little spider clamber through the black and gray hair of the woman in front of me, returning to the topmost hairs after every downward foray. Instinctively upward, up to where a web can be useful, up to where it won't be crushed on the ground. But what good is that instinct when the spider is climbing on an erect, movable island?

Rich explored the need to invent what we desire: "To track your own desire, in your own language, is not an isolated task. You yourself are marked by family, gender, caste, landscape, the struggle to make a living, or the absence of such a struggle.... Look into the images."

I will track my own desire, I swear, my brother's desire. I will read familiar marks of gender and landscape, look into the images that mark us. I wish I were Adrienne Rich.

12 NOVEMBER 1993, PROVO

A noisy beetle of a backhoe rumbled past as I rode my bike to work this morning. In its wake I felt the pressure and heat and smell of a diesel motor, sensations that took me back to the Arizona desert between Phoenix and Tucson where I worked that one summer. Drilling through granite at a depth of two miles, it took several hours to drill down a thirty-foot length of pipe, several hours between the connections that required my presence. The desert cooled off in the hours before sunrise, and I often found my way to the shelf running along one of the draw-works' engines. I slept against the dragon's warmth, soothed by the steady rumblings in its bowels. When the driller revved the engine to raise the bit off bottom, the sound woke me, and I staggered up to the floor to help throw in the slips, break loose the tightly married pipes, swab the joint with pipe dope, add a length of pipe, spin it down with the chain, tighten it with the tongs, lift out the slips to recommence drilling. Then back to the diesel comfort of the draw-works' engine.

Our parents worked hard for what they had. One of Dad's favorite bits of advice: Always do more than the job requires.

19 NOVEMBER 1993, PROVO

I arrived at work this morning at seven thirty, just as a tinny national anthem blared from the roof of the library, giving notice that the flag was being hoisted in front of the administration building. Students and faculty and employees stopped walking and stood in patriotic deference. From where I was locking my bike, I could see the two uniformed ROTC cadets assigned to raise the flag. They had been marching from the administration building to the flagpole when the anthem began to play. They halted dutifully and stood at attention. Then it occurred to them that they were standing because the flag was being raised. They took a few more steps toward the flagpole, but the force of the anthem was too much for them, and they again drew themselves to attention. Inexplicably, one of them turned around and headed toward the administration building. The other called him back. The music ceased, mercifully, and they marched raggedly to the flagpole.

The university grounds crew has instructions from the board of trustees to make the campus look "clipped and controlled," a concept borrowed from the absolutist French landscape garden. I prefer the more natural English garden—botanically and metaphorically.

Last Sunday, in church for the first time in several months, I listened to a flat-topped, white-shirted buyer for BYU speak about the encroaching evils of the world. He had just been in Las Vegas for a purchasing convention, he said, and the university had supplied him with tickets for a show on the Strip. It turned out to be a girlie show, he reported grimly, all nine acts!

23 NOVEMBER 1993, PROVO

When I left home at seven thirty this morning, it was cloudy, still, and warm. Five minutes later I was pedaling through a snowstorm. I bent my head to keep the snow out of my eyes, and my world shrank to the motion of my legs, the beating of my heart, and the patch of wet asphalt directly in front of the hissing front tire. Now I sit in my office and watch flakes sift onto tree branches, rooftops.

Dream this morning: I was playing tennis with John. We had only one racket, so we practiced serving. I was chasing balls John had hit when a couple of guys moved onto our court. They pushed John out of the way. I argued with them, but they wouldn't listen. I ran at the nearest of them. He saw me coming, but before he could move I slammed into him with enormous force, threw him to the ground, and savagely attacked his face.

The BYU Board of Trustees is continuing its retreat from the idea of a university. Active Mormon, Pulitzer Prize winner, and MacArthur Fellow Laurel Thatcher Ulrich has been named persona non grata on campus. Her crime? She was once involved with the Mormon feminist publication *Exponent II.*

13 DECEMBER 1993, OREM

The last time I visited home before the accident, Dad let me drive his first new car in almost thirty years. After a block or two he told me I was shifting gears too late. Irritated, I said something about how I drove my Volkswagen. This is no Volkswagen, he said sharply.

Stretching a weekend by driving all night from New Mexico to northern Colorado, anxious to see his dying mother one more time, battling a spring snowstorm, thirty miles short of the destination, Dad miscalculated (or dozed off?) and sent the new car into a spin. An abandoned car on the shoulder of the road did the damage.

I wasn't there. The four who were are reluctant to remember. The sleepy darkness, the sudden awakening, the shattering loss of warmth when snow gusted into the car and blood flowed, Dad's shouts to Mom and the children, Christy and Paul and Jeff frantic on the road until someone finally stopped, noise and lights and confusion, Mom watching Dad die while her own ruptured spleen went unnoticed, the helicopter, the ambulance, the irrevocable loss.

17 DECEMBER 1993, PROVO

I pull at my eyebrows and collect a little pile of curved hairs on a sheet of white paper. I bite my fingernails and add the little crescents to the pile. Inert parts of myself on paper. How is my list of John's personal effects any different from these remnants? The photos I have gathered? The sentences I have written? As a mammal with a large neocortex, I can manipulate symbols. To what end?

Although I think your judgment is sometimes skewed, I ought to tell you that your rambling thoughts are important to me. So you're not going to find the Holy Grail. Big deal.

19 DECEMBER 1993, OREM

John's Civitan trip to Colorado. What happened in the dorm room with the roommate? The closest I can approximate that event would be my seventh grade trip to band camp at BYU. During the week in the dormitory, my roommate showed me how to play strip poker. We played behind closed blinds. It was the first time I had an erection in the presence of another person. It was playful and secret and more memorable than anything else that happened there that week. The other boy claimed he could hold up a towel on his stiff penis, and that became our goal. Looking back it feels a bit like (don't laugh) a manifestation of Kant's purposefulness without a purpose, a nonteleological playfulness, no orgasms anticipated or experienced. There was no longing for hands or lips. Making out with my girlfriend as late as my first year in college, I was still (incredibly) in the dark about the exact physical goal of all our kissing and hugging. But there was that erection again.

What if the roommate and I had been a year or two older? What if I had found him attractive? Weren't the erections proof of attraction? Proof at least of an ambiguous position on the sexual continuum? The experience didn't trouble me at all (although the fact that I remember it thirty years later means something). It felt natural. It promised later responses to intimate encounters (always with women, it turned out) in the years that followed.

23 DECEMBER 1993, OREM

After Carol moved her little family from Boise to Las Cruces, John thought about moving to Nashville. One of Carol's letters was in his briefcase: "Hope you're getting enough money to move. Wish there was a cheaper way to get to Tennessee. Bet Scott is thrilled to have you move to Nashville. You two have so much in common that you'll have fun." Maybe we would have. And maybe not. I remember being apprehensive at the time. What kinds of demands would John put on my time? Would he ask me for money? For some reason he never made the move. Was it my lack of response?

28 DECEMBER 1993, OREM

New snow this morning. I woke up with thoughts settled overnight into the elegant line of a telemark turn. They moved on to the familial chaos in Loren Eiseley's essay "The Star Thrower." Unable to sleep, the troubled Eiseley walks along the dark shore to find a man throwing stranded starfish back into the surf. He remembers a photo of his mother at the age of six: "The eyes in the photograph were already remote and shadowed by some inner turmoil."

At lunch Sam Rushforth says that his own father, near death, called Nurse Ratchett over. She covered the tracheotomy hole in his throat, and he rasped what were nearly his last words: I'd like to give you a carbolic-acid enema.

Our parents were less troubled, more conventional than Eiseley's mother or Sam's father. I don't get up before dawn, tormented, to walk the beach. I have been secure in a family whose aggressions are strictly civilized. (Freud made predictions about the likely consequences of this.) In middle age I stumble through my own ruins like an amateur archaeologist. I find internal structures reeking of conformity and control, unsettled by desire.

These are predictable and understandable responses to the slowing pace and diminishing hopes middle age brings.

Do you really think it's this predictable? This easily understood? Nothing but a midlife crisis?

29 DECEMBER 1993, OREM

Mormon family stories, gathered and written by zealous amateur genealogists, are generically faith promoting. We tell tales of "Latter-day Saints." Isaiah's admonition is stamped on my "Book of Remembrance": "Now go, write it before them in a table, and note it in a book, that it may be for the time to come for ever and ever." For ever and ever. Family chains promise eternal relationships. Pedigree charts and hagiographic stories make that abstraction flesh.

How is it that genealogies so often begin with coats of arms? "The Hilton Family is the most ancient in England, the oldest entitled to bear arms in England," writes my grandfather Hilton's brother in his history of the family. He is doubly proud when he can establish racial nobility based on biblical covenant:

> As believers in modern revelation, we know that in some way— probably from the invaders from northern Europe—there came to England some of the blood of Israel, especially that of Ephraim. The descendants of these people of "the blood that believes" have demonstrated this by their glad and ready acceptance of the message and authority of the restored gospel. They have furnished the dominating strength and leadership of the Church and Kingdom of God in these latter days.
>
> With almost complete unanimity...descendants of Hugh and Isabella Hilton are still proving faithful, as were their ancient forebears, to the truth that they had the opportunity to receive...from the racial mixture of the freedom-loving people of England.

With almost complete unanimity, he claims, we continue to prove through faithfulness that we have the literal blood of believers and are destined to be authoritative church leaders. If the racial force is so powerful, what happened to John? Or to me? What about the rest of the descendants of Anglo-Saxon "Ephraimites"? Thousands fled nineteenth-century industrial slavery for the promise of a new communitarian Zion on the American frontier. Millions didn't.

In 1978 the leader of the Mormon Church reversed the policy of denying the priesthood to men "of African descent," and that might have ended our religious racism. But even in a hierarchical religion, it's not that easy. When the only Native American general authority of the church was excommunicated a few years ago, Mom lamented the tragedy. While he rose in the hierarchy, she recalled, he sat up there with the other authorities and was no longer dark, just like the Book of Mormon promises: "And many generations shall not pass away among them, save they shall be a white and delightsome people."

The Book of Mormon has been changed, I told her. It now says "pure" and delightsome. The "white" was meant metaphorically. That has been made clear for literalists.

I would think twice, she answered tersely, before I changed the Book of Mormon.

Mom's favorite family story is about her great-grandmother Maria Jackson Normington Parker:

> At last, on July 28, 1856, the Martin Handcart Company started westward from Iowa City.... With brave hearts they traveled on, often singing:
>
> > For some must push, and some must pull,
> > As we go marching up the hill,
> > And merrily on the way we go
> > Until we reach the Valley, O.
>
> Soon after leaving Fort Laramie it became necessary to cut down the rations. The pound of flour was reduced to ¾ of a pound, and after to ½ a pound, and still later to something less, or nothing at all. Still the company toiled cheerfully on through the Black Hills country.
>
> About this time, the baby boy, one and a half years old, died, and grandmother was permitted to ride one half day with her dead child, until the company stopped and it could be buried. Soon after, a new baby was born to her which also died.
>
> On the morning of October 19 the beds of the company were covered with four inches of snow. The storm continued for several days until the snow was 15 inches deep on the level. But still they struggled on, strong in their faith in the glorious gospel, and their hopes for a new life in Zion.

It was about this time when cholera visited the starved, suffering camp, and one night Grandpa Normington and sixteen others died and were buried in the same grave.

Grandma walked until her feet were so terribly frozen and sore she could walk no more. Then she crawled along on her hands and knees, and when her hands were so frozen she could use them no more, she went on her knees and elbows, until even after many years, at the time of her death, there were great scars on her knees and elbows from this awful experience. She remembered nothing of the last part of the journey.

Grandmother was a most faithful Latter-day Saint, and felt that the Gospel, for which she had endured so many trials, was the most glorious of all blessings.... She lived and taught the gospel and raised her family to be good, staunch, honorable Latter-day Saints. She was a loving, affectionate mother, but was firm and strict in having her children obey. (Annie Hilton Bishop, granddaughter, 1929).

Holy smokes! Elbows and knees at the Sweetwater! It doesn't get much wilder. Brave. Cheerful. Staunch! We live out the heavily freighted past they hand down. This story ought to be accompanied by an account of the impatient zeal that pushed the Willie-Martin group out onto the plains much later in the year than experience deemed wise. Brigham Young was livid at the reckless, heedless stupidity of those zealots.

Or so he postured. It was, after all, his plan of migration.

At the age of eighty-five, my grandfather recorded memories of his mother:

I was born in 1902 so wasn't part of Virgin City, but to think of mother and the hardships they had moving up from Virgin City to Abraham, they were terrible.

Sometimes when the kids had necessary things to do, they would end up in a quarrel. Mother would say, Oh, I think I'll go crazy.

Mother grew up in a bishop's home. I don't ever remember her bearing her testimony in Sacrament meeting but I don't doubt but what she bore her testimony. She was a very faith actuated woman and I have no question but what her faith was as sound as any of her family, and they have grown up and all married in the temple.

I had no question about my mother's faith. She fit into her area and fulfilled her requirements whatever they were. She was constantly busy with such a big family. Every day had its constant needs. There were times I know that mother had the feeling of depression, but I never heard her complain for lack of anything. I never felt that mother felt that she was a burdened woman in that sense.

As far as I can remember my love for my mother was never in question nor her love for me, and that was true of the entire family. She and father were not an affectionate couple. I don't ever remember hearing them quarrel nor of ever hearing father tell her he loved her. He just wasn't that type of person. Mother would give us hugs when we had been away for a bit and I'm sure she must have told us she loved us. We had a good Mormon home.

Writing John's story against the gravity of this kind of history is like trying to fly with no wings. Sacred racist blood. Sound faith. Brave hearts. Cheerful toil. Good, staunch, honorable Latter-day Saints who fitted into their areas. But making history faith promoting isn't so easy, either. The phrase "good Mormon home" follows closely on the heels of emotional distance and repeated denials that love was lacking. There were scars on elbows and knees, and there were scarred psyches as well.

There is no place in faith-promoting stories like these for a moment I can pinpoint exactly: Princeton, New Jersey, April 21, 1979, 6:30 p.m. Walking home after a long day in the library, I experienced an epiphany, as close to revelation as I have ever come. I was brought up short, in midstep and midthought, by the abrupt awareness that I was no longer a believer. And then the surprising realization: the epistemological shift had little effect on my sense for right and wrong. The patterns of life that had proved so productive for me had been chosen pragmatically rather than superstitiously. I had good reasons for my actions, and those reasons remained valid.

What do you mean when you write: I was no longer a believer? Have you spent the next fifteen years as a hypocrite?

I no longer believed in God. I was left to accept, to admire, to practice—admittedly weak positions in a Mormonism dominated by certainty. Surely that doesn't mean my decades of trying to be a decent person, my volunteer work and tithes and the raising of my children as Mormons, my conscientious teaching at a Mormon university, have been hypocritical acts.

Agreed, but I also have some thoughts on patterns. I don't know how healthy it is to rip out a pattern that has helped to form oneself and one's family and heritage. The patterns are simplified and have a lot of blank spaces. If you retain the pattern and fill in the blank spaces, you create the complexity that allows for individuality, variation, and the joining of several patterns.

That's exactly how I have tried to live, as the years of church activity after my so-called epiphany demonstrate. Patterns become less useful, however, when their outlines begin to lose their clarity. For instance, the repeated admonition by Mormon leaders that transgressions lead to a loss of faith made little sense to me after the epiphany that came in the context of a devoted and faithful life.

30 DECEMBER 1993, 9:30 P.M., OREM

A cold wind gusting outside. I'm in the basement, a single light burning over my desk. When I walked in the door, seven-year-old Samuel ran to give me a big hug. He couldn't have known how much I needed the warmth of his little body. I tucked him into bed with Benjamin, and as I left the room it was to their combined and ritual assurance: *Ich liebe dich, schlaf wohl.* Then I made my way down to the study to work through the feelings that have collected over the last two hours. I'm just back from seeing the movie *Philadelphia.* I watched Tom Hanks die of AIDS while Denzel Washington conquered his homophobia and won their lawsuit. While he died, Hanks was surrounded and supported by a loving family, a faithful lover, a good lawyer, and friends. That's the part I'm having trouble with. John died unattended, vomiting and gasping for oxygen. He was alone in his extremity, just as he had been alone for much of his life. It was no Hollywood story, as I have noted before.

I can't embrace John, nor he me. I can't turn out the light for him or hand him his medicine or ask him what he thinks about Eiseley's "Star Thrower." I'm left to feel sorry for myself and to swear that the one world I will no longer inhabit is the one where love is not the god.

Dream: I entered a deep cave where John had been living with a beautiful woman. He was absent. At the back hung some of his framed paintings. I marveled at the beauty of his work, at the texture of the paper he used. His blue pack was lying on the floor. I emptied it and found charcoal sticks. The woman said, "His charcoals." We walked back to the front of the cave and exchanged glances; our hands brushed; we began to kiss. Someone came to take down the paintings. We ignored him and caressed one another intimately. I thought it right that I should take over my brother's duty in his absence. I exulted when she writhed under my touch.

31 DECEMBER 1993, OREM

The year draws to a close.

What else would I write on the last day of the year? "Draws to a close." Is the rest of what I've been writing that predictable? Is it stupid to try to assert the worth of a failed life? Is any life failed? Is it productive to construct believable fictions? To be sure of something and to be wrong? To be human? Thoughts harden into print and practice. Flights of fancy become reality. Metaphors reify. Reproductions distort and fix.

About the time John was practicing his backhand on the high school court, he and Dad got into a fight about something. I remember

watching them move bellig-
erently through the kitchen.
There were shouts and
shoves. John left the house
carrying a sleeping bag. It
grew dark, and Dad sat in
the kitchen with Mom. I
overheard scraps of their
conversation and still
remember Dad's heated
assertions that he should
step down as bishop of our
ward, citing Paul's counsel
to Titus: "Ordain elders in
every city, as I had appointed thee: If any be blameless,

the husband of one wife, having faithful children not accused of riot or
unruly. For a bishop must be blameless, as the steward of God." Mom
assured him that he was a good bishop. Dad and I went out looking
for John. He had been watering the neighbors' lawn while they were
on vacation, and we tried there first. The end of John's sleeping bag
was sticking out the door of their tool shed. Reassured, we returned
home and went to sleep (at least I went to sleep). Sometime the next
day John came home.

Why, I wonder, is Paul's portrait of a bishop so uncompromising?
Where are the half tones? And why the intemperate racial stereotyping
of the following verses? "For there are many...deceivers, specially
they of the circumcision...who subvert whole houses, teaching things
which they ought not, for filthy lucre's sake....Wherefore rebuke
them sharply."

*Paul does sound angry here, but it might help if you read some good
biblical criticism. What's being left unsaid? What assumptions, what
worldview, did Paul share that may have filled in between the lines?
You, by the way, are similarly intemperate every time you talk about
morticians, hierarchs, the pious. It makes for flat people.*

I'm not so sure. Why give Paul the benefit of the doubt? Following his lead, conditioned by his biases and by the prejudices of a conservative Christian nation, our parents helped pass along, part and parcel with their conservative stability, a racism related to Paul's. I had to confront this again a few weeks ago while waiting at a streetlight. Around the corner came a car driven by a black man. A white female passenger was snuggled up close to him. My stomach turned.

You actually felt nauseous?

There was always a bowl of nuts on our table for the holiday season: hazelnuts, peanuts, walnuts, pistachios, pecans, and nigger toes. That's what we grew up calling them.

Dad taught science and math at the junior high school before he became principal. As a science teacher he had access to mercury and to our delight brought home glass vials of it. We split it into quivering masses with our fingers and raced heavy blobs down inclines. Dimes, when rubbed with mercury, glistened like polished silver.

Families can be toxic with the best of intentions. Among John's things was *Love You Forever*, a children's book Mom had given him for Christmas in 1989. It's an inane little book that has gone through innumerable printings, perhaps because of its saccharine denial of mortality. In the front Mom wrote: "Dear John, This is how I feel about you and will always feel about you. You are my son forever and that's how long I will love you. Remember that all your life. I know Dad feels the same way. We both want you to be with our family forever. You can, you know. Love, Mom."

A song our children learn in church spells it out in similarly sweet verse:

Families can be together forever
Through Heavenly Father's plan,
I always want to be
With my own family
And the Lord has shown me how I can.

This is becoming hard to read. It makes you out as someone who hasn't a clue about normal human longing. These may be unsophisticated renderings, but can't you use your imagination—or some charity?

Families can also be ripped apart through "Heavenly Father's plan." How is John supposed to avoid that fate? By conforming to the rules of the church: no smoking, no drinking, no sex outside of marriage. He will need to live a stable, conservative life; have respectable friends; and be of service to the community. And, of course, attend church and not speak evil of the Lord's anointed and give 10 percent of what he earns to the church. And perhaps not eat too much meat and read the scriptures daily and hold a position in the church and pray often and repent of all his sins and have a family of his own and not be a homosexual and avoid depression and obey council from his leaders and sustain the prophet and not have a beard and see no R-rated movies. There's not much room for individuality or difference, but the rewards are eternal—and ironic. John spent his life fleeing the structured vision of his family and his faith, asserting his difference. What Mom offers, with all the love and faith she can muster, is a family blessing based on denial of difference.

But that's the framework she has. At least she didn't rip her clothes ritually and say he was dead for her. You are not seeing the whole picture.

A thought for the year's end from the final verses of the Hebrew Bible—Malachai's prediction of unspeakable violence: "For behold, the day comes, burning like an oven, when all the arrogant and all evildoers will be stubble; the day that comes shall burn them up, says the Lord of hosts, so that it will leave them neither root nor branch." Then the promise, couched between two more references to the curse: "Behold, I will send you Elijah the prophet before the great and terrible day of the Lord comes. And he will turn the hearts of fathers to their children and the hearts of children to their fathers, lest I come and smite the land with a curse."

As much as I despise the arrogant violence of the curse—this is true religion?—the image of a trunk without roots or branches works in me powerfully. It is, perhaps, a deep-seated fear of loneliness, of solipsism, of isolation that keeps me employed at a church university that would have attached electrodes to my brother's testicles to shock the hell out of him, that keeps me in a marriage that is, increasingly, not a marriage.

[John's Green and Tan Notebook #2]

A poem:
Rhapsody of Life
cacooned in solitude
holidays encrouch
naieve beliefs
in concrete
another religious myth
a time forced to remember
society dictates
open hearts

Secrets feed addictions
so share your secrets

You have to use (3) things to be successful
1. you use your mind to conceive
2.   "   "   "   eyes to perceive
3. and you use your hands to achieve

T.V. Doctors 377-2525 $10 Housecall

Etheral world,
euphoria present.
floating mediocrity
slows, each moment.

Reality fades
self-worth diminishes

a quagmire of being
sidles, down the road.

gamberone — gambe — 5 prawns
seafood primavera — s.f. prima — 2 prawns, fish, scallops
veal marsala — marsala — 4 pieces, mushroom
veal piccata — piccata — 4 pieces
carbanara — carb — bacon, pr
liver —   liver —   2 pieces, onions

Martin Luther King
Jesse
Reggie Jack
Michael

was in very bad
rushed
rifle refused to
He believed the firing pin might
break.   he said the telescopic sight
be properly aligned and
designed for a left-handed person
right handed   Oswald
him   poor marksmanship

Lime Marinade for fish
1/4 cup tequila
2 limes juiced
1 tbs chopped cilantro
1 tsp minced fresh herbs sage basil ecc.
salt pepper

Channel 2 11:30 Wed:
State employees bitching about not getting cost of living wage increase. What about us working people who have limited or no guarantees, health ins. ecc. Why give the above raises. They make more than most of us.

Shimmering nymph	Masocistic youth
Humanistic,	Aggressive soul
Elusive	Tennascious being
Rapturous,	Terrtierary man
Inception	

Life (is), in short, ridiculously easy, and for a while at least (we) are able to cope with the problems of aimlessness and isolation by deciding to ignore them...
The *Restaurant at the End of the Universe*, Douglas Adams

6

Our Feet
Are the Same

> Nothing stands still for us. This is the state which is ours
> by nature, yet to which we least incline: we burn to find
> solid ground, a final steady base on which to build a tower
> that rises to infinity; but the whole foundation cracks
> beneath us and the earth splits open down to the abyss.
>
> —PASCAL

1 JANUARY 1994, OREM, UTAH

His feet are livid, I wrote. Don't touch him, the mortician warned.
I wish I had touched him.

3 JANUARY 1994, OREM

"Why can't I be good?" Lou Reed sings this question in Wim
Wenders's film *Far Away, So Close!* "Why can't I act like a man? Why
can't I be good?" Was John good? Am I good? What does *good* mean?
The *American Heritage Dictionary* says that the root **ghedh-** means
"To unite, join, fit. 1. GOOD, from Germanic *godaz*, 'fitting, suitable.'"
You are good then, in the root sense, if you unite, join, or fit, if you
are fitting and suitable. But who decides what and who is suitable?
And what if that leaves you out?

John's first grade report card from Lincoln Elementary School in
Montpelier, Idaho, defines him as thoroughly good and satisfactory: he

has a first grade respect for law and order; he scores well in two categories of cleanliness.

Mrs. Anderson's comments on John's report card indicate that she found him a little gentleman and a hard worker. "Johnny is a very good student." His bright face in the class photo may be the result of getting to stand directly in front of her.

In his second grade picture he's got quite a different look on his face.

10 FEBRUARY 1994, PROVO, UTAH

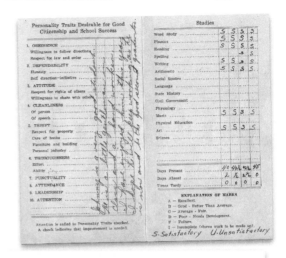

BYU's academic vice president, a man I have known for twenty years, asked me to come to his office this week. Scott, he said, I'm not sure what this is about, but your stake president called and said you were no longer worthy to teach at BYU. I asked if it was the *Sunstone* publication. He assured me it was not. Do you have any idea what this is about?

He's still angry that I have a mind of my own.

He claims there is more.

I haven't paid tithing for the last year. But you're not going to fire me because I don't pay tithing.

Yes, we will.

I'll pay up then.

Once again I sit in the stake president's office. A calendar from Berg Mortuary hangs on the wall. The last two times we met he shouted at me and told me that if I were obedient to everything church leaders require, I would never go astray.

Astray? Moved away from a group? I'm guilty already.

So now I sit and hold my tongue. Yes, I will pay tithing. Yes, I will attend all three church meetings each Sunday. Yes, I will accept any call to church service issued by the bishop. He smiles and shakes my hand and calls me Brother Abbott.

You drive a hard bargain, Roger, I reply.

This professor of religion once told assembled men of the priesthood that "the trouble with women in this stake is they aren't priesthood broke."

14 FEBRUARY 1994, OREM

When I started college in 1967, I bought a blue paperback edition of the Book of Mormon for my required religion class. Today I find it on a shelf and flip through pages illustrated by an artist obsessed with chiseled faces and massive muscles. I worked the book hard, highlighted passages, underlined ideas, made marginal notes on the chiastic structures Mormon scholars were claiming tied the authors to Hebrew patterns. Inside the back cover I copied a passage from Joseph Smith's "Lectures on Faith": "The man of faith hears the voice of the Lord and does what he says—no matter what."

15 FEBRUARY 1994, OREM

I dream that I'm sitting in Grandma Abbott's front room with several of my children and John, who lies on a couch reading a book. I explain to Nathan that I am willing to help execute John because the law requires it and John is willing to submit to what is required. It seems quite logical. Nathan goes away, and within the dream I fall into a light sleep. In that dreamed sleep, I am striking John's head with a heavy object. I wake up into the first dream and declare to myself and then to the others that I won't help execute John. They want an explanation.

20 FEBRUARY 1994, OREM

REBEL FILMMAKER DEREK JARMAN, 52, DIES OF AIDS.

23 FEBRUARY 1994, OREM

Ponavljanje (Repetitions) has been published in Belgrade. Our book recounts Žarko's and my trip into Slovenia, first my version in translation, then his. I can't read much of the Serbo-Croatian text, but I do recognize my name in Žarko's telling, often enhanced by declension: Scottom, Scottovih, Scotto Abbotto.

28 FEBRUARY 1994, OREM

This weekend an article in Boise's *Idaho Statesman* reported that "ex-gay ministries shove aside the genetics argument. They say a failure to bond with parents, child abuse and family immorality contribute to homosexuality."

That doesn't much resemble our family. It does, however, remind me of a favorite bumper sticker: UTAH, GUILT WITHOUT SIN.

3 MARCH 1994, AMERICAN FORK, UTAH

Mom and her older sister Marilyn have been recording memories of their stepmother, Vera. Marilyn's recollections, Mom tells me, are more positive than her own. Their stepmother had a heart condition, Mom remembers, and seldom left her couch. Mom felt she was ignored, for the most part, by her stepmother and by her chronically absent father ("I was not present at her birth because I was employed by the Hilton Brothers Motor Co. operating a one-man station in Hinkley, Utah").

6 MARCH 1994, OREM

I phoned Jill this morning. She said she had just made bread using John's bread pans. The bread pans! I forgot them when I listed John's things.

A few years ago we wrote and collected memories of Mom and gave them to her for Christmas.

Paul had fond memories of family backpacking trips. Christy wrote:

> The earliest thing I remember is asking Mom to read me Bible stories, stories of Jesus, so I wouldn't have scary dreams. I always remember Mom and Dad kneeling by their bed praying and also having family prayer in the morning and evening. Sometimes I was embarrassed if friends were visiting, but Dad always handled it like it was the most natural thing to do.

She included a note about an experience in the ninth grade:

> I really tried to read and study the scriptures and pray and do everything I should. One night as I was praying about John, a bright light came into my room and shone on the wall. I had a warm feeling come over me and I knew that John would be okay and we would all be a family forever.... From that time on, I have never doubted that John would be with us forever.

I read Christy's beautiful account and feel like an outsider gazing into what looks like a warmly lit room.

Carol wrote:

> When Lynn was strangled by the bars of his crib, Jill and I were in the bathtub. I remember sitting in the tub a long time before we got out.
>
> When you and Dad would go out for the evening I knew you would never come back. I spent hours looking and watching out the front window of the kitchen waiting for you to return. I could almost hide when I put the curtain over my head as I looked into the darkness. Tears streamed down my face while my mind raced 100 mph thinking of all the terrible things that might prevent you from coming home to me.

Jeff's memories were of comfort and security:

> Monday through Saturday, Mom would read from Tolkien's *Lord of the Rings* and on Sunday she would read a biography of a prophet. After reading to us she would put on a record for us to go to sleep by. My favorite was the "one with the birds" (Beethoven's 6th Symphony). The best thing about the inside of our house was the smell. Mom was always cooking cinnamon rolls, bread, or cookies.

John still had his copy of the collection, and although he hadn't contributed to it originally, his notes on my twelve pages reveal much. His first note is an answer to my question about place: "Junior Sunday School. Montpelier, Idaho. Or was it Paonia, Colorado? Sunday after Sunday she stood in front of us and taught us to sing. Filled with her warmth, basking in her love, bursting with pride that she was my mother, I told myself she was the most beautiful woman in the world."

Montpelier, John wrote.

I mentioned acting in a pageant, an ignominious role that required lipstick. John commented: *It was in Farmington for me, living at Grandpa's. I didn't go to school, because it took soap to wash the lipstick off. I'd already had my mouth washed out with soap.*

I remembered feigning cramps to avoid swimming lessons in the freezing water of Bear Lake. John noted: *never knew you pulled the same stunts. You were my idol.* I wrote about ice skating, and John responded: *frozen hands, no ability, too young, not as good as you—ever, till manhood.*

Manhood.

I mentioned happy memories in a less than pleasant physical environment (our little house out of place among the warehouses butted up against the railroad track): "Mom gave meaning to those early, potentially destructive years. What I <u>don't</u> remember from that time is a sense of shame." John drew a line from the word *destructive* to the margin and wrote: *for you, no! for me, yes!* For some reason, he crossed out the word *shame* and wrote *no humanity*.

John placed a cryptic *NS* after a paragraph about a photo of Mom as an object of desire. Did my mention of our parents' sexuality please him? Disturb him? Or does *NS* stand for a sarcastic "No Shit"?

Beside my description of a long family hike around Shiprock and the sleepy ride home made electric by the sight of our newly captured bull snake crawling up Mom's leg, John wrote: *I remember this. I didn't want to go.*

I recalled kneeling around the table for family prayer. John filled the margin: *Remember when Carol was saying the prayer and the phone rang. She hurried her prayer, jumped up, and grabbed the phone. "Heavenly Father," she said, and dropped the phone. Even Mom, next to the phone, was laughing and coughing so much that she could hardly answer the phone, which was for her.*

"One night," I wrote, "I woke to find Dad shaking my shoulder. He hurried me into Sunday clothes and rushed me off to the Elk's lodge where he and Mom had gone to hear an Australian boys' choir. I enjoyed the second half of the program, but my strongest memory is of gratitude that they had gone out of their way to share the experience with me." John commented, with an interesting choice of prepositions: *Never did this to me.*

I described Mom hobbling around the house with a broken toe, the victim of her temper, and asked, "How did the sides of her mouth survive those vicious chewings?" John's comment is *Ya!!*

Next to my statement about "the tender new mother (for the eighth time) with baby Jeff," John wrote: *Another brother.* A year after Jeff was born, John did a science-fair project nicely related to those family population pressures: "The Effects of Different Amounts of Space on the Number of Fruit Flies—*Drosophila melanogaster*—Produced in the F_1 Generation."

In response to my memory of hiking trips with Mom and Dad, John noted his own memory: *Mom a Cub Scout Den Mother while pregnant with Jeff. Pregnant lady followed by ten cub scouts. Very humorous.*

After my description of Mom as a fine and strict first grade teacher, ending with "I wonder how the children view Mrs. Abbott?" John noted: *An invigorating teacher like Mrs. Anderson, my 1st teacher. Teaches from love, not $. They viewed her as I viewed Mrs. A., a Goddess. I've seen her students introduce her to their parents. I've seen parents thank Mom for being their children's first grade teacher. Mom's a teacher like Dad was. Mom, they need you.*

More thoughts about Mom's class: "Each class day begins with a prayer. I warn Mom she might be taken to court by a disgruntled parent. Has she no respect for 'kings, rulers, magistrates, for honoring, obeying, and sustaining the law' as the Mormon article of faith states? Her answer is that she will continue to have prayer in her class." John was quick to defend: *No Scott. She obeyed what was right for her!*

I praised Mom's grit after Dad was killed: "The determined Mother and provider, back in school again at a ripe middle age. Surely an act of courage. But then again, she enjoyed it so much. Mom positively flourished." John wrote: *I disappeared for quite a few years. No help. No compassion. Nothing. Thanks Mom. I love you.*

After my criticism of Mom's frenetic walking habits, antithetical to contemplation and conversation, John again defended her: *No, she thinks more as she picks up speed. Give the woman credit. She's good at being a friend, even if she's herself. Scott, did you give her a chance to be herself? Probably not! Just you as her son yet intelligent? I spent*

2 months with my mother. She won't accept what I do, but we finally became friends.

John, how could you become friends if she won't accept what you do? You argue here for accepting her, for letting her be herself, but what if "herself" is antithetical to "yourself"?

I referred to Mom as a grandmother. John wrote: *I've never seen Mom as a grandmother. I guess it's because I have no family but the one I grew up with, except for Carol's kids.*

John had advice for me when I admitted that it's best for me not to talk politics with Mom: *You're afraid!! You have to make her be honest, and you have to be honest in discussion. It's not easy, but it works!*

"It's a pleasure to see how proud Mom is of us," I wrote, and John noted, with his trademark double exclamation points: *She's even proud of me!!*

In one paragraph I tried to analyze difficulties I have talking with Mom: "Those phone conversations when Mom asks: How are you doing?" *No!!* John wrote. *Scott, what's a mother to do? She loves us. We don't let her accept us and we don't accept her as her. We have to accept each other! Mom's a person herself. Share her right to believe! Are we friends, my brother?*

That question undoes me every time I read it.

My fragmentary essay ended with the words: "Merry Christmas, Mom. I love you dearly."

John added sentiments that quicken my heart: *Love you too my brother!*

It is a conversation of sorts. One text engenders another. Precious words, heartrending in their permanent paucity. If I didn't say those words to you then, John, I'm doing my best to say them now.

10 MARCH 1994, OREM

The man in the white turtleneck at the John Cage Memorial Service, Alex told me today, has died of AIDS.

14 MARCH 1994, AMERICAN FORK

Mom hands me a copy of Greenberry Boreing's story (as told by his son the Reverend John Boreing in the *Christian Advocate*, Nashville, August 15, 1874), recently unearthed in her genealogical research. I skim it and then read a paragraph aloud:

> He was the father of nine sons and three daughters, and although he and mother were not members of the Methodist Church in those days, every one of the children grew up united with the Methodist Church, professed faith in Christ, and started for the heavenly Canaan.... They both finally joined the Church of their children, and promised to go with them to heaven.

Isn't it wonderful? Mom responds.

Yes. But imagine the grief they would have felt if a Mormon missionary had converted Greenberry late in his life.

How is your work going, Scott? What are you teaching?

Mom! You don't get it, do you?

She answers suddenly, vehemently: What do you know? When I married Bob I took him from his Methodist family. They were mortified that their son became a Mormon during the war. They were very active and prominent in their church. It was embarrassing to them, even humiliating, and when I married him in the temple and they couldn't be present, they took it personally. Don't you ever say I don't understand!

I'm taken aback by the force of her reply, but awkwardly I forge on, for she has helped clarify the double thought I was getting at. It was a tragedy for Grandma and Grandpa, I say, but necessary, for some reason, for Dad. The family tradition was important, but Dad grew as he made choices of his own. I'm worried about your feeling that you have lost John and that you are losing me. Don't we all make choices based on our best sense for what will result in a good life?

I hope so, she replies.

15 MARCH 1994, OREM

Joseph, almost nineteen, has turned in his papers to go on a mission. Last night the ward bishop and a representative of the stake president came to our house to assist as I ordained Joseph an elder in the Melchizedek Priesthood. I was surprised the stake president would allow me to perform the ordinance. A carrot after the stick.

The stake president's representative read a couple of scriptures and gave a short speech. All you boys, he said, will receive the priesthood when you get older. And Maren, you will find a man with the priesthood to take you to the temple. While he continued, I remembered the canoe trip on Tennessee's Buffalo River, fathers with their priesthood-aged sons. I took both Joseph and Maren. I suspect there were priesthood leaders unhappy with my choice. Now the three of us laid our hands on Joseph's head. After stating that through our priesthood power we ordained him an elder, I gave my son some halting advice. I did my best not to paint him into any corners. I hope he heard my blessing and counsel as an admonition to be good on his own terms. I wish for him, as he continues his life, a sense of immense potential and opportunity. With equal fervor I would, if I could, grant that his productive, youthful feeling of immortality be tempered by a sense for the blessings of mortality.

Maren, I said later, I'm sorry for the way that man defined your role as a woman. What do you mean? she asked. It doesn't matter, but ten years from now I want you to remember that I mentioned it.

I hardly know where to start. I think of how your wife must have felt. She knows, surely, about your disbelief. Wouldn't this have felt like a mockery to her, like blasphemy? Isn't this a dishonest, or at least disingenuous, act on your part? And while I'm asking questions, do you realize that your wife is basically absent from this text?

There was no mockery. My only thought was to support my son and to express my love for him. I'm sorry, deeply sorry, that my choices are making life more difficult for my wife. As for her absence in this text—we have been absent from one another for a decade.

19 MARCH 1994, OREM
From British Columbia, where she is serving an eighteen-month mission, a letter from Mom:

Scott, last night I had a frightening dream. Someone was looking for you, so I went with that person to find you. As we came to the bathroom door, I had an overwhelming sense of dread. I opened the door and saw you wrapped in a shower curtain slumped against the washbasin and mirror. When I took off the shower curtain, your eyes flickered. I knew you were not dead but were close to it. I was so frightened, I woke right up. Are you becoming spiritually dead?

It's remarkable how she still has the power to unsettle me.

20 MARCH 1994, OREM

Why is Mom's vision so singular? And why does she cling to it so fiercely? She lost her mother early, her place taken by a chronically ill stepmother. Her father was a church official and businessman with little time for her. She lost an infant son in a tragic accident and then a second son to a shocking disease. If my life had been similarly marked, would the promise of eternal restitution and the threat of eternal loss have gripped me the way they have her?

You ought to be ashamed of this cheap psychological reduction.

I know it's a reduction. But it may help ease the anger that reduces my mother to a caricature in my mind. Mom has her reasons. The dream that felt like an act of religious terrorism now has a context that doesn't make me want to spit.

21 MARCH 1994, OREM

A letter today from Hans Schulz, a Marxist colleague at Vanderbilt, in response to a letter I sent him when I learned he is dying of cancer:

> ...It's been more than six weeks since I got your letter. I am only now coming out of the kind of hermetic self-referentiality which the news of my palpable finality engendered....Your letter has a tone that expresses a lot about a flux of beliefs and the sense of loss that comes with it. Difficult for me to empathize

because that is a whole field of beliefs I never entered and have always looked at as an indoor Hollywood landscape. But my own situation seems to subject a lot of things to revision too.

2 APRIL 1994, PROVO

I've never been entirely comfortable with my own sexuality. I spent decades dodging even the thought of a homosexuality I had learned to loathe. Now, after reading Derek Jarman, Tony Kushner, Levay's *The Sexual Brain*, and much more, after the introspection this writing facilitates, I am less fearful. I am, quite simply (quite complicatedly), heterosexual. Biology and cultural conditioning have forged that sexual identity. As they did John's.

11 APRIL 1994, PROVO

Back at my office after the weekend: 7:30 a.m. The cold-filtered clock reads 8:46. Permanently. The sweeping second hand has exchanged its steady circular motion for a spasmodic twitch. This is the moment I have been writing toward, the arbitrary end to my story. I'm not, however, quite ready to call this done. I'm planning to visit Santee, California, and Boise, listening, looking, hoping for echoes from John on his own ground.

16 APRIL 1994, HIGHWAY I-15

On the road. Not with Jack Kerouac. Not with Wim Wenders. But not without them either.

Winter semester is over, John, and I'm headed for San Diego, your notebooks in my bag.  The predawn mass of the Wasatch Mountain range looms over me to the east. The black sky leaches to gray, silhouettes the snowcapped mountains. I pull off in Cedar City for gas and breakfast. An hour later the freeway throws me centrifugally around the outskirts of St. George. The first Mormon temple completed in Utah gleams white against vivid redrock. Brigham Young had a winter home here.

I'm welcomed to Las Vegas by a screaming formation of low-flying jet fighters. An exit funnels me onto THE STRIP. The MGM Lion is a huge plastic pussycat. The LUXOR pyramid is fronted by a fiberglass sphinx and phallic obelisk. Sunburned tourists stagger along lethal sidewalks, their aging flesh sagging around bare kneecaps. I breathe easier west of the city among the straightforward mirages of the Mojave Desert.

It's 5:30 p.m. I'm in Santee, up the gorge from San Diego, parked in front of Van Winkle's. While collecting my thoughts and feelings, I make a rude sketch of your workplace in my notebook. I wish I had a better eye for things.

John, I don't know you. There's so much I don't know. You left what you called a self-portrait dated "89." Did you like the playful expression? The hint of light and dark personality?

How would I draw myself? It would be a set of awkward lines, fragments like my bits and pieces of self-awareness.

Day and Night Cook, you wrote. Twelve hundred dollars a month. And you lived on the premises.

I leave the restaurant and find a motel on Mission Gorge Road, the six-lane highway snaking up the canyon between the big city and this town dominated by trailer parks. I call Van Winkle's and ask for Van. My hands are shaking. A woman says he won't be in till ten thirty or eleven. I walk east from Van Winkle's, eager to see your neighborhood.

Sentry Storage. Santee Inn. Gun Shak—Discount Guns and Pawn. Kingdom Hall of Jehovah's Witnesses (cars arriving at a fast clip). A sign pointing north: Las Culinas Women's Detention Facility. Los Panchos Taco Shop—OPEN/ABIERTO. Bail Bonds. Santee Pioneer Little League: a big left-handed Chicano kid mows down skinny little long-haired gringos. The moon looks like a pared-off fingernail hanging just above Venus, neither body as bright as they were last night in Utah when I called the children out of the house to look.

I screw up the courage to go into Van Winkle's for dinner. I'm self-conscious. Will I be taken for you?

One side of the large room is a dance floor and stage flanked by a bar; the other side sports red carpet and Formica-topped tables set with paper place mats, forks and knives wrapped in paper napkins.

Photos and paintings of John Wayne crowd two walls. On a third wall, between signed photos of Pat Boone, Gene Autry, and Johnny Cash, hang two large photos of Santee in the old days and a huge painting of three San Diego Chargers annihilating an opposing quarterback.

One Sunday afternoon you called me from here, a Chargers game barking in the background. We talked about books, skirted the personal.

The menu suggests fried chicken or barbecued spare ribs. I tell the waitress I'd like the ribs. Blue cheese dressing on the salad. Baked potato.

It's karaoke night, and a bald man in jeans and western shirt is the host. He hands the cordless mike to an angular fifty-year-old woman he introduces as Debby. She stands at the back of the stage and sings "Stand by Your Man."

I dig into my potato.

A skinny nine- or ten-year-old boy lets his mother push him onto the stage. He stares into a monitor while he mouths the words to "Do You Think I'm Sexy?" The host doesn't have to look at the monitor while he sings "I Got You Babe." Not a bad voice. Nor is my salad too bad, although there's a lot of water in the bottom of the plastic bowl.

A man and woman wearing black cowboy hats sit at a table with a woman in pink polyester. At another table hunch an emaciated, chain-smoking woman and what I take to be her chain-smoking, even more emaciated mother. The older woman has dyed her limp hair at least three consecutive colors.

The woman with the black cowboy hat grabs the mike, bounces off the confining stage, and sings her way onto the dance floor. I can't help but pay attention to her red-skirted presence, especially when she skips her trim cowboy boots over to my corner table, stabs my eyes with hers, and sings "I want your body." Through the sauce of my spareribs I manage a half smile. She two-steps over to the bar and then swings her compact body back to my corner and sings: "I love your body."

Behind me the wall creaks open, and ten or twelve men and women come out of a room I hadn't noticed. They've been in a club meeting, or so I gather by the logo on their identical blue-satin jackets: "Fabulous Fifties—San Diego Chapter, Ford Club of America."

The kitchen is framed by a brightly lit door under a NO SMOKING sign. Your domain. Where did you smoke?

The bald man hands me a vinyl book: *SONGBOOK: BE THE STAR YOU ARE! D K KARAOKE.* I read through the list and fantasize about taking the stage and belting out Johnny Horton's "North to Alaska." I pay my bill and escape.

Eleven o'clock. Sitting in my motel room, I decide not to call Van. His version of things would divert me from the faint traces I'm following.

His version of things would be a pack of lies, Scott. Good choice.

17 APRIL 1994, SANTEE, CALIFORNIA

Nosing around your turf this morning, John. Did you have one of the three motel-like rooms stretched out under a flat roof in back of the restaurant? Rooms fronted by lemon trees and backed up to a row of tall cedars? At the west end of Mission Gorge, in Jack Murphy Stadium, there was a Pink Floyd concert last night. Would you have been interested? What did you do in your time off?

I drive into the parking lot of a shopping center just west of Van Winkle's: Purple Heart Veterans' Thrift Shop, Driftwood Lounge,

Fraternal Order of Eagles—Aerie 3973, Santee Chiropractic Clinic, Santee Coins and Jewelry, Rollerskateland—Classic Billiards, the Potter's House Christian Church, Pastor Chris A. Wendt: Jesus Christ: The Same Yesterday, Today—and Forever.

That's what we all want, I think. A fixed point. And many of us pin the assignment on Jesus.

I wander along a pleasant path, climb some rocks overlooking the river. A fat lizard does push-ups on a flat stone. Bees. A white butterfly. A deeply tanned man walks his big dog on the trail below. I imagine you a healthy brown after mornings spent walking in this peaceful gorge. Then I imagine you in bed until noon when you get up to work in the brightly lit but windowless kitchen. The one day you do lie on this rock in the sun, your lard-colored skin burns a cancerous red.

A lazuli bunting flaunts its colorful head and throat and white-barred wings on a bush just above me. A nomad on its way north. I lay back in the sun. A breeze keeps the flies away; when it abates, they drive me from the rocks.

During the afternoon I drive aimlessly around San Diego. In the evening, not far from Balboa Park, I stop at a Thai restaurant. I notice several male couples in the restaurant and more couples strolling along the sidewalk. Across the street at tables in front of a bar sit several dozen men.

Did you come here, John? Could I have seen you and your lover here in 1984, a year before his death?

Four men and a woman sit at the table opposite me. I picture you with them. A lively conversation, good food, friendships deepened by sexual attraction. You laugh about something. You care for one another. You meet every Sunday night for dinner.

But Sunday night, like every night, you are in the kitchen at Van Winkle's cooking ribs and frying chicken and making salads. You are proud of your soups. In your notebook you call your friends losers.

18 APRIL 1994, 10:30 P.M., PISMO BEACH, CALIFORNIA

Los Angeles behind me, I walk along a deserted beach under a half-moon. The waves break silver in triple and quadruple rows.

You left the tradition you must have felt held you captive. Did it feel like you were falling into empty space? You were throwing off the structure Mormonism had provided. The Kiwanis, the chiropractor, the Fraternal Order of Eagles, the Jehovah's Witnesses, the Potter's House, or even the Mormons could have supplied meaning and fellowship. But you had had enough of structured fellowship.

That's for damned sure!

Some of what you needed, John, was what you left behind.

And some of what I needed was waiting for me with open arms. I worry about you, Scott, about your inability to step away from a religion that encourages bigotry and punishes difference.

Chaos needs order, John, and order chaos.

20 APRIL 1994, MONTEREY, CALIFORNIA
Robinson Jeffers's Tor House overlooks the ocean in Carmel. A beautiful place to write poetry. To live. Clumps of delicate blue iris stand among the trees he planted.
One of the joys
of travel—rare
talk about an iris.
Basho

Basho defined haiku in words that may also describe these fragments of mine: "It is what is happening at this place in this moment of time." Down the road and around the bend sprawls the Basilica of Mission San Carlos Borradeo del Rio Carmelo, founded June 3, 1770. Inside is the tomb of the
BLESSED
JUNIPERO SERRA
1713–1784
+ ! + ! +

A pamphlet about the mission states that "the Indians lent themselves willingly to the Padres."

John, how willingly would you lend yourself to my story?

I don't really get to answer that, do I?

22 APRIL 1994, SAN FRANCISCO

I'll spend the night in the Amsterdam Hotel, just two blocks down from the Fairmont Hotel where my fiancée earned generous tips as a waitress in the Squire Room restaurant the summer we broke off our engagement.

I wake up in the night to a sound I recognize immediately: Squeak…squeak…squeak…squeak. A couple in the next room is having a good time. I'm happy for them. I slip into sweet dreams of my own and wake up later to hear them at it even more rapidly: squeaksqueak- squeak. I wonder if there is some sort of official endurance record. I wake again to the now ridiculous sound of a complaining bed. Don't these people understand the rhythm of the whole? At some point things speed up to a climax.

I get up to open the window of my stuffy room. A rectangular metal sign hangs by two wires from the top rail of the fire escape: WARNING / FOR FIRE ONLY. In the breeze from the bay the sign sways rhythmically: squeak, squeak, squeak.

I hear what I expect to hear. I hear what I know. I hear what I want.

Below my window is the Academy of Art College. In the morning there will be a steady stream of young men and women with oversize cases under their arms. Talented and hopeful and young. I'm forty-four.

I walk through the Haight in the early afternoon. In a small bookstore I find a paperback copy of *The Seth Material* and buy it, thinking of you and the excitement with which you once described its spiritualist breakthroughs over the phone. I thumb through the silly book until this section catches my eye: "There is the Mark which Mark has created, an actual physical construction. There is another, created by you, Joseph. There are two more physical Marks, one created by Ruburt, and one by your cat." Not a bad idea: multiple narrators, one of them a cat. E.

T. A. Hoffmann tried it once. And Cervantes used a couple of dogs.

You condescending son of a Neapolitan bitch.

Sorry. But I do like the idea of multiple voices.

Later, walking among an inventively dressed crowd, a store-window reflection brings me up short: button-down shirt, clipped hair, and a thin-lipped grimness under veiling sunglasses. In the context of Haight-Ashbury, even in its watered-down 1994 version, I see FBI, CIA, Secret Service, Establishment. Chagrined, I take off the sunglasses.

Doesn't change much, does it?

MIDNIGHT

I'm back from seeing Allie Light's film *Dialogues with Madwomen*. One of the women was a black law student at Stanford who found herself sleeping in toilet stalls at the airport. Others were abused by their fathers, their psychiatrists, their husbands—and then declared insane. One woman's life had been hijacked by her unrequited love for Bob Dylan. A Chinese American woman was brutally raped and murdered not long after Light spoke with her. And finally the film depicts a woman institutionalized for depression whose therapist discouraged her from going to college. Dr. Schwarz, she says, I hope you see this, because I did go to college, and I became a filmmaker and this is my film.

I saw Light's documentary in the Castro Theater. The Castro. For gays and lesbians what the Haight was for hippies. Walking from where I parked my car, I was the object of enough unwanted attention that I rounded my shoulders, pulled in my neck, stuck out my quills.

Inside the operatic theater, marveling as the gaudy theater organ rose dramatically from a pit, sitting with the animated audience, listening to the live music, watching the organist feel his uncertain way to the side of the theater when the lights dimmed, hearing a voice behind me say he's drunk again, hearing sympathetic responses to Light's cinematic stories, I felt, for all my prickly heterosexuality, part of a lively community.

Good for you.

23 APRIL 1994, WINNEMUCCA, NEVADA

Snow on Donners Pass, then down into the desert east of Reno. In just a few hours I have exchanged the human complexities of San Francisco for the spare, still forms of the Nevada desert. They aren't, however, as spare as they once were. I follow a trail of tattooed mountains: *S* for Sparks, *L* for Lovelock, *W* for Winnemucca. As a junior in high school, animated by school spirit, I helped whitewash the *F* for Farmington. Now it feels like domination, an insult to nature, desecration.

Take it easy, man.

WINNEMUCCA
AND WE'RE PROUD OF IT

Casinos, motels, restaurants, gas stations. I stay at a motel whose sign proclaims the LOWEST RAT S IN TOWN. The man who stumbles down a step to ask what I want is so drunk he can't make the credit-card machine work. I pay cash. Lying awake in the dismal room, I think about my reaction to how I was seen in the Castro. I thought I had worked through this. I have been trying to write my way out of the thicket of homophobia for nearly three years.

It's hard for me to understand this, Scott. Can't you just loosen your sphincter a bit?

24 APRIL 1994, BOISE

I find my way to the state capitol building where open green spaces frame the white neoclassical buildings in the afternoon sunshine. On West Jefferson I pass the law offices still in my memory from the trip three years ago and arrive at #425. Things change. You would have been kicked out.

Wouldn't have been the first time.

I check into a motel two blocks from the T&A Café and begin to call the people in your notebooks. I start with Candy. Hello, this is Scott Abbott. Could I speak with Candy? You have a wrong number. It becomes a litany of impermanence: Cheryl, Chad, Daniel, Erik, Kurt, Evonne, Kathy, Lisa, Pam, Phoebe. No longer at this number.

Hungry, I walk past the Cactus Bar on Main Street to the Renaissance restaurant. You worked here for more than three years. The menu, at least compared to the one at Van Winkle's, is a marvel of complexity and subtlety. You must have known the inner workings of Italian sauces and soups, fish and beef, pasta, vegetables. While you were here the owner died, and you had a chance to manage the place. You soon quit and went to work at the café.

I was a cook, not a manager.

Two women behind me talk about Christian marriage. They try to remember some sort of class they took, something about influencing people. Their gray-haired waiter suggests, in passing, Dale Carnegie. That's it! they say in chorus.

Each time a waiter bursts through the kitchen's swinging door, I get a partial view of stainless-steel pans, racks of utensils, long counters, and dark ovens. The two cooks wear floppy white hats and starched white jackets like the ones you had, the ones we buried you in.

I savor the handiwork of your colleagues.

25 APRIL 1994, BOISE

This morning I poke around town, trying to get a feel for your routines. The route from your rooms to work. From work to the bar. Did you come to this theater to see movies? Did you even like movies? On spring days did you frequent this park, this park bench? Was this where you got your used books? Did you buy newspapers along with your tobacco at Hannifin's? Did you read newspapers? What were your politics? Which of the current Boise bumper stickers would have caught your fancy?

SAVE THE BABY HUMANS

A LADY WITH A GUN HAS MORE FUN

JESUS LOVES YOU—EVERYONE ELSE THINKS YOU'RE AN ASSHOLE

WILD SEX FOR WILD FISH: FREE THE SOCKEYE

ECHOHAWK

Larry Echohawk, running for governor. The first Native American elected attorney general of a state. He and his brothers, John and Fred and Tom, grew up in Farmington in a house several blocks from ours. We went to the same schools. Fred married a girl I knew. John founded the Native American Rights Fund. Did you ever cross paths with Larry here in Boise?

You can probably answer that yourself.

The café is larger than I remembered. Naugahyde booths. Stools at a long counter. Formica-topped tables with wooden chairs. Some framed nature photographs for sale. A long slit of a window between kitchen and dining room. I remember the cigarette vending machine just inside the front door from one of my favorite photos. A man comes out of the kitchen to smoke a cigarette in the entryway. He's wearing a short apron like yours. He's tall, heavy, in his late forties.

The menu offers a good range of choices, most of them bearing a family resemblance to the hot beef sandwich with potatoes and gravy I order. It's plain fare served by thirty- and forty-year-old waitresses in black Levi's and pink or blue T&A Café T-shirts.

A big piece of warm lemon meringue pie follows the sandwich and potatoes. I want to ask the waitress who brings it about you, but ask instead about the chain hanging on the wall, the one with a steel hoop on one end and what looks like a nasty harpoon on the other.

I'll tell you in a minute, she says. She takes an order, pours some coffee, talks with another waitress. I'll tell you what that is, she says when she finally returns, but I'm not happy about it. It's a bull cinch. You hang the one end over a fence post and stick the other end up the bull's ass. It's a cinch he won't get away. The boss says we have to tell the story if anyone asks. And then she's gone.

> Love gets its name (amor) from the word for hook (amus) which means to capture or to be captured. (Andreas Capellanus, *The Art of Courtly Love*)

Walking off the lunch and a vague sense of disappointment, I stroll along Main Street. I'm a writer. Writers know things. They do research, ask questions, give explanations. My decision earlier in this trip to look for you where you are not feels like an evasion. I look up at faded letters on a blackened brick wall: MANITOU HOTEL / $7.54 A NIGHT. The sign has faded. What it meant is long gone.

Evening has come when I finally slow my steps in front of the Cactus Bar. It's not easy for me to enter a bar. I've had more than four decades of Mormon conditioning. I do it, John, for you.

And you do it for yourself. Let's be clear about that.

I climb onto one of the two empty stools at the bar and order a beer.

A pool table dominates the back third of the long room; a jukebox stands against one wall; small tables fill the rest of the space. Behind the bar a small TV is animated by miniature baseball players. The bartender is a bright-eyed, athletic young man, and about half the clientele, men and women of several races standing around the pool table or sitting at a table near the jukebox, are his approximate match. The rest of us line the bar, Caucasian gray beards mostly, neither bright-eyed nor muscular.

The man on the stool to my right has hollow cheeks and frightfully bony wrists.

Comes of sorrow, Scott, of sorrow and a liquid diet.

His thin hair looks like it hasn't been cut or combed or washed for
quite some time. He has a meager mustache and a week's thin stubble.
He wears a black polyester baseball cap with a grocery-store logo.
Around his pencil neck he has knotted a faded blue bandanna. His
polyester shirt and Windbreaker shade to a darker blue. Far too large
around the waist, his green slacks are cinched up by an ancient leather
belt. Black socks disappear into cheap red-and-white running shoes.
Between his nicotine-stained left index and middle fingers dances an
unlit cigarette. Turning to take a sip from the glass of beer in front
of him, he notices me. He straightens his stooped torso, switches his
cigarette to his right hand, holds it at arm's length, twists his hand,
and the cigarette disappears. He looks at me and raises his eyebrows.
Another twist, and the cigarette lies between his fingers.

How did you do that? I ask.

He lights his cigarette and leaves it burning in an ashtray on the bar
while he talks with people at a nearby table. The ash grows to finger
length. He turns back around in time for a last drag.

Do you have a good memory? he asks suddenly, his voice breathy,
raspy.

It's okay.

Is your memory good or bad? It's a simple question.

Good, I guess.

When I went to college, he says, they were amazed at my memory.
They did all kinds of tests. Memory tests. The sly brown fox jumped
over the lazy dog. What was the last word I said?

The jukebox is loud, and I can't quite hear what he is saying. I nod
my head.

The sly brown fox jumped over the lazy dog. What was the last
word I said?

Dog.

No, it was *said.*

Do you have a good head for math? he asks.

Not especially.

Can you do math? It's a yes-or-no question. Give me the courtesy of a straight answer to my simple question.

Yes.

Try this then. There were three people who checked into a hotel room that cost thirty dollars a night. Each one paid ten dollars. The clerk later figured out he had made a mistake and that it was a twenty-five-dollar room. He sent a bellboy up with five dollars in ones. The bellboy gave each of them a dollar back and kept two dollars as a tip. Each had originally paid ten dollars, and now with one back they had each paid nine dollars for the room. Three times nine is twenty-seven. That leaves three dollars from the original thirty. The bellboy kept two. How do you account mathematically for the missing dollar?

I don't know.

If that's how you do bookkeeping, they'd rob you blind.

He turns back to the man on his right. They are speaking some Slavic language. I order another beer and watch the baseball game. When he leans back to flick his ash into the ashtray, I ask what language they are speaking.

Polish. Do you know what city has the largest Polish-speaking population in the world?

Chicago.

That's right. He looks at me a little closer.

My friend here is an orphan, he says. He grew up in Chicago in a Polish orphanage. The Germans went to Wisconsin, the Poles to Chicago.

Where did you grow up? I ask.

You ask too many questions, he says.

I remember my reflection in the window on Haight Street. I'm interested in stories, I tell him. I like stories.

He leans his head in my direction, stares at me with watery eyes, and delivers himself of a bit of beery wisdom: Never answer a question with a question, and never ask a question for which you don't know the answer.

He pulls up the left sleeve of his Windbreaker and displays a tattooed wing. I got that in Hong Kong for two packs of American cigarettes.

In Hong Kong?

Yes. I spent years in the merchant marine. I've seen a lot of the world. I speak seven languages. I have knowledge of what I speak.

Seven languages?

Yes. English, Russian, Polish, Yugoslavian, French, German, and Spanish.

You learned them while you were in the merchant marine? I ask.

I was a cook for the merchant marine. I could have been an officer. I know how to handle a ship, but I hated all that yes-sir, no-sir shit. You probably wonder what I'm doing here, all fucked up, drunk, sitting in a bar.

I'm sitting at the same bar, I reply. And I speak German too. *Wo haben Sie Ihr Deutsch gelernt?*

Hier bin ich, he says, *total besoffen. Ein alter besoffener Scheißkopf. Aber ich war in Hamburg, auf einem deutschen Schiff. Ein Jahrlang in Hamburg.*

He sounds like he grew up in Hamburg.

My brother used to come in here, about three years ago.

That's before my time, he says. I've got a friend in Boise, dying of MS. It just gets worse, not better.

You've got real talent with languages, I say.

Those other languages are easy. English is the most difficult language on the earth. It's an amalgamation of all languages. Tell me a word, any word.

Dog.

If you look that up in a dictionary, you'll find "derived from." Not from German, that's *Hund*, but from Latin or something else. All the languages converge in American. Not English, I mean American. I know English. I've been in Blackpool, and I can speak their blimey buggered Cockney language. He begins to mumble Russian into his empty beer glass.

Can I buy you another beer? I ask.

He nods and turns to talk with a young woman who has come up beside him. I signal the bartender, then try to ask my neighbor what he wants. He likes Buds, the bartender says.

Turned back to me, a fresh beer before him, the thin man waxes eloquent: Two old maids opened a cathouse. One week later they had sold five cats. There were two whores, he says, one with hemorrhoids, one with adenoids. The one didn't give a hoot about her shitter; the other didn't give a shit about her hooter.

Some combination of the blaring jukebox, the baseball game, and shouts at the pool table keep me from hearing the whole thing. Would you repeat that? I ask.

I was in a ship once, he says, in the Baltic Sea. We must have slipped into Russian territory because they began jamming all our radar and sonar and everything. The captain called over the horn to see if there was anyone on the ship who spoke Russian. I took off my apron and went up onto the bridge and started talking Russian into the radio, trying to explain it was a mistake. There's no lines painted out on the Baltic Sea, so it's easy to be a few hundred yards into Russian territory. I talk a blue streak into the radio, and the captain slams down the throttle and we're flying outta there.

The jukebox blares "Cecilia, you're breakin' my heart," and he begins to drum on the bar with open hands, "I'm losing my confidence daily." I've got the gift of gab, he says, and a brilliant memory. That's why I can speak so many languages. I have knowledge of what I speak. The wise man can be a fool, but the fool can never be a wise man. You can't judge a book by its cover. But you look at me, and you think *besoffener Scheißkopf.* Isn't that right?

No, I say. We're sitting at the same bar.

You can't judge a book by its cover, he repeats. You look at me and don't know that I'm rich. I'm as rich as God. As rich as God. I believe in God. I do believe in God.

I nod.

He pauses for effect: But the God I believe in was standing too close when the Big Bang happened. Now he's blind and deaf.

He squints at me to see if I get it.

His white-haired friend comes by, and they speak Polish. The friend leaves, muttering bullshitbullshit.

It's time for me to leave as well. Good-bye, I say. He looks surprised.

Before I can move, he reaches over, takes my hand between his, looks into my eyes, and says through his crooked teeth: Our feet are the same.

I laugh, squeeze his thin hand, and say *auf Wiedersehen*.

What's your name? he asks.

Scott Abbott. What's yours?

Jay Allison. Jay Dexter Allison.

27 APRIL 1994, OREM

John, I just put new batteries in your Genuine Draft clock.

We <u>are</u> friends, my brother.

17 JULY 1994, ZION NATIONAL PARK, UTAH

Sitting alone on a sandstone boulder under the towering cliff called "Watchman." In the last sunlight the sandstone cliffs above me flush vermilion, maroon, magenta. Bright, white wisps of cloud. A sharply defined full moon.

The moon was in this phase when I stood with Žarko on a moonlit lakeshore in Slovenia. Awed by the moon's dark reflection in the still lake, we reflected on standing, on stasis, on being, on standing as a created moment of transition—the place between one movement and the next, on the brief moment when the moon is perfectly full, neither waxing nor waning, on the satisfying, fleeting interstice.

Darting swallows hunt high-flying insects. High above the chattering birds two tiny jet planes turn silently to the southeast. Down the slope from where I sit, Maren, Joseph, Nathan, and Thomas throw a Frisbee. Deer feed along the road, shyly pursued by a boy who wants to feed them and more deviously stalked by a woman with a camera. A buck stands to the side, his antlers heavy with velvet.

The moon grows steadily brighter. Bats join the swallows. The black and brown mammals flutter ragged lines through the sky. The birds wheel and sweep and dart. Insects have buzzed and clicked in the background all day long, but now, in the gathering darkness, as the colors fall silent, the chirpings and high hummings grow more insistent. The last faint colors coalesce into darkness. A stubby bat skims my forehead. Two deer race by, their quick, thrusting sounds more visible than their shapes.

Timothy, Samuel, and Benjamin return with their mother from the cool eddies of the Virgin River, dark forms trailing across the field. They join the other children, and I hear cheerful talk about dinner.

Below me rasps a single cricket. Like a dry pen on rough paper.

[John's Blue and Tan Notebook]

...I re-evaluated myself. I saw that I was from now on, forever, contemptible. I had been, and remained, intensely depressed, but I had also been, and always would be, intensely false; in existentialist terms, unauthentic. I knew I would never kill myself, I knew I would always want to go on living with myself, however hollow I became, however diseased. (John Fowles' *The Magus*, p. 58)

Basic Ingredients of BBQ sauce: Brown Sugar, Cayenne, Vinegar, Tomato Sauce.

Forever Living
re-evaluation of self
contemptible being,
depressed — existing.
intensely false,
existentially unauthentic.
living alone
forever hollow —,
or diseased.
till Charon I meet!
and death is sweet.

Re — Karman Larson
Thinking of her, off and on — through the years — w/o contact has kept me going at times. Was very happy when she made City Council.

Sorry you're not doing well. Your strength when I met you, going through cancer the first time. Thanx for strength, intelligence, courage, beauty, etc.

Sorry to hear of her in the news again, brain cancer. The first therapy worked, let's all pray that it'll work again because Karman

215

Larson is one of those rare people that come into our lives, touch us, and leave us so much better.

I knew her from cook to mayor. She changed all lives she came into contact with. One of the most alive, thriving honest women Boise has ever known is still fighting to continue living. Embodiment of Idaho.

being too tired
for thinking or anything
except dreaming
suppose at dusk
between the earth and the sea
mysteriously
and always floating

"My first Name is Steven" talking to mother while trying to self-destruct. I let him do it to me. I let him do it to my friends, so he wouldn't do it to me. They were my friends!

437

<u>20</u> Ted

4¹7

<u>100</u> Int

3¹7

<u>200</u> Rent

11⁷

<u>20</u> Bob

97

<u>30</u> Cig

77

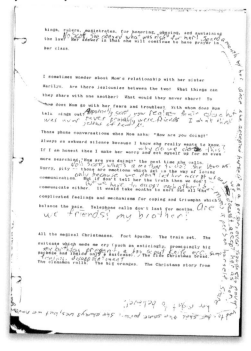

7

Denouncing the
Xenophobic Country
I Still Love

What a contradiction it is to search in reality for
memory's pictures.... The memory of a certain image
is but regret for a certain moment; and houses, roads,
avenues are as fleeting, alas, as the years.
—MARCEL PROUST

Nothing returns from what has been destroyed, nothing
is reborn, neither dead men, nor burned libraries, nor
submerged lighthouses, nor extinct species, despite
the museums commemorations statues books speeches
good will, of things that have gone only a vague memory
remains.

—MATHIAS ÉNARD

3 JUNE 1995, OREM, UTAH

His feet are livid, I wrote. The top of his skull had been sawed off.
He would have been forty-four today.

23 SEPTEMBER 1995, SALT LAKE CITY

The Family: A Proclamation to the World
We, the First Presidency and the Council of the Twelve

Apostles of The Church of Jesus Christ of Latter-day Saints, solemnly proclaim that marriage between a man and a woman is ordained of God and that the family is central to the Creator's plan for the eternal destiny of His children.

...Gender is an essential characteristic of individual premortal, mortal, and eternal identity and purpose....

We further declare that God has commanded that the sacred powers of procreation are to be employed only between man and woman, lawfully wedded as husband and wife....

We warn...that the disintegration of the family will bring upon individuals, communities, and nations the calamities foretold by ancient and modern prophets.

Since the 1978 revelation reversing more than a century of official LDS discrimination against men of African descent, this First Presidency focus on heterosexual marriages and condemnation of homosexuality is its most far-reaching doctrinal statement. It contrasts so starkly with the ideas and feelings you have expressed here that I predict difficult decisions for you in the near future. I wish you well.

I thank you.

Calamities foretold! Don't you wish they would turn their prophetic gaze inward to examine the personal calamities their solemn proclamations and declarations engender?

4 DECEMBER 1995, PROVO, UTAH

I just read a speech Boyd Packer gave to the BYU faculty and staff as this fall semester began. He used the results of the 1911 controversy at BYU over evolution and higher biblical criticism to warn us that our students are "snow-white birds" who will lose their faith if challenged with secular ideas and that like those earlier professors, we will lose our jobs if we don't submit ourselves to church authority.

What were the specific charges in 1911? Superintendent of church schools Horace Cummings reported that "the theory of evolution is treated as a demonstrated law..." and that the controversial professors claimed that "all truths change as we change. Nothing is fixed or reliable."

28 OCTOBER 1996, PROVO

On April 25 of this year, Merrill Bateman delivered his inaugural address as the new president of BYU. He focused on the moral relativism he sees as "eroding the moral fabric" of society in general and of universities in particular. Two months after his speech, finishing an essay about BYU for *Sunstone*, I discovered that the paragraphs about moral relativism had been plagiarized from a speech by Gertrude Himmelfarb published in the journal *First Things*. A plagiarized diatribe against moral relativism!

I added copious evidence of the plagiarism to the essay (Himmelfarb, for example: "The animating spirit of postmodernism is a radical relativism and skepticism that rejects any idea of truth, knowledge, or objectivity," and Bateman: "The driving theory is a radical relativism and skepticism that rejects any idea of truth or knowledge") and asked the editor to publish it without my name.

I had never considered anonymity, not in the *Sunstone* essay that drew the ire of my stake president and Elder Boyd Packer, not in my subsequent argument against BYU's new requirement of "ecclesiastical endorsement" for members of the faculty. But the revelation of plagiarism felt dangerous. As published in *Sunstone* in August, the essay's author was "Anonymous."

Then the shit hit the fan.

The plagiarism was reported in newspapers across the country and in the *Chronicle of Higher Education*. Merrill Bateman sent an apology to Gertrude Himmelfarb, he admitted to a careless lack of attribution but denied any major wrongdoing, and finally, in a thunderous speech to members of the BYU faculty, he denounced the cowardly writer whose intent was to undermine the Church of Jesus Christ and the Kingdom of God.

Just weeks later in the church's October conference, Boyd Packer interrupted his speech "The Twelve Apostles" to curse the anonymous writer (giving full credit to Isaiah):

Some few within the church, openly or perhaps far worse, in
the darkness of anonymity, reproach their leaders in the wards
and stakes and the church, seeking to make them "an offender
for a word," as Isaiah said. To them the Lord said, "Cursed are
all those that shall lift up the heel against mine anointed."

In the darkness of anonymity, an offender for pointing out plagiarism, having kicked against the pricks, I responded to the curse:
Holy shit!

Elder Packer purports to be holy. Does his curse feel threatening to you?

**His ponderous delivery was heavy with threat. But the evil eye works
only if the other person is superstitious.**

28 OCTOBER 1996, PROVO

Boyd Packer and Merrill Bateman are thinking on the same wave-
length as they worry about the dangers of moral relativism and as
they preach their Gospel of absolute truth. It is hard for me to trust
someone completely lacking in epistemological humility.

The comparison of students with snow-white birds is troubling.
University students who must be protected from ideas and church
leaders who must be protected from criticism? This is not the robust
Gospel Joseph Smith proclaimed in his thirteenth "Article of Faith,"
drawn in part from Paul's admonition: "We believe all things, we
hope all things, we have endured many things, and hope to be able
to endure all things. If there is anything virtuous, lovely, or of good
report or praiseworthy, we seek after these things."

30 OCTOBER 1996, OREM

A Cub Scout meeting in the church gymnasium. The boys and
their den mothers are wearing costumes for Halloween. Bishop
Gunderson, his trim Scout uniform just a little tight, asks us to rise
for the presenting of the colors. He salutes smartly. The rest of us
place our hands over our hearts. The first boy in the color guard

wears a blue-and-gold Cub Scout uniform. The third boy is dressed like a bloody but elegant vampire. Marching between the Cub Scout and the vampire, carrying the flag, is Samuel, got up in the dress and wig Benjamin wore last year. He levers the flag into the heavy brass stand. I pledge allegiance, the vampire begins. Samuel rips the wig from his head and holds it over his heart. To the flag of the United States of America.

3 JANUARY 1997, OREM

John, I turn to my notebook less often these days, but you'll be happy to know that your clock is still ticking, powered now by a third set of batteries.

I've been reading about birth order and creativity in Frank Sulloway's *Born to Rebel*. The first child is more apt to conform, Sulloway argues, the second more likely to rebel. I thought you would like these lines from the end of the book:

> Like Charles Darwin, who compared his belief in evolution to "confessing a murder," heterodox individuals have typically suffered for their revolutionary aspirations. Not every unorthodox thinker has succeeded, and not all of them have been right. But a surprising number of them have shared a deep and powerful bond. More often than not, they were born to rebel.

Scott, I do like the idea. I was no revolutionary, although I had some unpleasant times because of my "difference." I hardly succeeded. I was not especially right. But it's good to feel an unexpected bond with my first-born brother.

29 MAY 1997, PROVO

In our preparatory class for a trip to Tarahumara settlements in the Sierra Madre of north-central Mexico, we're having the students read Susan Griffin's *A Chorus of Stones*. One of the students objects to a text that thinks about violence against homosexuals in the context of Nazi hatred of Jews.

Why does the book disturb you? Sam Rushforth asks.

Because the book is pornographic, the student answers. And pornography, she explains, leads to masturbation, which leads to homosexuality, which leads to necrophilia.

Do you even know what necrophilia is?

Having sex with corpses.

How do you know that pornography leads so directly to necrophilia?

It's common knowledge.

She never comes back to class. Within a week we're notified she has filed an official complaint with the academic vice president. Our course, she claims, is not "God centered," as required by the university's mission statement.

Sam's wife, Nancy, defends us: At least it's not godawful.

23 MAY 1998, BELGRADE, FORMER YUGOSLAVIA

Where to begin this story of a trip along the Drina River, after the war, with Žarko Radaković and Austrian writer Peter Handke? Let it begin as a family story, perhaps, among the well-kept ruins of the Kalemegdan fortress that overlooks the confluence of the Sava and Danube Rivers. A barrel-chested man walks along a path with his two little girls. They lag behind. He shouts at them. They catch up. They turn aside to play among wildflowers. He threatens them. The girls join him momentarily, then disappear among the tall flowers. He roars a command. They return. The youngest girl begins to cry. The older girl takes her hand. The big man steps off the path. He rips a bunch of wildflowers from the high grass. He hands them to the crying girl. She stops crying. He shouts again. They walk away, all three of them, holding mismatched hands.

22 MAY 1998, BELGRADE

Žarko's mother, Ljubica, is seventy-two years old and not at all well. She refuses, however, to go to a doctor. At my age, she explains through her interpreter son, it's better to steer clear of potential disasters. Her hands spin and rub a six-inch cigarette holder. She smokes "Partners," a Macedonian brand. She snuggles up to Žarko, smooths his hair, and asks what barbarian cut it. She complains that she has but a single grandchild. Žarko tells her I have seven children. She nods her head approvingly. My son, she says, pointing her cigarette at Žarko, is lazy. Just one.

I picture Joe and Maren and Tom and Nate and Ben and Sam and Tim. How might they deal with a breakup of their parents' marriage?

Žarko's mother feeds us chicken soup, then new potatoes and carrots and chicken with gravy. While we eat, she smokes. You remind me of Greta Garbo, I tell her. Žarko translates. She shakes her head and says: Greta Garbo with diabetes.

A parliamentary debate on the education-reform law flickers on the TV. If the reform passes, Žarko explains, university deans will be appointed by the minister of education, faculty appointments will require ministerial approval, and all faculty members will have to sign new contracts affirming their support for the new policies.

That's how they do it where I work, I tell him. Not a healthy system, unless your main concern is to preserve an established way of thinking.

Ljubica, who has returned to her native orthodoxy, is surprised to learn that I work for a church university.

It's an odd fit, I explain. I grew up Mormon. I served as a Mormon missionary. I have a Mormon marriage. I raised my children to be Mormons. And now I'm no longer a believer. What should I do? Leave my job? Leave my marriage? Abandon my people?

No, Ljubica says. Be careful. Move slowly.

29 MAY 1998, VIŠEGRAD, REPUBLIKA SRPSKA

Was denkt in dir? Peter Handke asks.

What? I ask, unable to hear him over the noise of Milka and her band.

What is thinking in you?

Sorrow, I answer.

In 1992 there was intense fighting here. Marauding Muslims. Marauding Serbs. And now the town is devoid of Muslims. There remain only the roofless, windowless shells of their houses. Since we crossed the border into what is now the Republika Srpska, I have been imagining Muslims and Serbs lying in bed during the unrest, worrying, as they lay there, about possible futures. About a sudden end to possible futures.

Tonight we sit at a linen-covered table in the dining room of a large resort hotel tucked back into the forested hills above the town, guests of the mayor of Višegrad. A young man limps into the dining room with two women, one his girlfriend perhaps, or sister, the other old enough to be his mother. They sit at a table. They talk. They drink a bottle of wine. The young man twirls his box of cigarettes between the table and his finger.

Milka is a sultry lounge singer with a Serbian repertoire, traditional sad love songs sung in a Middle Eastern quaver. Her black-stockinged legs under a very brief skirt draw Žarko's and my attention until Peter points out that our mouths are open and couldn't we be more discreet? When she approaches our table and sings into Peter's ear while stroking his neck, we exact revenge by remarking on his adolescent smile.

A small man on crutches pushes past the waiter and approaches our table. He pulls two photographs out of a coat pocket. The waiter signals to Milka, and she skips toward us, cordless microphone in hand. The small man holds out two worn photos. The first is a glossy celebrity shot of Bosnian Serb leader Radovan Karadžić. The second is a snapshot. My brother, he says, killed in the war. At close range Milka belts out the song "Oh Višegrad!" The convalescing soldier puts away his photos and retreats slowly on his crutches. Milka hits three quick high notes, kicks up a shapely heel, and dances away.

14 JUNE 1998, OREM

> Dear Žarko,
>
> I taught my church class today, the younger brothers and sisters of the children in the class you visited four years ago. Do you remember?
>
> The assigned lesson was about Joshua and the battle of Jericho. I remembered the story from my own childhood Sunday School, the part about the circling army and the shouts that cause the city's wall to fall down. What I didn't remember was God's

command that Joshua and his army fulfilled when "they utterly destroyed all that was in the city, both man and woman, young and old, and ox, and sheep, and ass, with the edge of the sword." Joshua went on to the city of Ai, all of whose inhabitants he killed, men and women, and then he burned it. Next was the city of Hazor: "There was not any left to breathe: and he burnt Hazor with fire."

The lesson manual suggested that I emphasize how the Lord blesses those who follow his orders exactly. After our trip that was impossible. After our trip many things will be impossible.

16 JUNE 1998, PROVO

A couple of years ago, in response to the firings of our colleagues in English and anthropology, our BYU Chapter of the American Association of University Professors invited two AAUP investigators to campus. They wrote a draft report of their findings, and on that basis the AAUP attempted to negotiate with the BYU administration. Those negotiations failed, and now the AAUP has announced their decision:

> Dear President Bateman:
>
> The Association's 1998 Annual Meeting, on June 13, voted to place Brigham Young University on AAUP's list of Censured Administrations....
>
> The investigating committee...concluded that at Brigham Young University infringements on academic freedom are distressingly common and the climate for academic freedom is distressingly poor.

Reading the detailed and scathing account, I remember the moment I escorted President Bateman and two of his dark-suited vice presidents out of the room where they had met with the investigators. As their stiff, retreating backs passed through the door, one of the investigators looked at me in disbelief and rolled her eyes far back into her head.

Somehow the risks and experiments enabled by academic freedom have taken on the hue of moral relativism in the minds of an administration that supposes it acts unequivocally from an absolute moral center. It's too bad. When I was hired, the two vice presidents who interviewed me were more interested in what I was reading outside my discipline than in the orthodoxy of my beliefs. I put a new sign on my office door: CURB YOUR DOGMA.

15 OCTOBER 1998, PROVO

A couple of days ago, a Wyoming student named Matthew Shepard was beaten, tied to a fence, and left to die in Laramie. One of the killers was raised Mormon. Shepard was gay. Laramie has always reminded me of Farmington. Laramie residents deny that their town is a homophobic place. We live and let live here, they say, a western mantra that rings true until you bring homosexuals into the equation. Or Indians.

In 1974 thousands of Navajo marchers packed Farmington streets after high school boys tortured and killed three Navajo men. I ask Mom about that tense summer, and she says she didn't understand it: We had never had any trouble with the Indians before. Aside from the nervous night I spent on the reservation guarding the Cactus Drilling Company equipment, I have little memory of what happened.

Like the other good citizens of Farmington, you simply went to work? No impulse to march with the Navajo? No desire to end the violence and discrimination?

None whatsoever. I was a child of my time, of my place. Does that surprise you after everything else you know about me?

19 NOVEMBER 1998, PROVO

I've been reading Rodney Barker's *The Broken Circle*. He includes a 1975 Civil Rights Commission assessment of the murders and convictions and demonstrations called "The Farmington Report." He quotes Philip Reno's 1974 essay in the *Nation* to the effect that "various services have bound Indians and border towns together in the same 'relentless reciprocity' that Jean Paul Sartre saw binding colonized to colonizer in Africa." Sartre and Farmington in the same essay!

Reno argues that "now the old reciprocity, which was based on inequality and dependency, is breaking down and a new reciprocity, based on more equal rights and power, must be established." He's right about the need, I think, naive about the future.

Our family friend and church leader Marlo Webb was mayor of Farmington in 1974, just a few months in office when the marches began. He held meetings with the protesters. He tried to explain that the three boys didn't represent the rest of Farmington's Anglo population. Their families had moved in from elsewhere and didn't have a history with Navajo. Their abbreviated sentences to juvenile reform school were not evidence of racism, but unfortunate technicalities of the law.

"The Farmington Report" laid out ample evidence of racism, discrimination, and brutality against Navajo. Mayor Webb's frustration was manifest in his response, quoted in the report:

> This is a typical example of how the ever-growing cancer of bureaucracy is dominating and directing our country and the lives of its citizens.... This commission would appear to want to drag each of us down to the level of the lowest common denominator and obviously is advancing the cause of socialism in this country. They advocate that government fill all of the needs of the individual rather than achievement through individual effort. This would be impossible to finance and completely contrary to the American way of life, and the greatness achieved through the free enterprise system and self-achievement of the individual.

Sterling Black, chairman of the advisory committee, responded with frustrations of his own, also part of the report:

> There appears to be little awareness on the part of the general population or elected public officials of the complex social and economic problems.... Navajos are aware of the indignities and injustices, and want something done to better the situation.... Unfortunately, they hear only that there are no problems existing, people in this town get along very well with each other,

there are no indignities, there are no injustices, and there is
nothing to be done to remedy these complaints.

27 NOVEMBER 1998, PROVO

I've been studying a photo of a group of Mormon boys taken at
Lake Powell. We had been flown there for water skiing by several of
our church leaders the summer of 1966. I'm standing behind red-
shirted Larry Echohawk to the left of the photo. In the middle stand
the lawyer whose stepdaughter I knew, the Indian trader who gave
me his white dinner jacket, Marlo Webb, and, kneeling, a petroleum
engineer who was our bishop. We're a scraggly bunch of boys who
have had an adventure thanks to the well-to-do men who have taken
an interest in us. Other than Larry, we're all part of the Anglo establishment that will not, when the time comes, understand what has
gotten the Indians so riled up.

3 APRIL 1999, PROVO

Once again I have been denied promotion to the rank of professor.
That's not surprising, of course, but the details bear mentioning. To
prove the allegations of "contentious criticism" that were their justifica-
tion for denial, university officials cited the following statements from
my publications: "There is a virulent strain of anti-intellectualism in

the Mormon Church...and its purveyors are, among others, members of BYU's Board of Trustees"; "The Department of Religious Education has experienced the kind of inbreeding that weakens any academic department—they have hired teachers who fit the unctuous seminary teacher mold rather than teacher-scholars"; "BYU is a sanctimonious edifice, a formalistic, hyper-pious community."

Maybe I should have minced my words.

The professor of chemistry appointed university representative for the appeal wrote that my work had been "disruptive, manipulative, and contentious." The chemist pointed out that the university's new "Academic Freedom Statement," which I had argued against as an academic bondage policy, had been adopted by "people whom we sustain as prophets, seers, and revelators....BYU faculty 'assume an obligation of dealing with sensitive issues sensitively and with a civility that becomes believers.'"

The university representative, I responded in my appeal, has argued that I am a bad citizen because I used the word *unctuous* in reference to hires of nonscholars and because I called BYU sanctimonious, but he doesn't address the question of whether the words are appropriate. The dean has argued that I am a bad citizen because I held the university up to ridicule, but he doesn't ask whether the university has become ridiculous. The academic vice president writes that I should have made more affirmative contributions to the university, but doesn't address the affirmative contributions that even and perhaps especially stinging criticism can bring.

It is time to move on.

2 JUNE 1999, PROVO

John's birthday tomorrow. He would have been forty-nine.

Yesterday I signed papers resigning from Brigham Young University. For eleven years I worked for an increasingly coercive and distrustful organization sponsored by a church that despised my brother and his kind. When the regulations for continuing employment grew more severe, I found ways to subvert requirements I had complied with willingly for years. Forced to pay tithing, 10 percent of my earnings,

I quit paying all but a token. Forced to comply with dietary laws I had obeyed all my life, I began to imbibe. Forced to state my allegiance, I decided to shift allegiance. This fall I'll be a professor of integrated studies, philosophy, and humanities at Utah Valley State College (UVSC).

I have broached this topic before in the context of your revelations of desire, but now there is even more reason to point out that your use of the words "virulence" and "unctuous" and "sanctimonious" in print and these admissions that you have quit paying tithing and have started drinking coffee play right into the hands of those who will see them as proof, proof they predicted by the way, of your fall from righteousness.

You realize, by now, that that binary structure is deeply internalized in me: choices are either good or evil. And you know also that I have been trying to feel my way to a different kind of thinking. That some will see this as moral relativism is inevitable, but that doesn't make their judgment correct. I realized that the moment my belief in God fell away and I found I still had strong reasons to be good. In any case, I can't live my life afraid of what someone else might think.

4 JUNE 1999, BYU, PROVO

Dear Friends and Colleagues,

As many of you know, my second application for promotion to full professor was recently denied, as was my appeal of the decision. The Vice President who presided over the appeal of his own decision to deny promotion wrote that my actions over the last decade have been "injurious to both the university community and the institution." He added that he hoped "for a day in which you will be able to understand and appreciate the perspectives of all your colleagues here." To be a good citizen, according to his model, I should admit that I am alone in my criticism of the university and agree with my wiser colleagues.

What has kept me at BYU for a decade is the knowledge that we have done our best as university citizens to make BYU a better place. I'll miss working with you.

10 JANUARY 2000, MIDWAY, UTAH

A couple of days ago I moved out of our house. It is now her house. My sister Christy graciously invited me to use their place in Midway while they are in China. Standing in an aisle of a Midway grocery store at ten o'clock that first night, I marveled at the absurdity of this new beginning in an empty little store in the dark of the cold night.

It's not easy to adjust to the new rhythms of living alone. I wake up in the night and wonder what the hell I have done. It's not the empty bed—I slept alone on a futon in the basement for the past decade. It's the absence of sound.

12 MARCH 2000, STRAWBERRY PEAK, UTAH

I drive up Daniels Canyon, snow falling steadily, early Bob Dylan blaring from the tape deck: "Talkin' John Birch Society Blues," "I'm in the Mood for You," and a foreign song punctuated by a yodel he claims he learned in Utah: "Talkin' Hava Nagila." My boys are with their mother, and I've got an appointment with my therapist.

By eight I'm climbing through new snow with the rising sun at my back. Over the course of five hours, I hear the distant whine of two snowmobiles and the twin motors of an airplane. Otherwise, there are only natural sounds and profound solitude. The powder deepens as I climb. It's not long until I head for south-facing slopes where a solid crust under the new snow makes breaking trail a bit easier. The rhythm of skis and poles. The glow of my sweating body. The occasional chatter of birds. Hoarfrost on aspens. Icicles dangling from conifers. The snowshoe tracks of hares. A squirrel's scolding. Erotic folds of snow where a stream peeks out of a sinuous valley. The windblown snow at the top of the ridge is like powdered sugar. Clouds brush the ridge. Whiteouts alternate with sudden sunlit openings that reveal an immense landscape stretching from Mount Timpanogos to the Uintas, a vast and splendid mountainous expanse. I rip the skins from my skis, eat an orange—the brilliant color shocking in the white and blue landscape—gulp the last of my water, and shove off through aspens in swinging, bent-kneed turns that burn my legs and ease my mind. "Don't think twice," my therapist suggests. "It's all right."

21 MARCH 2000, PROVO

Our divorce became final today, in and by the wooden language of the law: "It is hereby ordered, adjudged and decreed: The bonds of matrimony and the marriage contract heretofore existing by and between the Petitioner and Respondent be, and the same are hereby dissolved, and the Petitioner is hereby awarded a Decree of Divorce from Defendant on the grounds of irreconcilable differences."

If I were the author of state law, I'd write an alternate text that petitioners could choose if they wished: After [twenty-five] years of marriage, remembering the richness of shared experiences, mindful of their [seven] wonderful children, regretting their sometimes bitter incompatibilities, these two human beings part ways.

7 APRIL 2000, MIDWAY, UTAH

PBS's *Religion and Ethics Newsweekly* just aired its program on intellectuals and the Mormon Church. Lucky Severson and his camera crew showed up at UVSC a few months ago to ask me some questions about academic freedom and BYU. While they were setting up the lighting equipment, Lucky made sure he had my credentials right: So, in 1981 you moved from a lectureship at Princeton to a tenure-track job at Vanderbilt. After being tenured there, you moved to BYU, and after eleven years moved to UVSC. Is that correct?

It is, I said.

I've never seen an academic career in such precipitous decline, he said.

Fair enough, I told him, but you should know that each step was carefully taken.

They filmed me saying something about how disappointing it was to leave a promising university that had lost its nerve. Then they hurried off for their next interview, the important one, with former

BYU and San Francisco quarterback Steve Young.

It left me thinking about choice. Which led to questions about truth. Conservative thinkers like Gertrude Himmelfarb are fond of quoting Nietzsche's "Nothing is true; everything is permitted." Mormons, including Himmelfarb's plagiarizing admirer at BYU, make the same point with a Dostoyevsky quote: "If God does not exist, everything is permitted." They conclude from this that truth and God must be defended at any cost. On this model, atheists and their epistemologically relativist friends are immoral (or at least amoral). But what if you look at Nietzsche's and Ivan Karamazov's claims through a less conservative lens? What if truth is a human invention, a human construct useful as a tool? What if "permitting everything" is a prerequisite for freedom? And what if that freedom makes choices possible, fosters innovation, and catalyzes change? Conservatives see only trouble in this scenario, but a pragmatist like Richard Rorty figures that we are better off making decisions on the basis of what we think will work best than we are when we claim to know what is true and what God wants.

I would have seemed like an alien if I had stood up in testimony meeting and said, in lieu of "I know the Gospel is true," something like "Best as I can tell, the Gospel is pretty good for me and my family." If I were to bear testimony today, I'd say that despite its positive influence on me over the years, the current Mormon emphasis on obedience and absolute truth and its narrow definition of the so-called natural family is no longer working for me.

23 APRIL 2000, PROVO

Lunch with a Navajo student today. She grew up on the reservation near Farmington and remembers her parents talking about the three Navajo men tortured and killed by students from my high school. I told her what "The Farmington Report" said about Anglo cluelessness. Does that surprise you? she asked.

Even though more than three decades have passed, I dredged up phrases I learned that summer working at the Four Corners Power Plant. Something like *hagaohnee howan cu*. She translated: Good-bye.

I'm going home now. Amazed that she could understand me, I tried the second phrase: *doh nah'l ish da.* She laughed and asked what I thought it meant. Good morning. How are you? I answered. No, she said. It means "I do no work." Your boss must have thought that was hilarious.

22 AUGUST 2000, PROVO

A year into my new job at UVSC and newly settled in a house in southeast Provo built the year my mother was born. I'm spending a lot of time with one of my colleagues, a professor of history named Lyn Bennett. And I'm as anxious as ever about my inadequacies as a father.

Dream: A phrase kept flitting through my mind that surely encompassed the secrets of the universe: "The coyote, evidently, will do anything to have a gloam sister." That's it! I thought. That's the answer. But what is a gloam sister? I went 'round and 'round with that question, knowing its answer would reveal everything. So close. Oh so close to transcendent knowledge.

2 OCTOBER 2000, PROVO CANYON

Sam Rushforth has left BYU to become the dean of science and health at UVSC. For four years he and I have been writing a column for the magazine *Catalyst* called "Wild Rides and Wildflowers." We feature botany, mountain biking, and whatever conversations arise between good friends while out on the mountain. Today, riding up the Great Western Trail just inside of Provo Canyon, I have a question for Sam: Do you believe in love?

What the hell are you talking about? he responds delicately.

Our philosophy students just read their prizewinning essays on love, I explain, and in the ensuing discussion I argued against any kind of pure love, against true love, against any Platonic absolute.

You've become an even worse cynic than I thought, Sam says. But since you raise the question, when intimacy and sex converge, it's what I call love.

I don't mean to downplay the importance of love in my life, I counter. But I get tied into knots if I start wondering about true love.

It's like wondering about God—just a potentially dangerous dead end.

Okay, Sam agrees. Enough simpering. We get paid to be botanical bikers, not to write a column for the lovelorn.

20 NOVEMBER 2002

> Church of Jesus Christ of Latter Day Saints / Membership Records Department
> 50 E. No. Temple / SLC, UT 84111
>
> To Whom It May Concern:
>   Please remove my name from the records of your church.
>   The critical issues that make me unwilling to remain a member are the Church's support of laws to limit the rights of gays and lesbians and the Church's focus on absolute obedience to patriarchal authority.
>
> Scott Hilton Abbott

The letter was straightforward enough. It was more difficult to explain the decision to my children, most of whom are still active in the religion I taught them. I don't believe I've found the one truth, I said. But the church that was so much a part of my life for a half century isn't good for me any longer.

6 APRIL 2003, AMERICAN FORK, UTAH

Mom fed me lunch today, and while we ate we worked a crossword puzzle. I tried to convince her that "Sicilian spouter" should be *Alex* (Caldiero). She insisted that I write *Etna*. We dug out a photo of you, John, in the arm of our great-grandfather "Grump" Boreing. As you know, his real name was Walter Thomas Boreing, and he was born in Butler, Missouri, in 1873. You were born in 1951, so you must have

been making this incredulous face late that year or early the next, three years before Grump shot himself with a shotgun in the enclosed porch just behind you in the photo. He was ill and tired of being a burden on Grandma Abbott. That's the story we tell one another.

John, the year before you died you sent a drawing to Mom. The sun reminds me of the stylized sun I had carved on your headstone. How did you draw the perfect spheres?

I smile when a penny fits the circles exactly. I trace around a penny myself and then scan your circles for the telling point where you had to shift your hand or where the angle forces the circle outward (caught you on the last circle on the bottom right, where it intersects the wall). I trace the wood grain with a pencil and learn some of your secrets. My pencil follows yours. I retrace patterns of your hand and eye and mind.

The small envelope into which you folded your drawing is addressed to J. H. Abbott. When you wrote your mother's initials, did you note that you too could be addressed as J. H. Abbott? It's true for all of us, if not that graphically: addressing your mother or father or brother, you address yourself.

Mom's address is 432 N. 800 E., not 732 N. The letter arrived anyway. You and I began crossing our sevens while serving missions in Europe. New languages began to speak us. Did you like that as much as I did?

I did, Scott. I had new ways to think about the definitions I had been handed. The language I learned from my gay friends was helpful in a similar way. Sorry you never learned that vocabulary, that syntax.

On the flap you wrote a thought complicated by a question mark: "I'm trying but I don't know why?" I am writing you in return, John, hoping to explore your question with questions of my own.

29 NOVEMBER 2003, FARMINGTON, NEW MEXICO

Lyn and I spent a quiet Thanksgiving in a rented casita in Abiquiu, that high-country town in the Chama River valley made famous by Georgia O'Keefe and her paintings. It's a New Mexico I never explored as a child, Hispanic to the core. Driving west from Chama, through Dulce, and then into Blanco, I wondered how the hell I could have grown up in Farmington with so little awareness of this dominant surrounding culture. Navajo populate my memories of the town, as do the West Texas oil-patch Anglos, and more intimately the Anglo Mormons. But Latinos?

In my fifty-fifth year, I'm still learning to see. That disturbs and pleases me.

The road into Farmington leads past an adult book and video store. A billboard with a huge picture of Jesus overlooks the store from the next lot: JESUS IS WATCHING YOU!

26 DECEMBER 2003, PROVO

For Christmas, Tom spanned the distance between Provo and Brooklyn with a CD of his Henry Jones Swing Trio. I've been listening to his sweet clarinet improvisations for hours. Nate sent me a deft sketch of a Hong Kong bridge and a lively description of an old man he was trying to proselytize. I had sent him Ed Abbey's response to a missionary: "So you're going to Christianize the savages. Aren't they savage enough already?" Dad, Nathan replied, I love you.

Ben and Sam and Tim joined Lyn and me for Christmas dinner. The boys seem to be adjusting well enough to the divorce (who knows what lurks beneath?) and have responded generously to the idea of their father with a new partner.

Maren and Brandon brought Kylie and Kadon to see their grandfather, and later Joe and Tracy stopped by with little Jake, adopted in November. We sat around a crackling fire, wary only when the children got too close.

6 OCTOBER 2004, PROVO

The *Deseret News* reported today on a speech given by the former director of the BYU Honors Program. Addressing a group called "Families under Fire," he said that traditional marriage brings significant benefits to individuals and to society. "The battle over marriage," he continued, is being lost because supporters of traditional marriage haven't clearly explained those benefits. (By traditional marriage, I suppose, he wasn't referring to the Hebrew tradition restored by Joseph Smith.) He laid out a set of ideals found in marriages between men and women but absent in same-sex marriages: "lifetime commitment, trust, fidelity, child-rearing, kindness, and sacrifice." The inspiring professor of philosophy who once recommended that I read Sartre's wonderful biography of Jean Genet repeats this same list several times. Each time I scratch my head.

I imagine how he would view the trajectory of my own life. In fact, I don't have to imagine. He sets up a "worldly" straw man whom he contrasts with "clusters of individuals who have each been reshaped so as to live together in love. These clusters are families." Worldly homosexuals and deluded defenders of marriage equality, however, are making of themselves "irresponsible and ineffectual persons" "in the name of a wildly misconceived freedom.... The deterioration in their chosen way of life and in the qualities of their selfhood is obvious and undeniable."

29 JUNE 2008, SALT LAKE CITY

Jumping headlong into the political arena, the First Presidency of the LDS Church has sent a letter to be read to all its congregations: "... We ask that you do all you can to support the proposed constitutional amendment [Proposition 8, California] by donating of your means and time to ensure that marriage in California is legally defined as being between a man and a woman."

4 NOVEMBER 2008

Proposition 8 passed, 52 percent to 48 percent.

14 NOVEMBER 2008

The *New York Times* reports today that "as much as half of the nearly $40 million raised on behalf of the measure was contributed by Mormons" and that "Mormons made up 80 percent to 90 percent of the early volunteers who walked door-to-door in election precincts."

6 DECEMBER 2008, PROVO

For a book of one-sentence autobiographies by Serbian writers (I am included because of my two books with Žarko), I wrote:

> After Ljubica Radakoviæ fed me chicken soup and taught me to say *Srbi su dobri ljudi*, after our Belgrade publisher realized I was not a figment of Žarko's fertile imagination, after translating Peter Handke's *Justice for Serbia*, after traveling up the Drina River between the wars, after the man in Bajina Bašta said he had read our book and I said "so you're the one," after the cruise missile bought with my tax dollars shook the stove that cooked the chicken soup, after I realized that my brother's death was not final, after I left the homophobic Mormon Church that inspired some of my best feelings and denounced the xenophobic country I still love, after my hair turned silver and the divorce was final and my children grew up and Lyn found her way into my heart, after sixty eventful years I still want to be a better person than I am.

[John's Yellow Notebook #2]

WE GUARANTEE FAST SERVICE
NO MATTER HOW LONG IT TAKES

I never knew the saint...but I was brought up in his very long shadow, and chilling it was until I read Voltaire, until I realized there was such a thing as glory in this world for the man who was not afraid to seize what he wanted, to create himself. *Burr, A Novel* Gore Vidal

The law is simply whatever is boldly asserted and plausibly maintained. Burr

Meridith, who had rarely come near a drunk and had never seen a drunken priest, was at first disgusted and then touched with a sharp compassion. This was what happened to some men when the terror of life caught up with them. *The Devil's Advocate*

He knew now how much he needed friendship, and he was prepared to go more than halfway to the making of it...For the first time in my life, I think, I am beginning to be close to people. It terrifies me to think how much time I've wasted, and how little there is left. The *Devil's Advocate*

"I admire your courage, Monsignor. I don't subscribe to the Roman faith, or to any faith for that matter, but I imagine you find it a great consolation at a time like this." (tumor, surgeon)
"I hope I may, Doctor," said Blaise Meredith simply, "but I've been a priest too long to expect it." Ibid p. 11–12

Don't blame malice for what stupidity can account for.

240

LOSERS
A NOVEL BY JOHN H. ABBOTT
WITNESSED AND EXPERIENCED
Fred — busboy Boise
Dino — cook, dad druggie ecc.
Bonnie — Santee
Victoria — Santee
Vince — Mexican Jumbo's
Mary — Boise Interlude
Sam — Farmington
Frank – Farmington

Creative
built weight bench for Scott
ski rack for Rambler
artistic
desks, bookends for Grandpa H.
plays
writing — Mr. Booton 10th Mental Health
fake science fair
fake play — 7th Grade
Cheated all through School, was too lazy to study but did good
on tests
cooking
foundry — Springville, Utah
Bank — Computer Center, SLC
Moving Company — Houston
walk out — Farmington High
minor little league — Home Runs ecc.

Think about becoming one of the cynical comedians?

Management needs to communicate with employees instead of
playing God. When there are problems (bad feelings ecc.) they need

to talk with everything and everyone and find out where the, or why the, unhappiness exists — refer to *Brave New World*, Aldous Huxley

Why I get pissed at waiters
No Memory — tortellini
Not Caring — lemons in water — Steve
Lazy — Not getting own parm
Loitering in kitchen
Not accepting when they fuck up, blaming the kitchen
Not garnishing with parsley
Not charging for extra plate (I forgot)
Believing their finances have nothing to do with the kitchen
Expecting kitchen to produce while they stand around and gossip
No respect
Being stupid (day after day)

As he struggled, he thought of something he had been told once, that personality exists only in interactions between people. That when a man's alone, he has no traits.

Neither choice had much appeal. Neither choice held much hope. *Magic Kingdom For Sale*, Terry Brooks

Death was the least final thing in the world. Marion Zimmer Bradley, *Web of Darkness*, p. 303

8

Home Again

> The circle of time drawn in this telling returns....[C]an
> there be an unraveling in the telling and another story
> that begins to reweave the strands, new on the loom once
> more? Are there earlier voices, older than the stories we
> have heard...interior language of the cell, standing stone
> of history, oddly familiar in our hands, making us lean
> toward what we have not yet perceived?
>
> —Susan Griffin

11 NOVEMBER 2012

I went into the LDS Third Ward in Farmington, New Mexico. I could
not tuck my long hair up under a cap as poet and environmental
activist Gary Snyder did when he "went into the Maverick Bar / In
Farmington, New Mexico." I had no earring to leave in the car. I
didn't drink double shots of bourbon backed with beer (although my
traveling bag held a flask of lowland single malt in case of emergency).
Unlike Snyder, I had an escort, an old friend who explained where I
was from. Instead of "We don't smoke Marijuana in Muskokie," the
organist played "For the Beauty of the Earth." There was no dancing.
Otherwise, my experience was exactly like Snyder's.

Snyder was in the Four Corners area to protest the rape of Black
Mesa, holy to Hopi and Navajo, black with coal. The corporations
prevailed, and the coal was strip-mined and slurried away with precious desert water. Coal smoke from various power plants, including

the one in whose warehouse I worked the summer after high school, so thoroughly fouls the air of these high, wild, open spaces that on Thursday, driving from Cortez to Shiprock, the dramatic volcanic core that lends the town its name was more clearly visible in memory than in actual fact. I had returned home to revisit my past, John's past, both of our histories veiled by time and distorted by intent.

Nearly four decades since I last attended church in my hometown, more than a decade since I left the Mormon Church, twenty years since I began writing after John's death, a week after Barack Obama was elected to a second term, I went into the LDS Third Ward in Farmington, New Mexico.

A billboard in southwestern Colorado had shouted at me as I drove past: SAVE GOD AND AMERICA. It proclaimed that OBAMA HATES BOTH. And it concluded that I should VOTE ROMNEY.

Utah County, where I live, had just given Mitt Romney 90 percent of its votes. San Juan County, New Mexico, where Farmington is located, awarded 63 percent of its votes to Romney (in contrast to Albuquerque's Bernalillo and Santa Fe Counties, which went 56 percent and 73 percent for Obama, respectively). With the exception of a few years in New Jersey's Mercer County (Obama 68 percent), I've spent my life among conservatives.

Farmington's citizens are conservatives of an isolated sort. It is 182 miles to Albuquerque, 208 to Santa Fe, 419 to Phoenix, 377 to Denver (the route my family took that fateful December), 425 to Salt Lake City (from where Brigham Young sent his son Brigham Young Jr. to colonize Kirtland, New Mexico, just west of Farmington); West Texas, origin of many of the town's oil-field specialists and workers, is about 500 miles distant. At the confluence of the La Plata, the Animas, and the San Juan Rivers, Farmington's Anglo culture is shoehorned between Latino New Mexico and the Navajo Reservation.

I haven't been politically conservative since I left Farmington. Or did the shift occur when I came home from my German mission? Or perhaps as I changed my major at BYU from premed to German literature and philosophy? Or when I headed east for graduate work at Princeton?

In any case, I went into the LDS Third Ward in Farmington, New Mexico, with my long gray hair pulled back into a ponytail just days after every voting member of this congregation (was there, perhaps, a single dissenter? two of them?) had voted for their fellow Mormon conservative and had done so after fasting and praying for him, sure, or at least hopeful, that he would save the Constitution and the Country from Socialism or worse. I live with a partner to whom I'm not married. There's that problematic flask of whiskey. I had coffee Saturday at Andrea Kristina's Bookstore in downtown Farmington. I swear like the roughneck I once was. I'm allergic to authority. I would gladly be gay if I had those inclinations.

I open the door and hold it for a gray-haired couple.

Thank you, they both say.

When I did this in the old days, people said thank you, young man, I reply.

You're not young any longer, the man says.

My friend Doug introduces me as the son of my father.

Your dad was our bishop, the man says. He was a fine man.

We're greeted by the current bishop's two councilors, men in dark suits and white shirts. Their firm handshakes and sincere smiles make me think they will not throw me out if they discover I'm a liberal environmentalist. Two young missionaries assess me avidly; my hair suggests the need for conversion. I almost stop to tell them I helped raise this building, home that summer from college, a laborer for the construction company hired by the church. But in deference to the gathering crowd behind us and with uncharacteristic good sense, I move on and enter the chapel.

Doug and I find seats in the back row next to our old friend Craig. He's the only man in the building not wearing a tie. I get too hot, he says.

Doug's wife, Tyra, plays opening chords on the organ, and we, maybe 150 white people, sing a hymn about the earth's beauty. Although I no longer believe there's a God to thank for that, I am thankful for the earth and smile when I realize I still remember many of the words. It feels good to sing again, to be part of this congregation. And they are not all white, as I supposed. A young Native American, twelve or thirteen, sits with the other deacons in front of the sacrament table.

A young woman rises to give the invocation. Women were not allowed to pray in sacrament meeting when I was young. Heads bow all around me. I watch the woman as she invokes "Our Dear Heavenly Father," her eyes screwed shut, focused intently on what she will say. She thanks the Lord for the veterans "who we honor on this Veterans Day." She slips into a well-worn groove to ask that God "bless the leaders of our church and the...and the leaders...and the leaders of our nation." Although the election is still very much with her, in the end, bless her heart, she fights through the disappointment and completes the blessing.

Quite a different Romney was running for president when I was growing up. In a 1964 letter to his friend Governor George Romney, Mormon apostle Delbert Stapley explained that Romney's support of the civil rights movement was contrary to the teaching of Joseph Smith and reminded Romney that Smith threatened dire consequences for "those who are determined to pursue a course, which shows an opposition, and a feverish restlessness against the decrees of the Lord." "The Negro is entitled to considerations," Stapley wrote, "but not full social benefits nor inter-marriage privileges with the Whites, nor should the Whites be forced to accept them into restricted White areas." The younger members of this congregation will have little experience with the racist beliefs that so colored my thinking. The Navajo deacon, I trust, can feel secure in his brown skin.

A master sergeant in splendid uniform speaks extemporaneously and emotionally about how his duty in Vietnam stripped him of religious beliefs, faith he regained slowly when he found the Mormons. I think about the flat plaque on my father's grave, paid for by the Veterans Administration, placed in a noisy corner below a busy highway in a sterile cemetery designed without gravestones to make grass cutting easier. The plaque declares BOB WALTER ABBOTT / 1ST LT US ARMY / WORLD WAR II / 1925–1977. That's it. No mention of loving father and husband. Of fine teacher and good principal and compassionate bishop. How did that happen? Dad's epitaph is elsewhere, I tell myself, in our "Books of Remembrance," in our collections of photographs, in our lives. John's gravestone stands in a more inviting spot atop a hill in American Fork, Utah. Fraternal hands are carved into bright gray granite—and into these meditations.

A woman sitting in front of us rubs her teenage son's back, a gesture repeated in other pews. A husband stretches an arm around his wife's back. Families snuggle together while a speaker drones on about a new, inspired curriculum for youth classes. I try to imagine John in this warm setting, a sixty-one-year-old arm around his husband's shoulder, happy to have rejoined the congregation that sent him on his mission to Italy.

I can't picture it. Not in my lifetime.

We sing "Count Your Blessings," one of Dad's favorites, and I chant the bass line that marches straightforward eighth notes ("count your many blessings") across the syncopated soprano line ("count...your blessings"). It's a song of trial and triumph: "tempest tossed," "all is lost," "load of care," "cross to bear," "Count your many blessings; angels will attend, / Help and comfort give you to your journey's end." Although no one but Tyra at the organ is watching her, the chorister signals for a slowing cadence at the end of each verse, adding the slightest of personal touches to the song.

Sacrament meeting over, I follow Doug across the gym into a large classroom. People still greet him formally as "Bishop," grateful for his service. The room fills with men and women, maybe sixty of us, almost everyone holding a fat set of scriptures. Christ's visit to the Americas after his Resurrection as told in the Book of Mormon will be the subject for today's class. Doug is a born teacher, as erudite as he is sensitive to the problem of too much erudition in this diverse and provincial setting.

Provincial. That's the word that best describes my sense for the town I drove into on Thursday. I was without sophistication when I left for college in 1967 and thus, logically, must have come from an unsophisticated town. Farmington is nearly twice the size it was then, approaching fifty thousand inhabitants, and it now has a two-year college. Still, over the years I have always thought that Doug was stuck in a backwater.

Cosmopolitan. That's the word that best describes the new sense
I have for Doug after having poked around in his downtown law
office. It's an insight I might well have expected had my thought not
coalesced around the word *provincial*. In high school we frequented
the school library in tandem, and as college roommates I was jealous
of Doug's passion for Shelley and Keats. I knew he had spent two
years speaking Quechua and Spanish as a missionary in Bolivia. He
had been a US marine for four years and had won two black belts in
karate. But until the revelation occasioned by seeing Doug's books,
I had him pegged as a small-town lawyer who had reverted to the
provinces. While I, in contrast...

The rooms of Doug's law office contain, of course, those leather-
bound books in glass-fronted cases meant to lend a sense of prosper-
ity and sagacity to their owners. There are shelves and shelves of law
books, various tools of the trade. The rest of the books, however,
testify to intellectual curiosity of the best sort. Most of them have
been read (excluding a pristine copy of Heidegger's *Being and Time*).
There is a long shelf of books about Navajo language and culture.
Several shelves of military history. Books about knots. Dozens of
books about knots! Innumerable field guides to birds and animals.
Entire bookcases devoted to philosophy and theology. A dozen
translations of the Bible. Mormon books, including twenty-two
volumes of the *Journal of Discourses*. Books by Meister Eckhart
and Saint John of the Cross and Thomas Merton and Martin Buber
and Bertrand Russell's *Why I Am Not a Christian*. There is a lot of
poetry. Shakespeare in abundance. Dictionaries galore: Spanish,
Spanish-English, Spanish-English Legal Dictionary, Spoken Spanish,
Navajo-English, French-English, Latin Verbs, a reverse dictionary,
a poet's dictionary, a usage dictionary, Bible dictionaries, a biblio-
phile's dictionary, a dictionary of literary terms, the *Oxford English
Dictionary*, law dictionaries, dictionaries of quotations, crossword-
puzzle dictionaries, dictionaries of etymology, and a whole raft
of thesauruses. Armed with such books, Doug has written three
dissertations: one for a doctorate of juridical science in taxation at
the Washington School of Law and two for doctorates in theology
and ministry at Faith Christian University.

Tyra says I'll do anything for a certificate, Doug told me. Look at my card:

F. D. Moeller
B.S., Th.B., M.S.M., M.A.(C.P.), Th.M., Th.D., D.Min., J.D., LL.M., DJ.S.
Farmington, New Mexico
424 W. Broadway

And it's not all academic. Tyra showed me dozens of film reviews printed in the local paper, a set of poems published in a weekly column, and numerous "Guest Commentaries" by "F. Douglas Moeller, a Farmington attorney and poet" or, alternately, "a Farmington attorney and writer."

This man in front of the adult Sunday-school class in the Farmington Third Ward, this man with the gentle mien and soft, precise voice, this father of four and advocate in various tribal and state and regional courts, this collector of knives and guns and canes and masks and books, this provincial friend of mine is no provincial.

The part of the Book of Mormon Doug is teaching today raises interesting questions related to the text—why, for instance, does Jesus quote the King James translation of Isaiah, or what about the multiple Isaiahs scholars of the Bible can identify?—but for the most part members of this class want direction for their lives, succor for their wounded souls, reassurance that they are God's children. That's exactly what they get. Doug asks for any last questions or comments, then bears his testimony of the truthfulness of the Gospel.

During the closing prayer, I remember Snyder's reference to "short-haired joy" and think, of the members of this American church, "I could almost love you again."

12 NOVEMBER 2012

It's ten degrees Fahrenheit when I begin my drive up the canyon, one degree as I drive through the little snowbound mining town of Rico, ten degrees again when I drive into Telluride, its streets busy with preparations for the ski season.

I spent the afternoon and night with my sister Carol at her home in Dolores, Colorado. She was just back from church when I arrived, returned from her duties as the ward Relief Society president. The years have been good to her, I thought as I looked into her lively eyes. She described the Veterans' Appreciation Assembly her fifth grade students will help with today. They have each interviewed a different veteran and have written three drafts of a short essay about the experience. They are lucky, I thought, to have this intelligent and vital woman as their teacher. Carol served us a tasty plate of spaghetti with sausage and a side dish of salad. Beer for Luther and me.

When I called her to arrange the visit, she asked me, "What's up?"

"I'm calling to urge you to vote for President Obama," I said.

"I've already sent in my early ballot," she answered.

Driving northeast from Telluride, the snow rapidly disappearing, I listen to Mose Allison sing a Duke Ellington–Bob Russell song whose refrain has always puzzled me: "do nothing till you hear from me / and you never will." I listen closely to Allison's lax, behind-the-beat swung performance of the story of separated lovers and the rumors that threaten to end the relationship permanently ("If you should take the words of others you've heard, / I haven't a chance"). He sings of new experiences ("other arms may hold a thrill") yet,

paradoxically, professes enduring faithfulness: "Do nothing till you hear *it* from me / And you never will." "It"—missing in the lines that perplex, but present in an emphatic final statement—would be the admission that he is untrue in his heart and that he no longer loves her. She will never hear that, he sings, because he will never speak it. (She, by the way, may decide she has had enough of this troubled relationship, but that's another story.) Love is complex. And perplexing. And swung.

In Paonia I find the little house we lived in until I was five, then eat lunch in a downtown diner. I tell the waitress I lived in the log house just up the street when I was four years old. That was a long time ago, she says. It seems like yesterday to me—the memories are not time bound—but I agree with her on principle. Sweet potato fries and a Reuben sandwich flavor another reading of Snyder's poem. He leaves Farmington "under the tough old stars," girding himself for "what is to be done."

Lyn and I have work to do as well. Most pressing is our interdisciplinary book about barbed wire, "Intimate Fences." In the late nineteenth century, barbed-wire advertisers promised protection from marauding savages, rapacious ex-slaves, and homosexual aesthetes like Oscar Wilde: "Glidden barbed wire is 'death on dudes.'" And barbed wire quickly became a literary motif. Steinbeck's Jim Casy, for example, quits preaching because women riled up by his sermons whip themselves with a "three-foot shag of bobwire." Flannery O'Connor's Hazel Motes, in contrast, wraps barbed wire around his torso because, he says, "I'm not clean." We'll end the book with Annie Proulx's story in which Ennis drives to Jack's parents' ranch to ask for the ashes he wants to spread on Brokeback Mountain. Jack's father refuses: "'Tell you what, we got a family plot and he's goin in it....' Bumping down the washboard road Ennis passed the country cemetery fenced with sagging sheep wire, a tiny fenced square on the welling prairie."

I barrel along the still ecstatic highway to Green River, savor the alkaline beauty of the northbound route between the San Rafael Swell and the Bookcliffs, and finally, after snaking down the now dark contours of Spanish Fork Canyon, ease down the steep driveway from which Lyn has shoveled a foot of heavy snow.

Home again.

Caro amico,

Come stai? Ti faccio sapere
che sono stato trasferito di nuovo.
Questa volta a San Giovanni al
Natisone, che si trova fra Udine
e Gorizia. È un paese di 1.500
abitante, cisca.

Sta piovendo adesso e stavo
pensando di tante cose, e ho pensato
di scriverti qualche riga. È difficile
di andare in avanti sempre. Tu mi
conosci un po, come penso, come sono
fatto, e lo sai che c'è un grande
tormento dentro di mi. Sono un
uomo e voglio abbandonarmi alle
piacere del corpo, della vita, ma allo
stesso momento la mia anima
mi dici che devo comportarmi in un
altro maniera.

Come può una persona vivere così?

Epilogue

This morning, looking through a drawer for a photo, I pulled out John's missionary notebook, the little black six-ring book from which I quoted when I was reading and writing about his letters. Between vocabulary lists and notes from missionary conferences, there were a couple of pages with paragraphs written in Italian. I always skipped over the foreign texts, figuring they were sketches for talks in church. Today I typed them into Google Translate. One was indeed a short sermon on the unique character of Jesus Christ. The other, however, was a letter written after John's final transfer. I asked Alex Caldiero if he would translate the letter. He sent me this:

> Dear Friend,
> How are you? I'm letting you know
> that I was transferred again.
> This time to San Giovanni al
> Natisone, situated between Udine
> and Gorizia. It is a town of about 1,500 inhabitants.
> It's raining right now and I was
> thinking of so many things, and I thought
> of writing you a few lines. It is difficult
> to always go forward. You know
> me a bit, how I think, how I am
> made, and you know that there is a great
> torment within me. I am a
> man and I want to abandon myself to the
> pleasures of the body, of life, but at the
> same time my soul
> tells me that I must behave in

253

another manner.
How can a person live this way?

I decide to reply.

Caro fratello, Caro amico,

Are we friends, my brother? You asked me that in a note
on my thoughts about our mother. It has become one of the
most important questions of my life. The answer is yes, yes my
brother, we are friends. Of all I have learned from you over the
twenty-five years I have followed your faint traces, friendship
may be the most important lesson. To have a friend. To be a
friend. Lover and friend share the same root, as does the phrase
"to set free." You have set me free, John. How I wish my much-
belated thoughts could have done the same for you.

This morning I found your letter—was it to Michele, whose
friendship so moved you?—and you ask another critical question: How can a person live this way? When I asked that question at perilous junctures of my life, the answer was that I could
not live that way. That left, of course, the more complicated
issue of how I should live. But back to your question, the one
raised by the way you were made. My dear friend Alex says
that your phrase "come sono fatto" reflects your sense for the
Italian idea of "how I am made, how I am in my essential
nature." Thinking about how you were made, you set the human
pleasures of the body or of life against the dictates of your soul.
I understand that dichotomy well, having been raised by our
parents, having been schooled by the church for which we
served missions. As time went on, we decided, if I may speak
for us both, that we were made as bawdy minds, as mindful
bodies, not as a mind that must wage vigilant war against its
body or as a body that must flee from its mind. That didn't
make us heroes. The gradual decision didn't lead to glorious
lives. It did free us, however, from having to ask the question:
How can a person live this way?

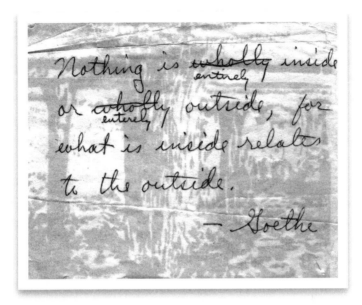

In the drawer where I found your letter, I discovered a scrap of paper with a quotation from Goethe, written in our father's rounded hand. Where did Dad come across the quotation? How was it that he reworded the translation? Dad didn't know German or Goethe's works. But somehow the lines from the poem "Epirrhema" were meaningful to him. In nature, Goethe thought, there is neither core nor shell. And for us, John, at least as I think about your youthful conundrum, the body/mind dichotomy has been destructive. We are whole creatures at our best.

That we are seldom at our best doesn't invalidate our attempts to be whole. And as we make sense of our richly flawed lives, humor sustains us. Alex told me that although your Italian was very good, you made a gender mistake of the sort that Freud taught us to understand. Your soul told you, you wrote, that you must behave in another manner—<u>altro</u> (masculine) <u>maniera</u> (feminine). Gender, like language, is many splendored and magnificently mutable. Even the emphatically definitive LDS Proclamation to the World on the Family can't quite nail down its prey. I heartily agree with the proclamation's assertion that "gender is an essential characteristic," essential in all its permutations.

Thank you, John, for helping me begin to understand. I love you.

Scott

Acknowledgments

My mother, Janice Hilton Abbott, inhabits these pages as she inhabits my life. My father, Bob Walter Abbott, absent now for decades, is present here as well. My love to Jill, Carol, Christy, Paul, and Jeff, sisters and brothers who certainly remember many of these events quite differently. Tim, Sam, Ben, Nate, Tom, Maren, and Joe are my reasons for living. To share my life with Lyn Bennett is a late, rich, and unexpected gift.

Heartfelt thanks to friends and others who have read and responded to versions of this book. They include Brooke Adams, Karin Anderson, Claudia Bushman, Alex Caldiero, Bill Davis, Steven Epperson, Brian Evenson, Larry Harper, Susan Howe, Thom Heine, Elaine Jarvik, Florence Krall, Monika Leßmann, Jeff Metcalf, Julia Nemirovskaya, Martha Nussbaum, Elbert Peck, Evan Richards, Žarko Radaković, Tom Rogers, Linda Haverty Rugg, Nancy Rushforth, Sam Rushforth, Hans Joachim Schulz, and Mary Karen Solomon.

Laraine Wilkins, Kristine Haglund, and Eric Robertson, editors of *Irreantum, Dialogue: A Journal of Mormon Thought,* and *saltfront* respectively, reworked my manuscript skillfully and generously as they published pieces of this work. John Alley and other consummate professionals at The University of Utah Press have supported and improved this book at every step.